JANE AUSTEN AND ANIMALS

To Darcy

Jane Austen and Animals

BARBARA K. SEEBER
Brock University, Canada

ASHGATE

Published by
Ashgate Publishing Limited
Wey Court East
Union Road
Farnham
Surrey, GU9 7PT
England

Ashgate Publishing Company
110 Cherry Street
Suite 3-1
Burlington, VT 05401-3818
USA

www.ashgate.com

British Library Cataloguing in Publication Data
Seeber, Barbara Karolina, 1968–
   Jane Austen and animals.
   1. Austen, Jane, 1775–1817 – Criticism and interpretation. 2. Human-animal relationships
   in literature. 3. Animals in literature.
   I. Title
   823.7-dc23

The Library of Congress has cataloged the printed edition as follows:
Seeber, Barbara Karolina, 1968–
   Jane Austen and animals / by Barbara K. Seeber.
      pages cm
   Includes bibliographical references and index.
   ISBN 978-1-4094-5604-9 (hardcover: alk. paper)—ISBN 978-1-4094-5605-6 (ebook)—
   ISBN 978-1-4094-7235-3 (epub)
   1. Austen, Jane, 1775–1817—Criticism and interpretation. 2. Animals in literature. I. Title.
PR4038.A625S44 2013
823'.7—dc23

2012045456

ISBN: 9781409456049 (hbk)
ISBN: 9781409456056 (ebk)
ISBN:9781409472353 (ePUB)

Printed and bound in Great Britain
MPG PRINTGROUP

Contents

Acknowledgments

In 1890 John Mackinnon Robertson claimed that "It is almost impossible ... to write a book on Jane Austen: you must not write treatises on miniatures" (qtd. in Southam, *The Critical Heritage* 2:193). Luckily for us, he was wrong. This acknowledgment page would not be complete without expressing gratitude for the richness of Austen studies and conversations with colleagues and students. Brock University provided the necessary conditions for scholarly work, granting me time to think and write during a sabbatical leave, and early on financially supporting a mind-opening trip to the British Library to read eighteenth- and nineteenth-century texts on animal welfare and rights. Ann Donahue, senior editor at Ashgate, has made the process of publishing this book run smoothly and I thank her for her warmth and wisdom. In addition, I am thankful to Seth F. Hibbert at Ashgate and the two anonymous readers, who made me do more work!

Peter Sabor, Elizabeth Sauer, John Sainsbury, Ann Howey, and Beth Lau offered helpful and generous comments on parts of this project. I also would like to express my gratitude to Mark Poulin for his enthusiasm and emotional support as well as his keen proof-reading eye. Maggie Berg's detailed commentary on an early draft of this manuscript was invaluable. She was a constant voice of encouragement from day one, and since this book has taken me a long time, I am also indebted to her for her patience.

Earlier versions of parts of this argument have appeared in print. "Nature, Animals, and Gender in Jane Austen's *Mansfield Park* and *Emma*" (*LIT: Literature Interpretation Theory* 13.4 [2002]: 269–85) is reprinted by permission of Taylor & Francis (http://tandfonline.com). I want to acknowledge the Canadian Society for Eighteenth-Century Studies for permission to reprint material appearing in "The Hunting Ideal, Animal Rights, and Feminism in *Northanger Abbey* and *Sense and Sensibility*" (*Lumen* XXIII [2004]: 295–308).

This book is dedicated to Darcy. He passed away in May 2012, and while he was not with me at the final manuscript preparation stage, he was a constant presence right up to then, cheerfully keeping me company in my study. Our friendship corroborated and made come alive all the texts I was reading about animal intelligence and emotion and the beautiful possibilities of interspecies connection.

Notes on Text

Austen's texts are cited from *The Cambridge Edition of the Works of Jane Austen*. The following abbreviations are included in parenthetical citations, when necessary for clarity, and correspond to the titles of individual volumes within the *Cambridge Edition*:

J *Juvenilia*, edited by Peter Sabor
NA *Northanger Abbey*, edited by Barbara M. Benedict and Deirdre Le Faye
S&S *Sense and Sensibility*, edited by Edward Copeland
P&P *Pride and Prejudice*, edited by Pat Rogers
MP *Mansfield Park*, edited by John Wiltshire
E *Emma*, edited by Richard Cronin and Dorothy McMillan
P *Persuasion*, edited by Janet Todd and Antje Blank
LM *Later Manuscripts*, edited by Janet Todd and Linda Bree

Austen's correspondence is cited from *Jane Austen's Letters*, edited by Deirdre Le Faye, and abbreviated in parenthetical references, when necessary for clarity, as *Letters*.

Preface

> The evergreen!—How beautiful, how welcome, how wonderful the evergreen!—
> When one thinks of it, how astonishing a variety of nature! (*MP* 244)

While *Mansfield Park*'s Fanny Price is often seen as an atypical heroine, her love of nature, quoted above, is shared by all of Austen's heroines. Think of Marianne Dashwood's passion for the trees at Norland in *Sense and Sensibility*, or Elizabeth Bennet's enthusiasm for "rocks and mountains" (*P&P* 175). In *Northanger Abbey*, the young Catherine Morland was "noisy and wild" (6) and "loved nothing so well in the world as rolling down the green slope at the back of the house" (7). In "training for a heroine" (7), she no longer tumbles down hills but still "never mind[s] dirt" (80) and loves the "out of doors" and "the pleasure of walking and breathing fresh air" (178). The heroine of *Emma* seeks "serenity" in "the exquisite sight, smell, sensation of nature, tranquil, warm, and brilliant after a storm" (462). *Persuasion*'s Anne Elliot "dread[s] the possible heats of September in all the white glare of Bath, and griev[es] to forego all the influence so sweet and so sad of the autumnal months in the country" (35). She "gloried in the sea" at Lyme and "sympathized in the delight of the fresh-feeling breeze" (110) which, in turn, "restored" her "bloom and freshness of youth" (112). Even in the early "Catherine, or the Bower," the heroine's favorite retreat is the "beloved" (*J* 243) arbor she built with her two friends, Cecilia and Mary, and the "shrubs they had planted" (*J* 245) in "days of happy Childhood" (*J* 243). Catherine "always wandered" to her green space to "restore her to herself": it "tranquillize[d] her mind and quiet[ed] her spirits" (*J* 242–43).

The nineteenth- and early twentieth-century critical tradition, which will be briefly surveyed in the Introduction, primarily saw Austen as a recorder of social life and removed her from her contemporaries' interest in nonhuman worlds. While nature in Austen still is usually read in exclusively human terms, I am interested in exploring the significance of the human relationship with nonhuman nature, including animals. Human–animal relations were contested from a variety of perspectives in the eighteenth and early nineteenth century, and an avid reader like Jane Austen would have been familiar with the arguments. This book demonstrates that Austen engages in a conversation with her contemporaries about nature and animals, and that she interrogates the human–animal divide from a feminist perspective. It is telling that in *Mansfield Park*, the outsider Fanny Price identifies with the "dear old grey pony" described as "her valued friend" (41) rather than viewing horses as a status symbol in the manner of her wealthy relatives, the Bertrams. It is significant that, quoting Edward in *Sense and Sensibility*, "every body does not hunt" (106): those who abuse women are keen hunters. And when Mr. Woodhouse's gruel inspires such heated responses in *Emma*, we know that its author was familiar with contemporary writings about the politics of consumption.

When I described my project early on to a colleague as "an examination of animals in Austen," he remarked, "but there are no animals in Jane Austen." While Austen does not center any of her texts on the treatment of animals, she weaves contemporary discourses about them into her narratives. Moreover, commodified animals are everywhere in Austen, whether as meat, prey, transportation, entertainment, or even decoration, such as the "monstrous curious stuffed fox … and … badger—any body would think they were alive" (*LM* 100) at Osborne Castle in "The Watsons." The view that there are no animals in Austen reflects, in part, our culture's disconnection between, on the one hand, the animals we love and want to protect and, on the other, the billions of animals in factory farms and laboratories, who have been made invisible in "un(ethical) geographies of Human/ Non-human relations" (Owain Jones 268). One of the main projects of Animal Studies is to make visible this bifurcation, and to challenge what Laurie Shannon calls a "double apartheid (a segregation in language and of bodies)" (477).

The interdisciplinary field of Animal Studies has emerged over the course of the last three decades. It is centrally concerned with studying the human–animal relationship, recognizing animals as subjects, and disrupting the predominant objectification of animals for a variety of human uses ranging from symbolic to material. In common with fields such as Women's Studies, which developed in conjunction with struggles for social justice in and outside of the academy, Animal Studies is connected to advocacy for the better treatment of animals and the animal rights movement.[1] In the foundational *Animal Liberation*, philosopher Peter Singer argues for the equal consideration of the interests of animals alongside humans. For Singer, the treatment of animals in Western culture is based on speciesism, "a prejudice or attitude of bias toward the interests of members of one's own species and against those of members of other species" (7). The position that the logic of speciesism is "identical" (9) to that of racism and sexism is supported by the fact that historically certain human groups have been denied rights by being marked as closer to the animal rather than the human in the great human– animal divide. Marjorie Spiegel in *The Dreaded Comparison*, for example, demonstrates the interconnectedness of racism and speciesism in eighteenth- and nineteenth-century slavery discourses. And a number of feminist theorists, building on ecofeminism's analysis of the "historical feminization of nature and the naturalization of women as part of the exploitation of nature" (Warren 144), have demonstrated the connections between the domination of women and the domination of animals, indeed the domination of women *as* animals. The question of who qualifies as fully human is an ongoing political struggle of crucial significance. Giorgio Agamben describes the human–animal divide as a "mobile border" (15) and argues that "in our culture, the decisive political conflict, which governs every other conflict, is that between the animality and the humanity of man" (80). Indeed, "the discourse of speciesism," as Cary Wolfe writes, "can be

---

[1]   For a particularly reader-friendly introduction to this political movement, see Paul Waldau's *Animal Rights: What Everyone Needs to Know*.

used to mark *any* social other": "We all, human and nonhuman alike, have a stake in the discourse and institution of speciesism; it is by no means limited to its overwhelmingly direct and disproportionate effect on animals" (7).

Animal Studies takes the critical stance that the opposition of the "human" and "animal" is socially constructed. Agamben argues that "*Homo sapiens ...* is neither a clearly defined species nor a substance; it is, rather, a machine or device for producing the recognition of the human" (26). This production is never complete. The maintenance of "that fantasy figure called 'the human'" necessitates the "sacrifice of the 'animal' and the animalistic" (Wolfe 6). It is in this sense that Wolfe argues for posthumanism, for the dethroning of the centrality of the human, a category that does not hold, since nonhuman animals are "not ... other-than-human but ... *infrahuman* ... part of us, *of* us" (17).[2] Posthumanist theory and Animal Studies as a whole draw on accumulating scientific evidence that capacities long considered unique to humans—cognition, tool use, language, altruism—are not exclusive to humans. These demonstrated continuities between humans and animals have implications for how we treat animals, since the use of animals for human ends without considering them as subjects in their own right is justified by the view of animals as inferior to humans. While most people today would not consider animals (at the very least, not their own pets) as Descartian machines, our society's use of animals is steeped in the assumption that their ability to experience suffering is significantly less than our own. Studies in animal behavior, field ecology, and ethology have problematized this assumption in significant ways, reinvigorating and, for some, legitimizing arguments for animal rights; Donna Haraway, for example, concludes, "movements for animal rights are not irrational denials of human uniqueness; they are a clear-sighted recognition of connection across the discredited breach of nature and culture" (152).

Literary critics working across the historical periods have adopted Animal Studies to examine representations of the human–animal relationship. This approach has been productive with a variety of texts, not only those which center on animal protagonists such as Anna Sewell's *Black Beauty* or Virginia Woolf's *Flush*. In many texts, animals (or animal products) might seem part of the background, but, looked at anew, they emerge as important in the texts' ideological work. Re-reading Austen through a lens informed by Animal Studies made visible to me passages that I had overlooked. I had not paused to think through the implications

---

[2]   I acknowledge the problem inherent in my textual distinction of humans and animals. We humans are animals, too. Some scholars prefer the term "nonhuman animals," but it is also "ideologically loaded," as Marianne Dekoven points out: "*Nonwhite, non-European*, and *non-Western* are parallel to *nonhuman* and reveal what is at stake in using it" (363). Jacques Derrida has critiqued the category of the "Animal" as overly reductive: "Whenever 'one' says 'The Animal,' ... in the singular and without further ado, claiming thus to designate every living thing that is held not be human ... this 'one,' this 'I' ... utters an *asinanity*" (31). Posthumanist theory suggests that the terms "human" and "animal" need to be put into quotation marks to alert the reader to their historical and ideological function. However, for reader ease only, I forego the repeated use of quotation marks.

of Austen's many references to hunting. Nor had I noticed what I now see as significant moments of destabilizing the human-animal boundary. Austen's work has long been appreciated for its attentiveness to the problems of women's social and economic standing. Looking at animals contributes to understanding Austen's project. Drawing on the insights of Animal Studies and feminist criticism, my book offers a new reading of Jane Austen that focuses on aspects such as rural sport, pets, and food, which have been largely relegated to "period detail." Attentiveness to nature and animals can deepen our understanding of Austen's feminism and her position in late eighteenth- and early nineteenth-century writing.

Introduction
A Nest of My Own

Regions of Wit, Elegance, fashion, Elephants & Kangaroons. (*Letters* 80)

When nineteenth- and early twentieth-century readers spoke of nature in the novels of Jane Austen, they usually meant human nature. *The Edinburgh Review* remarked on Austen's ability to "mak[e] people act and talk so exactly like the people … [readers] saw around them every day" (qtd. in Southam, *The Critical Heritage* 2:160). Similarly, Sir Walter Scott, in a letter to Joanna Baillie, writes that Austen's novels "have a great deal of nature in them" (qtd. in Southam 1:106), and in the *Quarterly Review* he commends Austen for "keeping close to common incidents, and to such characters as occupy the ordinary walks of life" (qtd. in Southam 1:63). This "truth of … description" (Scott qtd. in Southam 1:106) is one of the recurrent features of the paradox of homage and patronization that surrounds Austen: "She was a great little novelist," as Arnold Bennett puts it (qtd. in Southam 2:288). It is, then, not surprising that the natural metaphors employed in commentary on Austen's writing are of a domesticated nature. Austen's novel, according to Scott, is the world of "cornfields and cottages and meadows," not "the rugged sublimities of a mountain landscape" (qtd. in Southam 1:68). Charlotte Brontë likens *Pride and Prejudice* to "a carefully fenced, highly cultivated garden, with neat borders and delicate flowers; but … no open country, no fresh air, no blue hill" (qtd. in Southam 1:126). André Gide offers a similar appraisal in 1929: she "will never risk herself on heights exposed to too strong winds" (qtd. in Southam 2:14). A review dated 1823, comparing her with Frances Burney, commends Austen for "produc[ing] works of much fresher verdure" and "not … car[ing] to outstep the modesty of nature": "the stream of her Tale flows on in an easy, natural, but spring tide" (qtd. in Southam 1:109). The 1887 *Pen-Portraits of Literary Women* notes that her "enclosed spot of English ground is indeed little, but never was verdure brighter or more velvety than its trim grass" (qtd. in Southam 2:42). James Edward Austen-Leigh, in *A Memoir of Jane Austen*, sketched the biographical background for associating the novelist with the humble forms of nature. The "cradle of her genius" was Steventon, "the residence of Jane Austen for twenty-five years … which inspired her young heart with a sense of the beauties of nature" (23). These beauties are rather modest in his estimation, however. Jane Austen's mother, "one cannot be surprised," "thought" Steventon "unattractive, compared with the broad river, the rich valley, and the noble hills which she had been accustomed to behold" (20); Steventon "presents no grand or extensive views … the hills are not bold, nor the valleys deep; and though it is sufficiently well clothed with woods and hedgerows, yet the poverty of the soil in most places prevents the timber from attaining a large size. Still it has its beauties"

(19). Its "features are small rather than plain" (19); it is a landscape of "quiet charms" and "tame country" (20).[1]

A domestic Austen is further constructed through the animal metaphors employed in nineteenth-century commentary. These animal metaphors for Austen's work emphasize tameness, industry, and anonymity. J.E. Austen-Leigh likens Austen's novels to the "transformation" of "natural flowers" into honey by "that little insect," the bee (*Memoir* 156). In 1870, an unsigned article for *St. Paul's Magazine* postulates that Austen "was easily contented, a small modicum of general approbation satisfied her, and what she coveted most was that of her own family. She was willing, like the mole, to make her ingenious structures in the dark" (qtd. in Southam 1:237). J.E. Austen-Leigh "warn[s]" the reader "not to expect too much" from the letters included in the *Memoir*:

> the materials ... treat only of the details of domestic life. There is in them no notice of politics or public events; scarcely any discussions on literature, or other subjects of general interest. They may be said to resemble the nest which some little bird builds of the materials nearest at hand, of the twigs and mosses supplied by the tree in which it is placed; curiously constructed out of the simplest matters. (59–60)

Anne Thackeray, having read the *Memoir*, continues this image in a reverie that seamlessly blends Austen's domestic activities with her authorial ones:

> Aunt Jane ... makes play-houses for the children, helps them to dress up, invents imaginary conversations for them, supposing that they are all grown up the day after a ball. ... She built her nest, did this good woman, happily weaving it out of shreds, and ends, and scraps of daily duty, patiently put together; and it was from this nest that she sang the song, bright and brilliant, with quaint thrills and unexpected cadences, that reaches us even here through fifty years. The lesson her life seems to teach us is this: Don't let us despise our nests—life is as much made of minutes as of years; let us complete the daily duties; let us patiently gather the twigs and the little scraps of moss, of dried grass together; and see the result!—a whole, completed and coherent, beautiful even without the song. (qtd. in Southam 2:168–69)

The bird metaphor is used to create an Austen who worked purely by instinct. Alice King, writing in 1882, "see[s] only a sweet, modest woman. ... She began authorship almost without knowing what the dignity of authorship meant ... for writing had been, for her, so much like singing is for the songbird" (qtd. in Southam 2:38). Similarly, for Henry James, "Jane Austen, with all her light

---

[1]   See Kathryn Sutherland for the differences between the various "family production[s]" of Aunt Jane: for the Steventon or Hampshire Austens, as evident in Austen-Leigh's *Memoir*, discussed above, she is "nature loving, religious, dutifully domestic, and middle class" (77), while accounts from the Godmersham (Knight-Knatchbull) side of the family foreground the elevation of the Knight connection.

felicity, leaves us hardly more curious of her process, or of the experience in her that fed it, than the brown thrush who tells his story from the garden bough" (qtd. in Southam 2:229–30).

The metaphors of bee, mole, and bird, so often used to describe Austen's creative labor, are at odds with Austen's own gleeful delight in being a "wild beast" (*Letters* 212). Her letter to Cassandra from London on May 24, 1813, is filled with excitement about the success of *Pride and Prejudice*, evident in her playful searching for portraits of Mrs. Bingley and Mrs. Darcy at the London galleries. That her authorship was becoming more widely known seems not to have frightened her: "If I *am* a wild Beast, I cannot help it. It is not my own fault" (212–13). When she writes to Cassandra from Godmersham Park on September 23, 1813, she assures her that despite "my present Elegancies," "I am still a Cat if I see a Mouse" (225). Austen's own metaphors draw on sly, rapacious, and untamed animals. And while she employed the nest image in her writing, she did so in strikingly different ways from those of her commentators.

In *Mansfield Park*, the heroine's humble east attic, her retreat, is described as her "nest of comforts" (179). Filled with family cast-offs and without the benefit of heat, it marks Fanny's marginal status within the Bertram family. To liken the heroine's room to a nest is not a simple, cozy image. David Perkins, in *Romanticism and Animal Rights*, has shown that early nineteenth-century anti-cruelty discourses often focused on nests. Children's literature warned against the destruction of nests, and birds were vulnerable not only from children: nests were gathered for decoration, and birds were caged and consumed as food. The comparison of Fanny Price's room to a nest speaks to the heroine's closeness to nature as well as to women's and animals' desire for autonomy. Onno Oerlemans's point that in John Clare's poetry nests are "signs of animals' deliberate intelligence and their desire to remain undisturbed" (81) can be extended to the Romantic writers more generally. In that context, it is worth noting that all four visits to Fanny's "nest" are intrusions which disturb her peace. During the first visit, Edmund tells Fanny that he will participate in the theatricals—leaving Fanny "no composure" (183). In the second one, Mary Crawford and Edmund ask for Fanny's assistance in rehearsing lines: "*Her* spirits sank under the glow of theirs, and she felt herself becoming too nearly nothing to both" (199). Third, Edmund gifts Fanny a chain, leaving her "overpowered by a thousand feelings of pain and pleasure" (303), and then advises her to wear Mary Crawford's chain instead: "it was a stab" (306). And, finally, Sir Thomas's attempt to bully Fanny into accepting Henry Crawford's proposal takes place in her East Room and leaves her in utter despair: "the past, present, future, every thing was terrible" (370). The invasive quality of these visits is further highlighted by how carefully Fanny has constructed her nest: it, too, is a sign of her intelligence as she "worked herself" (177) into a space that "nobody else wanted" (177), gathering objects "thought unworthy of being anywhere else" (179), and thus transforming the old schoolroom into a room of her own, filled with "her plants, her books," and "her writing desk" (178).

Austen returned to the nest image in a letter dated on her birthday, December 16, 1816. Again, the nest is an image of deliberate creative endeavor, not instinct. She writes to her nephew, Edward, then an aspiring author:

> I am quite concerned for the loss your Mother mentions in her Letter; two Chapters & a half to be missing is monstrous! It is well that *I* have not been at Steventon lately, & therefore cannot be suspected of purloining them;—two strong twigs & a half towards a Nest of my own, would have been something.—I do not think however that any theft of that sort would be really useful to me. What should I do with your strong, manly, spirited Sketches, full of Variety & Glow?—How could I possibly join them on to the little bit (two Inches wide) of Ivory on which I work with so fine a brush, as produces little effect after much labour? (323)

At the time of this letter, Jane Austen had published *Sense and Sensibility*, *Pride and Prejudice*, *Mansfield Park*, and *Emma*, and for her to call any chapter a "something" surely would have cheered her nephew. The latter part of the passage is much quoted, but Austen's choice of image in the first part, the novel as nest, has received almost no attention. Austen does not offer the nest as the conventional image of domesticity and instinctual labor that we find in nineteenth-century commentary on Austen. Rather, she emphasizes strength and proprietorship—"two strong twigs & a half towards a Nest of my own"—and plays with the crossing of gender lines, the "theft ... of strong, manly, spirited Sketches." Jill Heydt-Stevenson argues that Austen's "grotesque image ... binding his unruly twigs, crude and stiff, with her finely delineated, painted ivory surface serves (quite politely) to reduce his work to nature and instinct and elevates her own to art and design" (*Subversive Laughter* 16–17). This overlooks, however, the negligible smallness of the ivory surface; clearly Austen did not believe that she worked on her "little bit ... of Ivory" with "little effect after much labour." Instead, she self-consciously performs feminine modesty. It is significant that for an image she chooses ivory, made from the tusks of elephants killed for this prized commodity. By comparing the female novelist's appropriately small canvas to ivory, Austen links the ideologies which dominate both women and animals: both are violently fashioned into objects. For her own novel, Austen chooses the nest, an image which she uses to not only invest nonhuman nature with intelligence but also connect human and nonhuman animals.

The fact that readers of Austen's letter have focused almost exclusively on the small piece of ivory is symptomatic of the critical tradition's tendency to locate Austen "inside" the country house (Williams 112). In his influential reading, Raymond Williams argues that nature "disappear[s]" in Austen: "most of the country ... becomes real only as it relates to the houses which are the real nodes; for the rest the country is weather or a place for a walk" (166). Peter Graham, in his recent *Jane Austen & Charles Darwin: Naturalists and Novelists* (2008), also maintains that Austen only treats a small segment of human society; he contrasts "Darwin's range of intellectual interests [which] was global, both geographically and figuratively" with Austen's attention to "an unusually narrow segment of the human world" (2). Readings which grant that Austen's novels do move outside have focused on landscape aesthetics, particularly the picturesque.[2]

Alistair Duckworth, in *The Improvement of the Estate*, posited that Austen embeds her argument for a conservative social order in landscape scenes. While this view continues to be influential, a number of critics have commented that Austen's treatment of landscape is, however, inflected by gender. Penny Gay maintains Austen's conservatism as argued by Duckworth, but qualifies that as "a woman (not a landowner), she views [the] workings" of the landed estate "in reality with a critical eye" ("Changing View" 47). Inger Sigrun Brodey notes that the debate surrounding improvements in *Mansfield Park* reflects "Austen's own ambivalence about authority" (91) and that its heroine is treated by her social superiors as a landscape to be improved. The significance of gender in Austen's depiction of landscape has been developed most fully by Barbara Britton Wenner in *Prospect and Refuge in the Landscape of Jane Austen*. Austen "recognizes ... that men controlled the landscape" (10), and her heroines seek the liminal spaces of bowers, hedgerows, and shrubberies to "subvert a male-dominated landscape" (12), to find "a way of being *in* the landscape without being *part* of it" (10). Like Duckworth and Gay, Britton Wenner concludes that Austen stays within the existing social structure: she "is neither 'radical' nor 'progressive'" for she "could imagine heroines creating a free space within existing society and transforming it, while clearly admiring what Burke felt English society ought to do: to preserve and to adapt existing institutions" (7). Articles by William Snyder and Jill Heydt-Stevenson argue that Austen's feminist concerns are interwoven with her treatment of landscape aesthetics: "the issue of how much control one should exert over a landscape is not a localized aesthetic issue, but instead directly impinges on the treatment of and expectations for women" (Heydt-Stevenson, "Liberty, Connection, and Tyranny" 264). The reading of Austen's landscapes as potentially subversive is opened up in an ecological sense by Robert Kern. He includes a reading of *Pride and Prejudice* in an article about the relevance of ecocriticism to a range of literary texts, not only those with an explicit environmentalist focus. While, for Kern, the descriptions of nature are "few and far between" and Austen is a "writer for whom the idea of the world as more-than-human must be close to unthinkable" (12), he grants that in Darcy's Pemberley Austen addresses the question of "wise use and management of ... natural resources": "there is even a sense in which Mr. Darcy may be regarded as a sort of neoclassical or preromantic environmentalist" (17).

---

[2]   See Edward Malins's *English Landscaping and Literature: 1660–1840* and Frank W. Bradbrook's chapter on "The Picturesque" in *Jane Austen and Her Predecessors* (pp. 50–68).

Arguments about nature in Austen hinge in part on whether or not she is seen as an Augustan or Romantic writer.[3] Rosemarie Bodenheimer, in her comprehensive "Looking at the Landscape in Jane Austen," puts forth Austen as a satirist of Romantic ideas about nature: "Jane Austen retains a self-conscious comparative stance toward the languages of response to nature, never entirely developing from a parodist to a practitioner of descriptive prose. In this sense, *Northanger Abbey* strikes an attitude which does not essentially change" (622). Arguments for Austen's interest in the natural world as Romantic have been advanced, but they usually construct Austen as a late bloomer. Walton A. Litz, for example, argues that in *Mansfield Park* "a new feeling for external nature begins to emerge" (151), but not until *Persuasion* does the attempt come to fruition: "nature has ceased to be a mere backdrop; landscape is a structure of feeling which can express, and also modify, the minds of those who view it" (153).[4]

The question of nature in Austen has implications, then, for not only her canonical position but also her politics. Austen's treatment of nature and landscape is connected by critics to her supposed politics. Penny Gay, for example, writes that Austen's view of nature is that of an "*intelligent* conservative," firmly planted in eighteenth-century notions of "care and stewardship" ("Changing View" 47), "*dulce et utile*" ("Changing View" 52), and a social hierarchy rooted in the estate, which "ensures that all people associated with the land, from the lowliest labourers to pensioned dependents, from tenant farmers to the members of the 'great house,' are kept in health and comfort" ("Changing View" 47). My contribution to this debate is a consideration of how the representation of nature and animals advances Austen's feminist argument and her critique of the conservative social order. My argument builds on the rich tradition of feminist studies of Austen, particularly Margaret Kirkham's *Jane Austen, Feminism and Fiction*, Alison Sulloway's *Jane Austen and the Province of Womanhood*, and Claudia L. Johnson's *Jane Austen: Women, Politics, and the Novel*. Both Kirkham and Sulloway situate Austen alongside Enlightenment feminists such as Catharine Macaulay and Mary Wollstonecraft, and argue that Austen also emphasized women's rational abilities and the detrimental effects of the existing system of education. Johnson's influential study revisits the grounds of Marilyn Butler's argument for Austen on the side of the anti-Jacobins in "the war of ideas," and instead concludes that Austen's novels interrogate family and marriage and debunk conservative patriarchal myths. I also

---

[3]   Austen's status within the Romantic canon has been a contested one. See Anne K. Mellor's "Why Women Didn't Like Romanticism: The Views of Jane Austen and Mary Shelley" for an influential articulation of Austen as an anti-Romantic writer. A number of critics, however, challenge such a view. For example, see the special issue of *The Wordsworth Circle* edited by Gene W. Ruoff and studies such as Edward Neill's *The Politics of Jane Austen*, William H. Galperin's *The Historical Jane Austen*, William Deresiewicz's *Jane Austen and the Romantic Poets*, and essays by Beth Lau.

[4]   Penny Gay also argues that while Austen's treatment of nature is Augustan, *Persuasion* "opens views on a different world" ("Changing View" 61). For a similar teleology, see Alistair Duckworth's "Nature."

am indebted to the work of William Deresiewicz and Beth Lau, who convincingly demonstrate Austen's participation in Romanticism.

The case for Austen as a Romantic writer provides a broader context for my argument that our understanding of Austen's novels benefits from situating them in the historical context of the changing human-animal relationship.[5] Christine Kenyon-Jones's *Kindred Brutes: Animals in Romantic-Period Writing*, David Perkins's *Romanticism and Animal Rights*, and Onno Oerlemans's *Romanticism and the Materiality of Nature* have illuminated the important context of animal welfare and rights arguments for late eighteenth- and early nineteenth-century literary texts. These groundbreaking studies provided an important counter to earlier readings, which tended to reduce animals merely to symbols or stand-ins for oppressed humans (slaves, women, children, working classes).[6] As Christine Kenyon-Jones demonstrates, "in the late eighteenth century ... the association of animals with oppressed human groups moved out of the purely symbolic realm and became much more direct" (40). David Perkins's notion of "interweav[ing]" (*Romanticism and Animal Rights* 107) is productive in that it suggests the connections between anti-cruelty discourses, feminism, and abolitionism without reducing animals to substitutes for more important, that is, human agents. Similarly, Onno Oerlemans cautions that the focus on the "overlap" between "gender, race, and animality" in theory and literary criticism can "obscure the history of our actual understanding and treatment of animals, and our overwhelming tendency to ignore them as living, independent beings with some claims to natural rights" (67–68). A brief reading of Samuel Taylor Coleridge's "To a Young Ass, Its Mother Being Tethered Near It" (1794) may serve as an example of the treatment of animal rights alongside human rights.

The speaker in Coleridge's poem sees the animal as an individuated being with whom he has formed a connection over time: "oft with gentle hand I give thee bread, / And clap thy ragged coat, and pat thy head" (3–4). The donkey is represented as experiencing physical and emotional pain: "But what thy dulled spirits hath dismay'd, / That never thou dost sport along the glade? / And ... / That earthward still thy moveless head is hung?" (5–8). Moreover, the speaker imagines a mutual exchange: "How *askingly* its footsteps hither bend? / It seems to say, 'And have I then *one* friend?'" (23–24). Rather than dismissing the poem for its anthropomorphism, Oerlemans argues that "the representation of animals in the romantic period can enable us to see that the concept of anthropomorphism, and the consequent prohibition of it, are inherently features of anthropocentrism" (70). For the insistence that animals are *not* like humans is usually in the service of

---

[5] See my essay, "'Does not it make you think of Cowper?': Rural Sport in Jane Austen and her Contemporaries" in Beth Lau's *Fellow Romantics: Male and Female British Writers, 1790–1835*.

[6] See Moira Ferguson's *Animal Advocacy and Englishwomen, 1780–1900: Patriots, Nation, and Empire*, for example, or G.J. Barker-Benfield, who describes animal reform as "surrogate feminism" (236) in *The Culture of Sensibility*.

reducing—rather than enlarging—animals' liberty. As Alexander Wilson suggests in *The Culture of Nature*, anthropomorphism "can be a radical strategy in a culture … where the frontier between the human and non-human is well policed" (68). The poem's anthropomorphism challenges not only the human-animal divide but also the social hierarchies which it legitimizes, indeed naturalizes. The speaker addresses the animal as a "poor little Foal of an oppressed race!" (1) and "hail[s]" it "*Brother*" (26). The language resonates with abolitionist politics, and the poem makes a parallel between the positions of animals, slaves, and the poor, since the speaker recognizes that the donkey's "piteous … lot" (15)—"Chain'd to a log within a narrow spot, / Where the close-eaten grass is scarcely seen, / While sweet around her waves the tempting green!" (16–18)—mirrors her owner's fate:

> Poor Ass! thy master should have learnt to show
> Pity—best taught by fellowship of Woe!
> For much I fear me that *He* lives like thee,
> Half famish'd in a land of Luxury! (19–22)

Rather than reading the donkey as a safe substitute for oppressed humans, Oerlemans claims that the "poem's sympathy for the foal is to be taken literally" (83) even though its "utopianism … will still appear to most of us, no doubt, as embarrassingly naive" (84). Indeed, this is precisely the response that the poem anticipates and repudiates: "I hail thee *Brother*—spite of the fool's scorn!" (26). When we read Austen in this context, Fanny Price's thinking of a horse as her "friend" (*MP* 41) takes on significant meaning. Such a moment participates in the literary conversations that recognized animals as subjects.

Kenyon-Jones, Perkins, and Oerlemans have opened up new ways of thinking about animals in Romantic-era writing. The topic of animals in eighteenth-century literature has been addressed in Frank Palmeri's edited collection *Humans and Other Animals in Eighteenth-Century British Culture* (2006) and Laura Brown's *Homeless Dogs and Melancholy Apes* (2010).[7] Brown, locating the "rise of the animal in the modern imagination" (1) in the eighteenth-century "discovery of the hominoid ape and the rise of widespread bourgeois pet keeping" (20), recognizes the profound instability of the human-animal relationship in a number of the period's literary texts, and "their tendency to surprise, to invert, to challenge, or to experiment with expected modes of order and stable structures of meaning" (17). Austen is not included in the above studies on animals. So far, there has been only one article on the topic treating *Mansfield Park*: Sally B. Palmer's "Slipping the Leash: Lady Bertram's Lapdog." Palmer situates the novel in the early nineteenth-century history of pets and explores the sociopolitical significance of Lady Bertram's pug. Our conclusions about animals in Austen, however, differ. Palmer argues that "Austen rejects the sentimental anthropomorphism of other Romantic-era writers that attributes noble characteristics and human emotions to animals and

---

[7]   Also see the special issue of *The Eighteenth Century: Theory and Interpretation* dedicated to animals in the eighteenth century, edited by Lucinda Cole.

attempts to enter into their lives and consciousness. She would be aghast at modern views of the animal kingdom suggesting that animals have rights" (par. 15).

J. David Grey's statement that Austen "pays little attention to pets and animals" (324) has remained largely unchallenged. In fact, the absence of the animal world has been cited as one of Austen's limitations. In an essay entitled "Jane Austen's Anthropocentrism," Joel Weinsheimer claims that "the central defect of Jane Austen's novels is that they study man in a vacuum" (138). Referring to Austen's description of *Pride and Prejudice* as "too light & bright & sparkling" and "want[ing] ... a long Chapter —of sense if it could be had, if not, of solemn specious nonsense—about something unconnected with the story" (*Letters* 203), Weinsheimer suggests that "Perhaps what we lack in reading Jane Austen is a chapter on whales, one that would establish the otherness of things, their primal indifference to human feelings and judgments" (134). It is difficult to imagine the introduction of whales in landlocked novels such as *Emma*, *Northanger Abbey*, and *Sense and Sensibility*. Certainly, Austen was aware of an animal world beyond the one indigenous to her corner of England. In a letter dated February 11, 1802, she characterized London as "the Regions of Wit, Elegance, fashion, Elephants & Kangaroons" (80). In April 1811, Austen wrote to her sister Cassandra of her visit to London, in particular the British Gallery and the Liverpool Museum, which was "then on display at 22 Piccadilly" (*Letters* 402, n1). The Liverpool Museum boasted among its natural history exhibits "the mighty cameleopard (stuffed), thirty-two species of monkeys (from the pig-tailed baboon to the Palatine monkey), the head of a rhinoceros, a striped hyena, a termites' nest (ten feet in height)" (Nokes 375). Austen reports the visit to the gallery and the museum with some distance: "I had some amusement at each, tho' my preference for Men & Women, always inclines me to attend more to the company than the sight" (179). Weinsheimer quotes this passage in support of his argument that what is "missing" (134) from Austen is "the nonhuman" (133), but Austen shifts her focus from the "sight" to the "company" at both the gallery and the museum. Moreover, read in the context of John Berger's *About Looking*, we might see in Austen's letter not disinterest in the nonhuman but a recognition that the "sight" of a collection of imperial specimens reveals more about the spectator, the "company." Berger argues that "the zoo cannot but disappoint" (26). "In the accompanying ideology" of the zoo, "animals are always the observed": "What we know about them is an index of our power, and thus an index of what separates us from them. The more we know, the further away they are" (Berger 14). Austen, in looking at the observers, dismantles the relations of power between human and nonhuman animals.

Austen's correspondence registers her interest in the nonhuman. Alison Sulloway notes that "one of Austen's most charming techniques for disrupting depression was her habit of personification" (106). Her letters to Cassandra personified "various household goods" (Sulloway 107) and, in letters to nieces and nephews, she personified animals: "Edw:ᵈ desires his Love to You, to Grandpapa, to Anna, to little Edw:ᵈ, to Aunt James & Uncle James, & he hopes all your Turkies & Ducks & Chicken & Guinea Fowls are very well" (45). These personifications also suggest that Austen considered animals as feeling beings and that she had affection for them. When she writes of horses stalling on a journey through London, she does not speak in terms of animal obstinacy demanding a firm human hand; rather she sympathetically attributes the behavior to the difficulty of the road and the animal's pain: "a load of fresh gravel made it a formidable Hill to them, & they refused the collar;—I beleive there was a sore shoulder to irritate" (184). Austen also identified with animals' objectification. In a letter updating Cassandra on the preparations to move from Steventon to Bath, Austen comments, "My father's old Ministers are already deserting him to pay their court to his Son; the brown Mare, which as well as the black was to devolve on James at our removal, has not had patience to wait for that, & has settled herself even now at Deane" (71). Making it seem as if the horses enthusiastically participate in the dispersion of themselves as property, Austen's joke gives vent to her feelings about her own lack of choice in the move to Bath.[8] Another letter to Cassandra reports, "James went to Winchester fair yesterday, & bought a new horse; & Mary has got a new maid—two great acquisitions, one comes from Folly Farm, is about five years old, used to draw, & thought very pretty; & the other is neice to Dinah at Kintbury" (50). Both horse and servant are objects to be "acquired" and Austen plays with the interchangeability of horse and girl: pretty and familiar with drawing can describe the workhorse as well as an accomplished girl!

Even at a young age Austen treated the topic of animal cruelty. In "The Generous Curate," a "moral tale" in the first volume of the juvenilia, the Curate is remiss in providing Young Williams with the promised education. Young Williams "knew nothing more at the age of 18 than what a twopenny Dame's School in the village could teach him." Austen connects Williams's ignorance with animal abuse, and the Curate's inadequacy as an educator with his failure to treat animal cruelty seriously: Williams entertains himself by "flinging Stones at a Duck or putting brickbats into his Benefactor's bed, but these innocent efforts of wit were considered by that good Man rather the effects of a lively imagination, than of anything bad in his Nature" (*J* 95). The Curate fails to recognize one of the prime eighteenth-century lessons: cruelty to animals leads to cruelty to humans, as per William Hogarth's *The Four Stages of Cruelty*. The narrator underscores the lesson with the pointed contrast of Williams, the eldest brother, a sailor "destined for Newfoundland, where his promising and amiable disposition had procured him many freinds among the Natives, and from whence he regularly sent home a large Newfoundland Dog every Month to his family" (*J* 94). The brother's good nature is marked not only by his friendship with people but also his recognition of an affectionate bond between humans and pets. As demonstrated by Keith Thomas and J.H. Plumb, pet-keeping gained prominence in the eighteenth century. Living with pets opened up new ways of thinking about

---

[8]   See Claire Tomalin's biography (Chapter 16) on Austen's reaction to the announcement of the move.

the human-animal relationship and the proximity, rather than the inseparable gulf, between humans and animals.

Austen would have been aware that the status of animals was a question of considerable political and literary import. She likely would have heard about the parliamentary debates surrounding anti-bullbaiting in 1800 and 1802 and the proposed anti-cruelty bill in 1809, which "was widely reported in the press and subsequently published as a pamphlet" (Kenyon-Jones 80). We can be certain that Austen was conversant with anti-cruelty arguments through her reading of William Cowper, one of her favorite poets, who was also a favorite with writers of animal rights discourses like Joseph Ritson (90–91, 220) and Thomas Young (36, 85, 91), who invoked his poetry in support of their position. Being familiar with "the richness of the present age" of poetry (*P* 108), in the manner of *Persuasion*'s Captain Benwick and Anne Elliot, would have included a familiarity with Romantic ideas of animals. And Austen would have known a tradition of women's writing on the treatment of animals. Sylvia Bowerbank's *Speaking for Nature* traces the beginnings of ecological and ecofeminist movements in texts by seventeenth- and eighteenth- century women writers, and demonstrates that "during the late eighteenth century, women produced an important body of texts that ... denounced the oppression of animals" (21). These literary sources of influence (Cowper, the Romantic poets, and women writers) are addressed in more detail in the subsequent chapters. This book is the first full-length study of animals in Austen's writing. I argue that Austen aligns the objectification of nature with the objectification of women and, more specifically, the hunting, shooting, and racing of animals with the domination of women. Austen draws parallels between the positions of women and animals, and her uneasy marriage plots critique women's subordination as part of nature.

William Deresiewicz, in his perceptive *Jane Austen and the Romantic Poets*, demonstrates that Fanny Price's, Emma Woodhouse's, and Anne Elliot's "spontaneous emotional responsiveness to nature ... is in no way criticized or ironized" (20), but, I would add, neither is it in the earlier novels. While Deresiewicz distinguishes *Mansfield Park*, *Emma*, and *Persuasion* from Austen's early "Augustan" phase (*Northanger Abbey*, *Sense and Sensibility*, and *Pride and Prejudice*), I see Austen's representation of nature as consistent. Fanny Price's love of the "evergreen" (244) in *Mansfield Park*, for example, is strikingly similar to Marianne Dashwood's mourning of the trees at Norland in *Sense and Sensibility*, and Austen's criticism of rural sport, rooted in a connection to nature, is consistent from her earliest to her final work. Accordingly, the following chapters do not discuss each novel in chronological turn; rather, I have chosen a structure of patterns: the satire of sportsmen; male characters who conversely are distanced from sport; the heroines' closeness to animals and nature; and food as a marker of class and sexual politics. The book's examination of these patterns includes Austen's correspondence, early writings, short fiction, and poetry alongside the six novels. I also offer brief analyses of specific films or televisuals treating an aspect of the patterns I see operating in Austen's work. In looking at changes made to Austen's originals, my intention is not to invoke the problematic "fidelity" standard.[9] Rather, I turn to specific choices made in adapting a scene or character which allow me to draw out something in Austen's argument about nature and animals. Sometimes, the changes made to the original text throw into relief elements of Austen's texts that have been previously overlooked. For example, what is at stake when Mr. Woodhouse is transformed into an enthusiastic eater in Amy Heckerling's *Clueless*? Or when the 1995 *Pride and Prejudice*, directed by Simon Langton, adds scenes of Mr. Darcy shooting with Mr. Bingley?

Chapter 1 examines eighteenth- and early nineteenth-century animal rights discourses. In particular, I focus on the connections made between the human-animal hierarchy and other social hierarchies. While male writers tended not to interrogate the gender hierarchy, instead re-inscribing female subordination as natural, Enlightenment women writers such as Catharine Macaulay and Mary Wollstonecraft drew attention to the system of education shaping women's so-called nature. It is significant that texts on education by Macaulay and Wollstonecraft protest the treatment of women as well as the treatment of animals. Recognizing that the subordination of women within patriarchy is rooted in the ideology of women's proximity to the natural and physical realms, rather than the rational (masculine), both Macaulay and Wollstonecraft rethink the social construction of not only women's but also animals' "nature." I conclude the chapter by turning to Austen's anxieties about the "natural" roles of marriage and motherhood. The marriage plot which structures the novels also is counterpointed in significant ways: Austen suggestively casts marriage and maternity as animalizing, and thus disempowering, women.

Chapter 2 places *Northanger Abbey*, *Sense and Sensibility*, and *Mansfield Park* in the context of eighteenth- and early nineteenth-century debates on rural sport and argues for Austen's development of William Cowper's anti-sport position. Austen consistently satirizes what Stephen Deuchar has called the "sporting ideal" (25). Rather than presenting hunters as noble, patriotic, physically and mentally strong, as did defenders of sport, she characterizes them as indulgent and unintelligent, and she pits hunting against reading and domestic affection. For example, *Northanger Abbey*'s John Thorpe boasts of "never read[ing] novels" (43) and "shooting parties, in which he had killed more birds (though without having one good shot) than all his companions together" (63), and *Mansfield Park*'s Mr. Rushworth, "ignorant in … books" (233), bores Maria Bertram with "repeated details of his day's sport, good or bad" (135). Austen has her heroines appreciate nature, and contradicts the idea that it is sport which brings its practitioners closer to nature. Austen's work clearly is aligned with the anti-sport position which

---

[9]   George Bluestone reminds us: "The filmist becomes not a translator for an established author, but a new author in his own right" (62). Brian McFarlane argues that the fidelity criterion is problematic in its privileging of the literary text above the film, its "depend[ing] on a notion of the text as having … a single, correct 'meaning'" (8), and its limiting of the film's intertextuality to the literary text.

critiques sport for reifying class hierarchies. Further, Austen establishes parallels between the positions of women and animals in patriarchy. We see this clearly in the predatory actions of Willoughby in *Sense and Sensibility* and Henry Crawford in *Mansfield Park*, and there are also implications for the courtship plots as a whole, troubling their conclusions.

Chapter 3 focuses on *Persuasion* and *Pride and Prejudice*. While both novels develop the patterns established in Chapter 2, they also contain male characters who are "too cool about sporting" (*P* 236), preferring books instead. In *Persuasion*, Captain Benwick plays a significant role in the novel: he "never shot" (141) and is aligned with the heroine through their joint discussion of Romantic poetry and their roles as healers of emotional and physical trauma. The novel's emphasis on the beauties and restorative influence of nature contributes to its anti-sport argument. But while the concluding marriage between Anne and Captain Wentworth stays within the hierarchies of the sporting world, the relationship between Elizabeth and Darcy in *Pride and Prejudice* evades this world and its attendant social hierarchies. The novel's narrative of education is one of ethics, moving beyond narrow self-interest to consideration for others. These ethical values shape the hero and heroine's relationship, and are reflected in their connection to nature. Elizabeth longs to see the Lake District. Darcy is distanced from the hunting and shooting worlds; instead the novel depicts him as sharing the privileges of fishing with Mr. Gardiner at Pemberley, an estate whose harmony with the natural environment is emphasized: Elizabeth "had never seen a place for which nature had done more, or where natural beauty had been so little counteracted by an awkward taste" (271). It is in this natural setting, their joint future home, that Elizabeth and Darcy's relationship begins to transform. And while Bingley and Jane's plot is resolved by a drawing-room proposal in tandem with a shooting expedition with Mr. Bennet, Darcy and Elizabeth come to a full understanding of each other in fully reciprocal conversation during two long walks.

Chapter 4, "Evergreen," takes as its point of departure recent postcolonial readings of *Mansfield Park*. Edward Said's argument that both Austen and Fanny Price "finally subscribe" (62) to Sir Thomas's imperialist project has been faulted by a number of critics for overestimating "the order, the beauties" (Said 79) of the Bertram family home at Mansfield Park. Recent postcolonial readings arguably fall into a similar error when they posit Fanny Price as a national heroine, whose rejoicing in the trees at Mansfield is seen as a celebration of England's imperial might. Nature in *Mansfield Park* is hardly one of simple poise and harmony. The novel is filled with references to rural sport debates, as Chapter 2 demonstrates, and nature is used and abused by everyone except the heroine. Fanny Price is consistently associated with nature, also there to be used by others at their convenience or ignored. Feminist criticism has demonstrated that she is treated like a slave by the Bertrams, but it needs to be added that Fanny is also treated as an animal. The only Austen novel which includes a pet among its cast of characters, *Mansfield Park* charts the ideological connections between women, slaves, and animals. Fanny Price's rejoicing in the "evergreen" is not to be taken synonymously with "Green England," but rather is in opposition to the nation. The chapter contextualizes its argument about *Mansfield Park* with a comparative analysis of *Sense and Sensibility*.

Describing the 31-year old Louisa Bridges, a baronet's daughter, Austen writes, "She looked remarkably well (legacies are very wholesome diet)" (*Letters* 126). Chapter 5, "Legacies and Diets," examines Austen's representations of food. For Austen, food demarcates social status based on wealth, class, and gender. The production and consumption of food is one of the most direct ways in which humans interact with nonhuman nature. Onno Oerlemans argues that early nineteenth-century debates about diet and vegetarianism are also debates "about the place of humankind in nature" (103). Austen drew on late eighteenth- and early nineteenth-century dietary discourses and uses food in her novels to comment on the construction of the human-nature dualism and associated male dominance and social inequities. That the human-nature dualism relegates to object status not only nature but also women is developed most thoroughly in *Emma*. The only novel which does not include hunters, *Emma*'s exploration of the human relationship to nature is focused instead on agriculture. Here the marriage plot is framed by an agricultural, rather than sporting, plot; that both women and nature yield to men— that is, submit and produce—is suggested by the novel's time scheme, which, as Juliet McMaster has noted, is "in harmony with woman's biological rhythms in conception, gestation and childbirth" ("Children in *Emma*" 62). Significantly, as we will see in the next chapter, the absence of the marriage plot in "Sanditon" is matched by an independence of nature; the overturning of the carriage in the famous opening is one of the ways in which the fragment destabilizes the human-nature relationship and associated hierarchies.

Chapter 6 focuses on Austen's final texts: "Sanditon," abandoned in March 1817, and "When Winchester races first took their beginning," a poem written a few days before her death. "Sanditon" has long been seen as radically different in terms of landscape, while the poem largely has been ignored. In my view, Austen's final texts are the culmination of her argument about nature. Jane Austen, writing with the consciousness of time running out, perhaps is more overt in her critique, but she treats the agency of animals and nature throughout her oeuvre. Further, the oppression of nature and animals is implicitly critiqued by its connection to the heroines, who are rational, feeling beings but are treated as objects by patriarchal society. Austen recognized that to write the human is also to write the animal, and that "the discourse of speciesism ... can be used to mark *any* social other" (Wolfe 7).

Chapter 1
The Animal Question and Women

Poor Animal, she will be worn out before she is thirty.

(*Letters* 336)

William Hogarth's *The Four Stages of Cruelty* (1751) figures prominently in cultural histories of the human–animal relationship in the eighteenth century. In Kathryn Shevelow's *For the Love of Animals: The Rise of the Animal Protection Movement*, Hogarth's engravings mark a "point of transition," the "moment at which earlier, scattered, individual expressions of concern for the abuse of animals began to coalesce into a large collectivity" (146). Hogarth spelled out his didactic intention in the "Autobiographical Notes":

> The four stages of cruelty, were done in hopes of preventing in some degree that cruel treatment of poor Animals which makes the streets of London more disagreeable to the human mind, than any thing what ever, the very describing of which gives pain. … it could not be done in too strong a manner, as the most stony hearts were meant to be affected by them. (Qtd. in *Engravings by Hogarth* n.pag.)

The narrative charts Tom Nero's progression from torturing animals as a boy ("The First Stage") to abusing animals as an adult in his work as a coachman ("The Second Stage") to thieving and murder ("Cruelty in Perfection"). The final engraving, "Cruelty Rewarded," focuses on Tom Nero's executed body as the object of medical dissection. Scalpels and knives, variations of the instruments of torture used on animals in the first and second engravings, are now turned on him. And, in a reversal of the human–animal hierarchy, a human body becomes meat as a dog feasts on Tom Nero's heart. Given the text's emphasis on the protagonist's corruption, this latter reversal seems more of a comment on Tom's brutishness rather than a leveling of the human–animal hierarchy. Hogarth's series is exemplary of the eighteenth-century moralist argument for humans' indirect obligation to animals, since it vividly suggests that cruelty to animals leads to cruelty to humans. While animals are similar to humans in their sentience—"the describing" of "the Creature's pain" in turn "gives pain"—Hogarth's primary focus is on the human agents and the debasement of their humanity. The class dimensions of Hogarth's print have received much commentary. The male figure who seeks to intervene in the animal abuse in the first engraving is markedly middle-class in opposition to Tom Nero and the other participants in cruelty.[1]

---

[1]   Robert Malcolmson, among others, has argued that anti-cruelty discourses mask class politics. However, "the continuity of the modern humane movement with seventeenth- and eighteenth-century thought on the ethics of human relationships with animals should not

However, as Shevelow argues, "Although those who physically perpetrate the acts depicted in the first and second stages are all members of the laboring classes, the upper classes share culpability for the violence on their behalf" (131). Members of the professional classes overcrowd Tom Nero's hackney coach, presumably to save money, without regard for the consequences—the excessive burden on the horse, who, "subdu'd by Labour," collapses, and is then subjected to his "cruel Master's rage." Similarly, while the "tender Lamb," already "faint" from exhaustion, "dies beneath the Blows" of an "inhuman Wretch," its death implicates the much larger system of food production. And in the final engraving Hogarth expands the scope of cruelty to the "state-sanctioned violence of the executioner and the surgeons" (Shevelow 139). Cruelty pervades and implicates the lower as well as the upper ranks of society in Hogarth's engravings.

Of particular interest to this study is that Tom Nero's progression of cruelty from animal to human victims takes a gendered form. Tom murders his pregnant girlfriend; the maid was "betray'd" into "lawless Love" and "soon Crime to Crime succeeds": she steals from her Mistress for her lover, who then kills her. Eighteenth-century women writers developed the connections between violence towards animals and violence towards women. For example, in Mary Wollstonecraft's *The Wrongs of Woman: or, Maria*, the heroine's brother advances along lines similar to those in Hogarth's didactic tale: "from tormenting insects and animals … [he] became the despot of his brothers, and still more of his sisters" (1:124). In Frances Burney's *Camilla*, a novel to which Jane Austen subscribed, the heroine is confronted with the spectacle of monkeys who, with the aid of "fierce blows" (429), are trained to play music, and bullfinches who are similarly beaten into "learn[ing]"(492). When Camilla, "pained" by the bullfinch keeper's "sever[ity]," "inquired by what means he had obtained such authority," the man "with a significant wag of the head, brutally answered": "By the true old way, Miss; I licks him. … everything's the better for a little beating, as I tells my wife" (492). The parallel between the treatment of animals and women is made explicit, and the animal abuse sheds disturbing light on the heroine's painful education plot. Austen was aware of animal welfare discourses and, I argue, drew on them in her work.

The status of animals, or the Animal Question, to use Paola Cavalieri's coinage, was the subject of rigorous scientific, philosophical, and political debate during Austen's lifetime. Discussions of animals in cultural history, contemporary theory, and literary criticism locate in the eighteenth century a significant shift in the human–animal relationship. The founding of animal protection organizations such as the Society for the Prevention of Cruelty to Animals in 1824 (which became the Royal Society for the Prevention of Cruelty to Animals in 1840) and, closer to our own day, the Great Ape Project in 1993 are connected to the animal

---

be forgotten" (Maehle 100). Similarly, literary critic David Perkins states, "No important argument has yet been adduced, on the question of right conduct toward animals, that was not already urged in the eighteenth century" ("Cowper's Hares" 58). Diana Donald (224) also challenges the argument that anti-cruelty discourses are class politics in disguise, as does Hilda Kean (31–32, 36).

welfare and rights movements of the eighteenth century and to the early steps towards legal protection of animals that took place during this time.[2] In 1800 and 1802 William Wilberforce put forth anti-bullbaiting bills, both defeated in the House of Commons, while 1809 saw the introduction of an anti-cruelty bill by Lord Erskine in the House of Lords, "the first of its kind ever to be debated in any Western legislature" (Kenyon-Jones 79). Given that Erskine's "address was widely reported in the press and subsequently published as a pamphlet" (Kenyon-Jones 80), we may assume that Austen would have read or heard about it. While Erskine was defeated, and it took until 1822 for the passing of the Martin's Act, the first anti-cruelty bill (specifically to "Prevent Cruel and Improper Treatment of Cattle"), its ultimate success is inseparable from the history of animal welfare and rights in the eighteenth century.[3]

The seventeenth-century philosopher René Descartes's categorization of animals as machines, without souls or reasoning and feeling capacities and, hence, exempt from claims to moral consideration, was challenged on a number of fronts in the eighteenth century.[4] For example, Richard Dean, in *An Essay on the Future Life of Brutes. Introduced with Observations upon Evil, its Nature and Origin* (1768), sought to "confute ... De Carte" and "the Absurdity of the Doctrine, which teaches that Brutes are unintelligent Machines" (2:xix–xx): "dumb Animals are liable to Infelicity as well as Men: ... they have their Pains and Sicknesses, suffer many Sorrows from internal Disorders, and many Pangs from external Injuries, and finally languish, decay, and die as he himself does" (1:2–3). Man should "consider, that as Brutes have Sensibility, they are capable of Pain, feel every Bang, and Cut, and Stab, as much as he himself does, some of them perhaps more" (2:104). Dean also argues for animal souls: "Certain it is, that a future Life of Brutes cannot be absolutely denied, without impeaching the Attributes of God. It reflects upon his Goodness, to suppose that he subjects to Pains, and Sorrows, such a Number of Beings, whom he never designs to beatify" (2:73).[5] Arguments

---

[2]   The Great Ape Project seeks to establish a United Nations Declaration granting nonhuman great apes the status of individuals, with basic legal rights of life, liberty, and freedom from torture. Legal rights for great apes have been successfully advanced in Spain (2008). See similar advocacy for whales and dolphins in the 2010 Declaration of Rights for Cetaceans.

[3]   See Chapter 3 in Kenyon-Jones's *Kindred Brutes* for a detailed account, and also Hilda Kean's *Animal Rights: Political and Social Change in Britain since 1800*.

[4]   There are excellent overviews of this history by Shevelow, Keith Thomas, Andreas Holger Maehle, Aaron Garrett, and John Simons.

[5]   John Hildrop, in *Free Thoughts upon the Brute Creation* (1742–43), also argued for animal souls and kindness to animals. In contrast, Humphrey Primatt contended that animals had a right to just treatment on earth *because* they were barred from the justice of the afterlife: "as we have no authority to declare, and no testimony from heaven to assure us, that there is a state of recompence for suffering Brutality, we will suppose there is none; and from this very supposition, we rationally infer that cruelty to a brute is an injury irreparable" (42–43).

for animal souls, animal sentience, and animal language were advanced, all with important implications for the question of the ethical treatment of animals, ranging from indirect to direct obligation to animals. Andreas Holger Maehle summarizes this debate: "Either *indirect* obligations towards animals were constructed on the basis of direct duties to God, to other human beings or to oneself; or animal rights were conceded by analogy to human rights, the consequence being *direct* obligations towards animals. Whereas the latter argument appeared after 1750, the former can be traced back to the early eighteenth century" (91).

Harriet Ritvo reminds us that "Wherever we look in nineteenth-century British culture … the role of animals appears not only multiple but contested. … the search for a single generalization or a single unfolding narrative may be intrinsically misguided" ("Animals in Nineteenth-Century Britain" 122). It is beyond the scope of this study to do justice to the complex history of the human–animal relationship. My aim here is to pursue two interrelated strands in this history—sentience as the basis for direct ethical obligation to animals and the connections drawn between cruelty to animals and cruelty to humans—and to read Jane Austen within this context. Markman Ellis writes, "Just as abolitionists sought to reposition Africans as thinking and feeling people, the animal-cruelty campaigners sought to refigure the cultural construction of brute creation, showing them to be not things but animals possessed with feeling and thus endowed with certain rights" (107). I argue that Austen's novels resonate with late eighteenth- and early nineteenth-century discourses about animals as thinking, feeling beings and with discourses which connect the animal question to abolitionism and feminism. Fanny Price in *Mansfield Park* is neglected and abused, treated without feeling by her family. All of Austen's heroines, even those whose immediate contexts are more loving, find themselves perilously close to the status of animals in a culture which denied women citizenship, and the novels explore the pain of their subordination and vindicate their feeling, thinking natures. Focusing on discourses about animals, I seek to contribute to the discussion of Austen as engaged with the revolutionary politics of her time. Christine Kenyon-Jones argues that at the end of the eighteenth century, "the issue of animal cruelty became associated with questions of rights and citizenship": "Since animals could be seen to be metonymically or synecdochically linked to … oppressed human groups, they were drawn into the debate, and the continuum of better treatment and rights was also, to some extent, applied to them" (40).

Eighteenth-century discourses of animal welfare and rights emphasized animal sentience. We see this clearly in Humphrey Primatt, one of the first to present an "alternative to the concept of a merely indirect obligation towards animals" (Maehle 94). In *A Dissertation on the Duty of Mercy and Sin of Cruelty to Brute Animals* (first published in 1776 and reprinted in the 1820s), he argues that "a man can have no natural right to abuse and torment a beast, merely because a beast has not the *mental* powers of a man" (12). He dethrones reason as the central determinant of human–animal relations, and, instead, emphasizes the commonality of sentience: "Pain is pain, whether it be inflicted on man or on beast" (7). The ability to feel pain entitles animals to "FOOD, REST, and TENDER USAGE"

(147), but "not only their necessary Wants, and what is absolutely their Demand on the principles of strict Justice, but also their Ease and Comfort, and what they have a reasonable and equitable Claim to, on the principles of Mercy and Compassion" (202). Animals, according to Primatt, have a right to "Happiness" (202).[6] Similarly, Thomas Young's *An Essay on Humanity to Animals* (1798) emphasizes that "animals are endued with a capability of perceiving pleasure and pain" (8). The most frequently invoked challenge to the Cartesian mind-body and human–animal duality is that of Jeremy Bentham in his 1789 *Introduction to the Principles of Morals and Legislation*: "a full-grown horse or dog, is beyond comparison a more rational, as well as a more conversible animal, than an infant of a day, or a week, or even a month, old. But suppose the case were otherwise, what would it avail? the question is not, Can they *reason*? nor, Can they *talk*? but, Can they *suffer*?" (283). Some eighteenth-century writers on the ethical treatment of animals extend their arguments to vegetarianism. Joseph Ritson, in *An Essay on Abstinence from Animal Food as a Moral Duty* (1802), links the cruelty of rural sport to meat consumption: the prior is a prejudice and a "custom" (97, 220), just as "animal food [is] not natural to man" (41). John Oswald's *The Cry of Nature; Or, An Appeal to Mercy and to Justice, on Behalf of the Persecuted Animals* (1791) also includes a case for vegetarianism alongside a denunciation of rural sport. These texts "provided ways of showing how human behaviour could be mediated through temperance and non-violence" (Morton, *Shelley and the Revolution in Taste* 41).

In these texts, animal suffering matters in and of itself, but is also seen as intersecting with other forms of oppression. Primatt protests human slavery alongside animal suffering: "the *white* man (notwithstanding the barbarity of custom and prejudice) can have no right … to enslave and tyrannize over a *black* man" (11). Slavery is also included by George Nicholson (*On the Primeval Diet* 223) and John Lawrence in *A Philosophical and Practical Treatise on Horses and on the Moral Duties of Men towards the Brute Creation* (127). The title page of *The Cry of Nature* announces its author, John Oswald, as a "Member of the Club des Jacobines," aligning the animal cause with other revolutionary causes. And Ritson links cruelty to animals to social hierarchies:

> Man, who is every-where a tyrant or a slave, delights to inflict on each sensible being within his power the treatment he receives from his own superiors: as the negro revenges the cruelty of his owner upon the innocent dog. Every animal, wild or tame, of which he becomes the possessor, is his property, his prisoner, his slave; to be treated with caprice and cruelty, and put to death at his pleasure. (100)

---

[6]   Primatt's text contravenes the claim that all anti-cruelty discourses are more about social regulation and "effective labour discipline" (Malcolmson 89). Primatt explicitly draws attention to cruelty "of every class and denomination" (77): his examples include sport associated with the lower classes (cockfighting and bullbaiting) as well as the sport of the upper classes ("to chace a Stag, to hunt a Fox, or course a Hare"), the mistreatment of horses, and upper-class culinary privileges ("to roast a Lobster, or to crimp a Fish") (75). See footnote 1.

Thomas Young, in *An Essay on Humanity to Animals* (1798), writes that "cruelty to animals ... tends to render those who practise it, cruel towards their own species": "humanity towards animals" has "an important connection with humanity towards mankind" (3). He situates animal welfare alongside other claims for social justice, "the sufferings of the prisoner ... the condition of the poor ... [and] the abolition of the slave trade" (2).

While these writers draw connections between the treatment of animals and other systems of oppression, they tend to overlook women's subordination. Oswald "hope[s]" for the "day ... when the growing sentiment of peace and good-will towards men will also embrace, in a wide circle of benevolence, the lower orders of life" (ii), but the dawn he envisions does not bring gender equality. The frontispiece engraving to *The Cry of Nature* shows a deer mourning a fawn while Nature, in young and naked female form, averts her eyes in sorrow: "The butcher's knife hath laid low the delight of a fond dam & the darling of Nature is now stretched in gore upon the ground." The speaker has "listen[ed]" to the "plea[s]" (38) of the "mother of every living thing" (44), and mediates her appeal to the reader. "Nefarious science" with "ruffian violence interrogate[s] trembling nature; ... plunge[s] into her maternal bosom the butcher knife" (Oswald 33), and Mother Nature is dependent on male intervention to save her. Moreover, while Oswald links carnivorism to the class hierarchy, his vegetarianism does not challenge the gender hierarchy. Nature is an eroticized temptress and offers herself for male consumption:

> And innocently mayest thou indulge the desires which Nature so potently provokes; for see! the trees are overcharged with fruit; the bending branches seem to supplicate for relief; the mature orange, the ripe apple, the mellow peach invoke thee, as it were, to save them from falling to the ground, from dropping into corruption. They will smile in thy hand; and, blooming as the rosy witchcraft of thy bride, they will sue thee to press them to thy lip; in thy mouth they will melt not inferior the famed ambrosia of the gods. (22–23)

Conventional gender roles also are at work in John Frank Newton's *The Return to Nature*, as evident in the domestic scene he sketches to dramatize carnivorism's fateful consequences of illness and death:

> Recently has he lost his best companion; the spotless mother of his children; her who was the repository of his cares and his secrets; who at each return to his threshold found no words but kind ones for him. Has she then suddenly disappeared, who so late was the cheerful and affectionate centre around which the whole family revolved; and who has left the question forever undecided whether she contributed more largely to the comfort and pleasure of the father, or of the children. (153)

For Newton, the "Return to Nature" entails a return to a clearly delineated gender system:

The male broad-shouldered, dignified, erect; his muscles every where strongly pronounced; his sinewy form gradually lessening from the shoulders to the feet; in every limb, vigour and elasticity. The woman more than beautiful; her eyes sparkling with mirth, or brimming with sweetness; happy in her own existence, and increasing the happiness of all around her. (147–48)

Similarly, in the work of Jean-Jacques Rousseau, liberty from social prejudice and a return to natural principles, including ethical concern for animals, does not translate into equality of men and women. Rather, "it is part of the order of nature that the woman obey the man" (*Emile* 407) and, in accordance with nature, the animal kingdom reflects the gender system. For example, Rousseau supports his point that woman is by nature sexually coy: "I have already noticed that affected and provocative refusals are common to almost all females, even among animals, even when they are most disposed to give themselves. One has to have never observed their wiles not to agree with this" (*Emile* 359). Similarly, male sexual jealousy "appears to depend so closely on nature that it is hard to believe that it does not come from it. And the example of the animals, several of whom are jealous to the point of fury, seems unanswerably to establish that it does come from nature. Is it men's opinion which teaches cocks to tear one another apart and bulls to fight to the death?" (*Emile* 429). While animal welfare writers focus on human agents shaping blood sports, Rousseau here recruits sport into the service of the gender system. This is surprising since, in *Discourse on the Origin and Foundations of Inequality Among Men*, Rousseau's ethical system does include animals: "since [animals] share to some extent in our nature by virtue of the sentient quality with which they are endowed, one will judge that they should also participate in natural right, and that man is subject to some sort of duties towards them" (36). Rod Preece credits Rousseau as one of the leading voices on behalf of animals in the Enlightenment period. However, Rousseau's philosophy, as Nathaniel Wolloch emphasizes, prescribes limits to duties towards nonhuman beings. According to Rousseau, animals have "the right not to be needlessly mistreated" ("Discourse" 36), except "in the legitimate instance where, if [man's] preservation being involved, he is obliged to give preference to himself" ("Discourse" 35). Legitimacy and need are not clearly defined and, hence, as Tristram Stuart comments, "it is difficult to see ... where exactly Rousseau thought people's compassion ought to outweigh their self-interest" (199). For example, he did not propose a consistent vegetarianism (even though he theorized meat-eating as unnatural),[7] nor did he develop a consistent position on hunting. In fact, in *Emile or On Education*, he recommends it (for men) as a distraction from sexual passion:

Emile has everything needed to succeed at it. He is robust, adroit, patient, indefatigable ... . He will lose in it—at least for a time—the dangerous

---

[7]   For a comprehensive discussion of vegetarianism in Rousseau, see David Boonin-Vail and Chapter 15 in Stuart's *The Bloodless Revolution*. For the influence of Rousseau on educational writings for children, see Kenyon-Jones, pp. 53–65.

> inclinations born of softness. The hunt hardens the heart as well as the body … .
> I do not want Emile's whole youth to be spent in killing animals, and I do not
> even pretend to justify in every respect this ferocious passion. It is enough for
> me that it serves to suspend a more dangerous passion. (320–21)

This passage, in particular, exemplifies Wolloch's point that for Rousseau,
"sensitivity to animal suffering was … a concomitant of the 'weak sex'" (297).

Rousseau's philosophy of gender is most vividly cast in *Emile or On
Education*, which sets out in detail that man and woman "ought not to have the
same education" (363). The title character's female counterpart, Sophie, is raised
only to become a wife and mother:

> the whole education of women ought to relate to men. To please men, to be
> useful to them, to make herself loved and honored by them, to raise them when
> young, to care for them when grown, to counsel them, to console them, to make
> their lives agreeable and sweet—these are the duties of women at all times, and
> they ought to be taught from childhood. (365)

Rousseau roots this gendered education in the "law … of nature": "In the union of
the sexes each contributes equally to the common aim, but not in the same way.
From this diversity arises the first assignable difference in the moral relations of
the two sexes. One ought to be active and strong, the other passive and weak"
(358). Woman "is made to yield to man and to endure even his injustice. You
will never reduce young boys to the same point. The inner sentiment in them
rises and revolts against injustice. Nature did not constitute them to tolerate it"
(396). Woman's "proper purpose is to produce" children (362). Rousseau sees
maternity as the determining factor of women's lives and character ("the timidity
of women is another instinct of nature against the double risk they run during their
pregnancy" [362]):

> The female is female her whole life or at least during her whole youth. Everything
> constantly recalls her sex to her; and, to fulfill its functions well, she needs a
> constitution which corresponds to it. She needs care during her pregnancy; she
> needs rest at the time of childbirth; she needs a soft and sedentary life to suckle
> her children; she needs patience and gentleness, a zeal and an affection that
> nothing can rebuff in order to raise her children. She serves as the link between
> them and their father. (361)

As Susan Moller Okin argues, Rousseau "defines woman's nature, unlike man's,
in terms of her function—that is, her sexual and procreative purpose in life … .
Woman's function is seen as physical and sensual, whereas man's potential is seen
as creative and intellectual" (99–100). Given women's "functional" role, they are
excluded from citizenship.

The educational plan set out in *Emile*, published within a month of *The
Social Contract*, supports its limiting of citizenship to men. *The Social Contract*
"excluded women from citizenship and consigned them emphatically to private

life" (Canovan 84) on the basis of nature. Women's role in Rousseau's envisaged republic was to be subordinate to men: as Okin writes, "It was ... only through their domestic influence on their husbands, exerted through making full use of the latter's feelings for them, that women were to have any power in Rousseau's ideal republic. No contract-based civic equality was to replace the natural differences bestowed upon women" (Okin 145). Rousseau "never envisaged that women should be enfranchised citizens whose voices contribute to the formulation of the general will" (Okin 144). In Rousseau's view, the nonparticipation of women is not ideological; rather, women are incapable of participation. Her childbearing role precludes participation in the public world and, secondly, "the quest of abstract and speculative truths, principles, and axioms in the sciences, for everything that tends to generalize ideas, is not within the competence of women. All their studies ought to be related to practice. It is for them to apply the principles man has found, and to make the observations which lead man to the establishment of principles" (*Emile* 386).[8] While Rousseau is known for his advocacy of the natural over the social, his notion of citizenship is based on a (masculine) transcendence of the personal, the material, and the emotional realms. Rousseau exemplifies the "distinction" Kenyon-Jones notes

> in the liberal, republican ideology of the eighteenth century between property-holding, politically-participating, male citizens, with both the ability to bear arms and the capacity to own land and thus to have a physical stake in the welfare of the state, and the groups of subjects who mediated between the citizen and nature, providing their material needs. These latter groups—who shared to a greater or lesser degree in a feminized representation of nature and who were therefore characterized ambivalently ... were women, the working classes, and colonized races. (156)

Enlightenment feminists interrogated this inscription of sexual difference and the subordination of women as part of nature. Catharine Macaulay and Mary Wollstonecraft challenged what they perceived as a "false system of education

---

[8]   Without purporting to recuperate all of Rousseau's ideas for feminism, Joel Schwartz argues that "there are feminist elements within his thought" (9). Rousseau "also emphasizes the dependence of men upon women" (3) and grants the importance of women's influence over men, and through this influence, over civil society and the political world (5). Lynda Lange writes that in Rousseau "Familial, domestic, and sexual practices were brought under the same type of scrutiny as more commonly considered questions in modern political philosophy. This was a basic theoretical move that was necessary for feminist political philosophy to be possible" (2). Lange does add, "arguably, this gives Rousseau too much credit" (7). Rousseau has received a very divided reception among feminists, as is evident in the essay collection *Feminist Interpretations of Jean-Jacques Rousseau*. Some critics suggest the feminist potential of his work, while others argue that it subordinates women. A number of essays in the collection explore the ambiguities and paradoxes which make Rousseau's work more hospitable to contemporary thinking about gender and sexuality.

… consider[ing] females rather as women than human creatures" (5:73), such as the one set out by Rousseau.[9] And, as we will see, their challenge of woman's so-called "nature" has important implications for the human–animal hierarchy.

Enlightenment feminists protested that women's so-called "nature" is, rather, a product of education. Catharine Macaulay, in *Letters on Education*, writes: "all those vices and imperfections which have been generally regarded as inseparable from the female character, do not in any manner proceed from sexual causes, but are entirely the effects of situation and education" (202). Claims about women's innate "nature" serve to legitimize women's subordination. Macaulay speaks of women's inferiority as a consequence of man's "prejudice" (49). In *Vindication of the Rights of Woman*, Mary Wollstonecraft, an enthusiastic reader of Macaulay's treatise, also declared that the state of women is anything but natural: "I am unable to comprehend what either [Dr. Gregory] or Rousseau mean, when they frequently use this indefinite term" (5:97). Wollstonecraft expounds the pernicious effects of this "indefinite term" (natural sexual difference) and argues that women are made to be weak and kept in a state of "perpetual childhood" (5:75). Given that Rousseau repeatedly speaks of the importance of women's "docility" and "gentleness" (*Emile* 370), Wollstonecraft concludes that women are to be raised as "gentle, domestic brutes" (5:89). In effect, women are excluded from humanity, Wollstonecraft argues: "they are treated as a kind of subordinate being, and not as part of the human species" (5:73). In response, she adopts the "firm tone of humanity" and repeatedly speaks of "the whole human race" (5:65). Both Macaulay and Wollstonecraft argued for co-education as part of their overall argument that women's subordination is ideological, not natural.

Recognizing that the disenfranchisement of women was legitimized by their alleged closeness to nature, rather than culture, Enlightenment feminist texts insist on women's rational capacity: women are not creatures of the body, emotion, and instinct; like men, they are "rational creatures" (Wollstonecraft 5:75). Austen clearly draws on this argument in her novels. Responding to the persistent Mr. Collins's marriage proposal, Elizabeth Bennet entreats him, "consider me … a rational creature speaking the truth from her heart" (*P&P* 122). And Mrs. Croft objects to her brother's notion that women belong at home, not on ships: "I hate to hear you talking so, like a fine gentleman, and as if women were all fine ladies, instead of rational creatures" (*P* 75). In *Emma*, Mrs. Elton speaks of possessing the discretion of "a minister of state" (495), but her avenues of expression are woefully limited. Mrs. Elton attempts to make the best of her small lot: her husband is "engaged from morning to night" with "magistrates, and overseers, and churchwardens," and she tells him, "rather you than I.—I do not know what would become of my crayons and my instrument, if I had half so many applicants" (497). But it is clear that Mrs. Elton's life lacks purpose and, with her pearls and lace, Austen colors her like the accomplished ladies of Wollstonecraft's *Vindication*

---

[9]   For arguments linking Wollstonecraft and Macaulay, see Devoney Looser ("Those Historical Laurels"), Bridget Hill, and Catherine Gardner.

of the Rights of Woman who, "confined … in cages like the feathered race, have nothing to do but to plume themselves, and stalk with mock majesty from perch to perch" (5:125).

For Macaulay and Wollstonecraft, what came to be termed the Woman Question was connected to the Animal Question. Their arguments for gender equality and co-education, while emphasizing women's rational capacity, also proposed better treatment of animals. They recognized that the way animals were treated within patriarchy was connected to the way women were treated; to protest the oppression of women was to protest the other. As ecofeminist theorist Val Plumwood argues, in the Western tradition,

> the human essence is often seen as lying in maximizing control over the natural sphere (both within and without) and in qualities such as rationality, freedom, and transcendence of the material sphere. These qualities are also identified as masculine, and hence the *oppositional* model of the human coincides or converges with a masculine model, in which the characteristics attributed are those of the masculine ideal. (17)

The treatment of animals is thus an integral part of Macaulay's argument about women's education: "If brutes were to draw a character of man … do you think they would call him a benevolent being? No; their representations would be somewhat of the same kind as the fabled furies and other infernals in ancient mythology" (121). Macaulay, as we have seen, speaks of women's subordination as man's "prejudice" (49). She also characterizes humans' attitudes to animals in these terms. Already in the first letter Macaulay recasts the inferiority of animals as the "fond prejudices and pride of our species" (1). Macaulay uses the same language as animal welfare and rights texts, which frequently denaturalize human attitudes to animals as a form of prejudice. For example, George Nicholson's *On the Primeval Diet of Man; Arguments in Favour of Vegetable Food; On Man's Conduct to Animals* (1801) casts human superiority to animals as "deep-rooted prejudices" (2). Similarly, Lawrence speaks of "human pride, prejudice, and cruelty" (1:78). Macaulay examines the ideological underpinnings of human violence towards animals: "There are very few of the insect or reptile tribes which belong to this country, that can be said to be personally injurious to man; yet we are brought up with such prejudices, that they never escape our violence whenever they come within our reach" (122). This example is particularly striking, as she includes species which continue to receive little moral consideration. Her program for early childhood education advocates pet-keeping as a way of countering received ideas about animals: "by the knowledge [children] will thus acquire of brute nature, they will be cured of prejudices founded on ignorance, and in the vanity and conceit of man" (125). Just as the gender system is culturally produced and should be subject to rational interrogation, so is the human–animal system. Macaulay asks for more than "mercy" to animals, for mercy, after all, is the prerogative of those in power. Instead, she argues for a more fundamental shift in how humans think of and treat animals, including legal protection.[10] In common with writers such as Primatt and Oswald, Macaulay connects "the abuse of power which the brute creation suffer from our hands" (268) to other systems of oppression, such as slavery (190), and, going beyond Primatt and Oswald, she includes patriarchy in her analysis.

Macaulay identifies virtue with sympathy; our ability to imagine ourselves in someone else's plight, to sympathize with them, leads us to the ethical value of equity, that is, to not impose our will on others: "it was the movements of sympathy which first inclined man to a forbearance of his own gratifications, in respect to the feelings of his fellow creatures; and his reason soon approved the dictates of his inclination" (275). In this ethical system, animals matter:

> In order … to impress the more strongly on the people's minds the superiority of benevolence, to that of any other virtue; No statue, bust, or monument, should be permitted a place in the church, but of those citizens who have been especially useful in mitigating the woes attendant on animal life; or who have been the authors of any invention, by which the happiness of man, or brute, may be rationally improved. (336)

Macaulay's "benevolence" is put to political work; she develops what Sylvia Bowerbank calls a "radicalized concept of compassion" (5).

The importance of compassion to animals also is consistently addressed in Wollstonecraft's educational writings.[11] In *Thoughts on the Education of Daughters* (1787), Wollstonecraft observes that children are raised to "think man the only thing of consequence in the creation," and she counters that children should be "led to take an interest in [animals'] welfare and occupations" (4:44). The first three chapters of *Original Stories from Real Life; With Conversations, Calculated to Regulate the Affections, and Form the Mind to Truth and Goodness* (1788) are titled "The Treatment of Animals," and they ground ethics in the shared sentience of humans and animals. Mrs. Mason defines "Goodness" as "first, to avoid hurting any thing; and then, to contrive to give as much pleasure as you can" (4:368). The narrative of education is the inverse of Hogarth's. The female pupils, Mary and Caroline, mature from running "eagerly after some insects to destroy them" (4:367) to nursing wounded birds shot at by an "idle boy" (4:368): "Look at it [a wounded bird] … do you not see [that] it suffers as much, and more than you did when you had the small-pox, [when] you were so tenderly nursed" (4:369). Moreover, the emotional lives of animals, their ability to feel "affection,"

---

[10]   "Were government to act on so liberal a sentiment of benevolence, as to take under the protection of law the happiness of the brute species, so far as to punish in offenders that rigorous, that barbarous treatment they meet with in the course of their useful services, would it not tend to encrease sympathy" (Macaulay 277). Lawrence also makes the case for legal protection: "Experience plainly demonstrates the inefficacy of mere morality to prevent aggression, and the necessity of coercive laws for the security of rights" (1:123).

[11]   For a full discussion of Wollstonecraft's views on animals, see my essay in *Animal Subjects: An Ethical Reader in a Posthuman World*.

are recognized: "if you take away their young, it almost kills them" (4:373). *Original Stories*, as Bowerbank argues, "is designed to stimulate relational ways of thinking" (152), and "the animal is granted status as a feeling subject requiring ethical consideration" (149). Similarly, in *Lessons* (1798), published posthumously by William Godwin, the mother explains to her child:

> Oh! the poor puppy has tumbled off the stool. Run and stroke him. Put a little milk in a saucer to comfort him … . You are wiser than the dog, you must help him. The dog will love you for it, and run after you. I feed you and take care of you: you love me and follow me for it. When the book fell down on your foot, it gave you great pain. The poor dog felt the same pain just now. (4:473)

The child is "wiser than the dog," but the experiences of pain and love cross species lines. And in *Vindication of the Rights of Woman*, Wollstonecraft argues that "Humanity to animals should be particularly inculcated as a part of national education" (5:243):

> habitual cruelty is first caught at school, where it is one of the rare sports of the boys to torment the miserable brutes that fall in their way. The transition, as they grow up, from barbarity to brutes to domestic tyranny over wives, children, and servants, is very easy. Justice, or even benevolence, will not be a powerful spring of action unless it extend to the whole creation; nay, I believe that it may be delivered as an axiom, that those who can see pain, unmoved, will soon learn to inflict it. (5:244)

George Nicholson, in *The Primeval Diet of Man*, noted this passage with approval: "Mrs. Wollstonecraft humanely observes that tenderness to animals should be particularly inculcated as a part of national education" (216). It is clear that Wollstonecraft participated in eighteenth-century discussions of animal welfare and rights, and she was recognized as doing so by her contemporaries. As in the case of Macaulay, compassion to animals is "radicalized" (Bowerbank 159). The subjugation of animals is paradigmatic of oppression in general, and the lesson of kindness to animals carries with it a lesson about social justice.

Wollstonecraft's fiction dramatizes the connections between the human–animal hierarchy and other social hierarchies. Alison Sulloway notes that feminist writers used "metaphors of morally maimed, blinded, or fettered women; of creatures fluttering in vain, like caged birds" (62). Wollstonecraft's *The Wrongs of Woman, or Maria* offers a particularly rich example. Its heroine describes herself as a bird "caught in a trap, and caged for life" (1:138) and "hunted, like an infected beast" (1:165). The novel treats the suffering of women across class lines. Jemima, the laboring-class servant with whom the imprisoned upper-class Maria forms a friendship, tells her life story as one of being "treated like a creature of another species" (1:108). Illegitimate, orphaned, and poor, Jemima suffered a childhood of abuse: "It seemed indeed the privilege of their superior nature to kick me about, like the dog or cat. If I were attentive, I was called fawning, if refractory, an obstinate mule, and like a mule I received their censure on my loaded back"

(1:109); "I was the filching cat, the ravenous dog, the dumb brute, who must bear all" (1:109–10). These tropes open up a space in which the reader is encouraged to critique not only the abuse of women across class lines but also the abuse of animals. Since cruelty to animals paves the way for cruelty to humans, and since animals, like humans, are sentient beings (both points repeatedly made in the early educational writings), the treatment of animals is of ethical and political import in Wollstonecraft. The novel connects the ideologies that oppress along the gender, class, and species lines, and interrogates "perversions of the understanding, which systematize oppression" (1:88). The role of the animal is crucial in the systemizing of oppression. Because Jemima is "view[ed] ... as a creature of another species" (1:111), she is treated cruelly and excluded from moral consideration.

We know that Austen was familiar with the tradition of Enlightenment feminism.[12] Thus, she would have encountered texts which included the animal question alongside feminism. This study demonstrates that Austen likened women's state in patriarchy to that of animals, whether as hunted prey or as pets. The marriage plot, often seen as defining Austen's oeuvre, also carries significant anxiety. Mary Crawford calls marriage "a manoeuvring business" (*MP* 53), a perspective not wholly rejected by her author. The novels' conclusions often are perfunctory, and self-consciously drawing attention to their artifice, they reflect Austen's ambivalence towards marriage. At the end of *Northanger Abbey*, "the bells rang and every body smiled" (261). The narrator of *Emma* is similarly circumspect: "She spoke then, on being so entreated.—What did she say?—Just what she ought, of course. A lady always does" (470). Emma jokes that she will call Mr. Knightley "once by [his] Christian name ... in the building in which N. takes M. for better, for worse" (505), but her comment also irreverently suggests the formulaic quality of the marriage plot. The marriage closure does bring her heroines degrees of economic security and social integration, but it compromises their liberty. In "Sanditon," Lady Denham boasts, "I do not think I was ever over-reached in my life; and that is a good deal for a woman to say that has been married twice" (*LM* 178). Austen skillfully negotiated a variety of expectations and audiences in her novels, and they continue to appeal to a range of communities of readers. Her marriage plots enjoy the status of romances, but also sustain contrapuntal readings, particularly by feminist and queer critics. In the latter school, Austen's marriage plots are far from tidy. Deborah Kaplan has argued that Austen's work can be characterized by "divided loyalties" to the "culture of the gentry" and to "women's culture" (*Among Women* 14). Alison Sulloway acknowledges moments of "Austenian joy" (84), but sees Austen first and foremost as a satirist. The ideological fissures in Austen's novels trouble, to quote the narrator in *Northanger Abbey*, the "hastening ... to perfect felicity" (259) which marriage is supposed to signal. In a provocative reading of Austen's famous characterization of *Pride and Prejudice* as "too light & bright & sparkling" (*Letters* 203), Joseph Litvak

---

[12]   See Mary Spongberg's article on Wollstonecraft, Macaulay, and Austen and their treatment of English history.

suggests that Austen was critical of the "marriage plot, whereby the traditional novel idealizes heterosexuality and its reproduction" (22). Austen "may in fact be seen as at once authorizing and enacting an *ill-mannered reading* of her own text" (22). I argue that Austen's consistent alignment of women with animals is one of the ways in which she "authorize[s] and enact[s]" counter-readings of the very marriage plot that structures her novels; Austen's ambivalence towards marriage is expressed in the joint subordination of women and animals. Austen suggests the subordination of women within marriage by consistently drawing connections between the subordination of nature, animals, and women. We might relate this to Austen's references in her letters to maternity and childbirth as a type of breeding.

Austen's correspondence registers an anxiety that women's participation in marriage and motherhood reduces them to the status of animals, subject to ownership and mistreatment by men. When we look at Austen's letters to her sister and nieces, births are announced in rather lukewarm tones: "Mrs Clement is very welcome to her little Boy & to my Congratulations into the bargain, if ever you think of giving them" (224). Childbirth, of course, came with grave dangers, as recorded in a letter to Cassandra in 1798: "I believe I never told you that Mrs Coulthard and Anne, late of Manydown, are both dead, and both died in childbed. We have not regaled Mary [pregnant at the time] with this news" (20). But even if tragedy was averted, childbirth carried certain costs. Austen advises her niece Fanny Knight that "by not beginning the business of Mothering quite so early in life, you will be young in Constitution, spirits, figure & countenance, while Mrs Wm Hammond is growing old by confinements & nursing" (332). A letter to Cassandra of October 1, 1808, opens with congratulations on the birth of Edward and Elizabeth Austen Knight's sixth son:

> We are extremely glad to hear of the birth of the Child, & trust everything will proceed as well as it begins—his Mama has our best wishes, & he our second best for health & comfort—tho' I suppose unless *he* has our best too, we do nothing for *her*. (139)

Austen recasts childbirth here as a loss of identity: there is no "she" without the child, significantly a boy. In the same letter, Austen records her pity of Mrs. Tilson: "poor Woman! how can she be honestly breeding again?" (140). Given that her sister-in-law's sixth son makes a total of 11 children, this acerbic comment might equally apply to her; indeed, in manuscript form the line is "roughly cancelled—probably by Lord Brabourne (the grandson of Edward and Elizabeth Austen Knight)—but still legible" as noted by Deirdre Le Faye (391, n6). Furthermore, the same letter resentfully registers hospitality as another specifically female labor: "About an hour & half after your toils on Wednesday ended, ours began;—at seven o'clock, Mrs Harrison, her two daughters & two Visitors, with Mr Debary & his eldest sister walked in; & our Labour was not a great deal shorter than poor Elizabeth's, for it was past eleven before we were delivered" (140). Female labor, epitomized in childbirth, is a burden. In a letter to Fanny Knight of March 23, 1817, she writes of her niece Anna: "Poor Animal, she will be worn out before she is thirty.—I am very sorry for her.—Mrs Clement too is in that way again. I am quite tired of so many Children.—Mrs Benn has a 13th" (336). Austen conducted a lively literary correspondence with Anna, and celebrated her "charms of flesh and bone," "mind," "fancy," "wit," and "judgement" in the poem "In measured verse."[13] But Austen clearly fears that the aspiring novelist will sacrifice her writing for domestic duties once she marries on November 8, 1814. A telling letter composed in December 1815 spells out the exchange of book for child: "As I wish very much to see *your* Jemima, I am sure you will like to see *my* Emma, & have therefore great pleasure in sending it for your perusal" (310). Jemima was Anna's first baby, born October 20, 1815, rapidly followed by a second on September 27, 1816; all together Anna had seven children between 1815 and 1827.[14]

Austen's embrace of *Emma* as *her* baby is in keeping with other letters. She is "never too busy to think of S&S. I can no more forget it, than a mother can forget her sucking child" (182). *Pride and Prejudice* is "my own darling Child" (201), and she speaks of her heroine with motherly adulation: "I must confess that *I* think her as delightful a creature as ever appeared in print, & how I shall be able to tolerate those who do not like *her* ... I do not know" (201). While Austen sees childbirth as detrimental to women's independence, the writing of books is life-affirming, allowing her to participate in the public sphere as a professional author. *Sense and Sensibility* was announced to be "By a Lady," but this signature was quickly supplanted. *Pride and Prejudice* was by "By the Author of 'Sense and Sensibility'" and all other lifetime publications were announced as being "By the Author of 'Pride and Prejudice,'" including the second edition of *Sense and Sensibility* in 1813. Kathryn Sutherland makes the compelling point that Austen's title pages, rather than reflecting a desire for anonymity as is commonly argued, "map a knowable fictional space or estate" (*Textual Lives* 232). That is, Austen's signature foregrounds her literary progeny.

At the end of *Sense and Sensibility,* the happy Elinor and Edward "had ... nothing to wish for, but the marriage of Colonel Brandon and Marianne, and rather better pasturage for their cows" (425). This casual yoking together of marriage and milk production is strikingly suggestive. It parallels women's domestic role to the subordination of nature for human ends, and registers the anxiety that marriage and maternity animalize women. The novel hesitates to cast Marianne's marriage to Brandon in romantic light, instead emphasizing Marianne's utility: Edward, Elinor, and Mrs. Dashwood "each felt [Colonel Brandon's] sorrows, and

---

[13] See *Letters* pp. 195, 266, 267, 274, 276, 282, 284, 289.

[14] While Anna did not fulfil her literary aspirations, she did not completely give up on them. See *Jane Austen: A Family Record*: "Although *Which is the Heroine?* [the subject of her correspondence with her aunt] had been destroyed unfinished, Anna had earned herself a little money by publishing a novella, *Mary Hamilton*, in *The Literary Souvenir* for 1833, and followed this up by two small books for children—*The Winter's Tale* (1841) and *Springtide* (1842); at some time after the manuscript of *Sanditon* came into her possession she attempted to continue the story, but gave up after writing about 20,000 words" (William Austen-Leigh, Richard Austen-Leigh, and Deirdre Le Faye 244–45).

their own obligations, and Marianne, by general consent, was to be the reward" (429) for Colonel Brandon. The objectification of Marianne in the marriage plot is reiterated when we see her cast into a passive role through marriage: "she found herself at nineteen, submitting to new attachments, entering on new duties, placed in a new home, a wife, the mistress of a family, and the patroness of a village" (429–30). John Alexander's 2008 adaptation of *Sense and Sensibility*, a vivid example of what Deborah Kaplan has termed the "harlequinization of Jane Austen's novels" ("Mass Marketing" 178), is intent on amplifying the Colonel Brandon and Marianne plot as romance. The script even has Marianne spell it out for us: "What sadness he has known … . He is the true romantic, I think." The film's glamorization of Colonel Brandon in part relies on his mastery of animals. With Colonel Brandon on horseback in the background, Elinor compares his style of courtship to the breaking in of horses: "the great tamers of horses do it by being gentle and then walking away. Nine times out of ten the wild horse will follow." And sure enough, this Marianne does. The film also invents a scene of Colonel Brandon as falconer—with a suitably impressed Marianne looking on: the falcon has been tamed and trained, and so has Marianne. While the film casts this in a romantic light, Austen is less sanguine about the animalization of women and their subordination in marriage.

Chapter 2
Making a Hole in Her Heart

It was such a dead time of year, no wild-fowl, no game, and the Lady Frasers were not in the country. (*NA* 215)

In *Mansfield Park*, Mr. Rushworth's plan to "have the avenue at Sotherton down" leads Fanny Price to comment to Edmund "in a low voice" (65): "Cut down an avenue! What a pity! Does not it make you think of Cowper? 'Ye fallen avenues, once more I mourn your fate unmerited'" (66). John Wiltshire, in his introduction to the Cambridge edition of *Mansfield Park*, suggests that one of Austen's reasons for setting the novel in Northamptonshire is because of its geographic proximity to places associated with William Cowper: "Jane Austen would … have known that William Cowper had lived in Olney, where poems remembered by Fanny Price, 'The Task' and 'Tirocinium,' were both composed" (xlix). While Wiltshire links "the sober and repressive morality of Sir Thomas Bertram" to "the piety of Cowper" (l), I associate Cowper with Fanny, and focus on the influence of his animal welfare position on Austen's work. Cowper ranked highly in Jane Austen's estimation; Henry Austen's "Biographical Notice of the Author" states that her "favourite moral writers were Johnson in prose, and Cowper in verse" (330), and in the *Memoir*, J.E. Austen-Leigh records: "Amongst her favourite writers, Johnson in prose, Crabbe in verse, and Cowper in both, stood high" (89).[1] It is surprising, then, as William Deresiewicz points out, that Cowper, "whom virtually everyone acknowledges as a major influence, has scarcely ever been investigated as such," an oversight which he attributes to the "bias … against … poetry" (*Romantic Poets* 162).[2] This chapter follows Fanny Price's lead, thinking through her question and Cowper's influence on Austen. Sylvia Bowerbank and Richard Pickard have shown that to "question … the right of landed gentlemen to

---

[1]   Planning the garden at the Castle Square house, Austen writes to her sister: "I could not do without a Syringa, for the sake of Cowper's Line" (119).

[2]   Deresiewicz reads *Mansfield Park*, *Emma*, and *Persuasion* in the context of Coleridge, Wordsworth, Scott, and Byron, but does not include Cowper. While in Deresiewicz's account of Austen's "early" versus "major" phase, Cowper is an influence Austen eventually outgrew, he is neglected by critics situating the novelist in relation to women's writing and feminist thought. There are brief references to Cowper in studies on Austen's influences, such as Jocelyn Harris's *Jane Austen's Art of Memory*, Frank Bradbrook's *Jane Austen and Her Predecessors*, and Mary Lascelles's *Jane Austen and Her Art*, but there appears to be only one detailed examination of Austen's allusions to Cowper: John Halperin's "The Worlds of *Emma*: Jane Austen and Cowper." Most recently, Gabrielle White examines the influence of Cowper's abolitionist stance on Austen. See also Emily Auerbach (193–96).

cut trees" is to "question the structures of power which give upper-class men all their privileges, not just the privilege of controlling their own landscape" (Pickard, "Sexual Politics").[3] Cowper questioned tree-cutting and the sporting prerogative, and Austen further developed this argument by establishing parallels between the positions of women and animals in patriarchal society.

Rural sport was far from uncontested in the eighteenth century. As Stephen Deuchar explains, the defence of rural sport was that it "was healthy, virtuous, brought beneficial contact with nature, provided either a restorative rest from work or an admirable substitute for it, was royal, noble, manly and even patriotic" (57). While in the mid-eighteenth century "the English public had a firm and almost unanimous view of the social and moral irresponsibility of the behaviour of those at the heart of the sporting world" (94), Deuchar argues that by the end of the century, the threat of the French Revolution and its Jacobin politics led to a resurgence of the "sporting ideal":

> For the first time in many decades sport could be seen to be associated with (even to be symptomatic of) a greater, stronger, English past—one from which men might draw inspiration and example at a moment when, thanks to the French Revolution and the subsequent wars with Catholic France, the national way of life seemed to be under severe threat. (155)

A renewed emphasis was placed on the English "country sportsmen's robust physical health, warlike capabilities, hospitality, national loyalty and personal generosity" (155). David C. Itzkowitz similarly explains that hunting was justified as providing "healthy, invigorating exercise" and "keeping gentlemen resident in the country where they could carry out their duties to their tenantry and to the country at large" (19). Hunting was "associated with the hardy virtues" of country life and "believed to be excellent training for war" (20); in short, it was "conducive to manliness" (21). Rural sports also were attacked as leading to gambling and sexual vice. Certain sports, such as foxhunting, were perceived as dangerous by blurring class distinctions, and others as causing social unrest because of their exclusive nature and the divisiveness of the Game Laws.[4] Anti-cruelty arguments also were articulated. I share Diana Donald's position that "the strength of moral opposition to hunting in the eighteenth and early nineteenth centuries … has been underestimated by historians" (362, n1), and see my study as part of an effort to redress the balance by focusing on texts which explicitly are concerned with the welfare of animals.[5] For example, Joseph Ritson's *An Essay on Abstinence from*

---

[3]   Also see Pickard's "Environmentalism and 'Best Husbandry.'"

[4]   For a concise summary of pro- and anti-hunting arguments, see Richard H. Thomas's *The Politics of Hunting* (232–47). Also see P.B. Munsche's *Gentlemen and Poachers: The English Game Laws, 1671–1831.*

[5]   See Donald, Chapters 7 and 8, for excellent analysis of the hunting controversy in visual culture.

Animal Food as a Moral Duty (1802) links the cruelty of rural sport to the cruelty of meat consumption:

> The barbarous and unfeeling sports (as they are call'd) of the Engleish, their horse-raceing, hunting, shooting, bul and bear-baiting, cock-fighting, boxing-matches, and the like, all proceed from their immoderate addiction to animal food. (88)

Given that animals are capable of a "high degree of mental with bodily pain" (189), Catharine Macaulay also depicts hunting as cruel and counter to the virtue of "benevolence" (65); even fishing—"putting worms on a hook as baits"—is "hardened barbarity" (122).

Anti-cruelty arguments are treated explicitly in the works of William Cowper, William Wordsworth, S.T. Coleridge, Percy Bysshe Shelley, and Lord Byron. Given Cowper's status as one of Austen's favorite writers, we can be certain that she was very familiar with the anti-sport argument and, I will argue, influenced by it. Cowper's emphasis on the sentience and individuality of animals is characteristic of the emerging discourse of animal rights in the eighteenth century. The anti-sport argument of *The Task* is based on three major points, the chief of which is animals' ability to feel pain: rural sport is "detested" because it "owes its pleasures to another's pain" and "feeds upon the sobs and dying shrieks / Of harmless nature" (3.326–29). Animals "suffer torture" (6.390) to "make … [man] sport" (6.386). Secondly, *The Task* depicts rural sport as unthinking activity, for "a mind / Cultur'd and capable of sober thought" (3.323–24) will "love the country … for … its silence and its shade" (3.321–22), not the "clamours of the field" (3.326). It is the hunter's "supreme delight / To fill with riot, and defile with blood" (3.306–307) the "scenes form'd for contemplation, and to nurse / The growing seeds of wisdom" (3.301–302). And thirdly, Cowper implies that rural sport leads to cruelty towards humans:

> The heart is hard in nature, and unfit
> For human fellowship, as being void
> Of sympathy, and therefore dead alike
> To love and friendship both, that is not pleased
> With sight of animals enjoying life,
> Nor feels their happiness augment his own. (6.321–26)

While the hunter "gratif[ies] the frenzy of his wrath" (6.387), the poet imagines an animal world where "the bounding fawn … darts across the glade / When none pursues, through mere delight of heart, / And spirits buoyant with excess of glee" (6.327–29) and the horse "skims the spacious meadow at full speed, / Then stops and snorts, and, throwing high his heels, / Starts to the voluntary race again" (6.331–33). *The Task* endows the treatment of animals with ethical and poetic significance: the speaker "deem[s] the toils / Of poetry not lost, if verse of mine / May stand between an animal and woe, / And teach one tyrant pity for his drudge" (6.725–28).

Cowper attempts to represent animals as individuals in several of his works. In an essay published in *The Gentleman's Magazine*, he describes his three pet hares, Puss, Tiney, and Bess, "as having each a character of his own" (42): "We know indeed that the hare is good to hunt and good to eat, but in all other respects poor Puss is a neglected subject" (40). After observing and recording the behavior of the three animals, Cowper concludes, "my intimate acquaintance with these specimens of the kind has taught me to hold the sportsman's amusement in abhorrence; he little knows what amiable creatures he persecutes, of what gratitude they are capable, how cheerful they are in their spirits, what enjoyment they have of life" (43). Cowper's attribution of individuality to animals also is evident in "Epitaph on a Hare." Tiney was "surliest of his kind":

> Though duly from my hand he took
> His pittance ev'ry night,
> He did it with a jealous look,
> And, when he could, would bite. (9–12)

The poem is notable for not sentimentalizing the hare, and its memorializing of Tiney's habits and pleasures contributes to an anti-sport argument. In her survey of the evolving attitudes towards animals revealed in pet epitaphs and elegies, Ingrid H. Tague cites Cowper's epitaph among those in which "pets themselves increasingly took center stage, with the owner's affection for the animal as the primary emotion" (300).[6] "Epitaphium Alterum," evoking ancient epitaphs and asking the reader to reflect on her own mortality, gives seriousness to the life and death of Puss, one of Cowper's hares. Austen referred to Cowper's pets when describing William, Henry Thomas Austen's manservant, in a letter: "An inclination for the Country is a venial fault.—He has more of Cowper than of Johnson in him, fonder of Tame Hares & Blank verse than all of the full tide of human Existence at Charing Cross" (250).

While David Perkins suggests that Cowper identified with "persecuted animals and in protesting on their behalf, he was using them as surrogates" ("Cowper's Hares" 58), he also states that "no writer in the eighteenth century had more effect than William Cowper in transforming attitudes to animals and stimulating reform. He was quoted over and over in sermons, pamphlets, and in Parliament" (*Romanticism and Animal Rights* 44).[7] For example, Lord Erskine

---

[6]   Kenyon-Jones offers a contrasting view on animal epitaphs of the period: they "move quite swiftly away from commemoration of the dead animal to the concern of the living poet, and use the animal's death as a pretext for exploring differences—rather than similarities—between human beings and animals" (27).

[7]   Donna Landry takes an unsympathetic view of Cowper: "Seeing animals at leisure, expressing themselves and demonstrating the pleasure of freedom, especially freedom from human constraints, does nothing for Cowper so much as consolidate his sense of rational superiority to other humans as well as animals, his own humane benevolence …. Cowper's advocacy ends with inviting the benevolent … to feel pleased with themselves" (*Invention of the Countryside* 123–24).

quoted *The Task* in Parliament when introducing a bill against animal cruelty in 1809 (Kenyon-Jones 90), and Joseph Ritson quotes the poem to support his *Essay on the Abstinence from Animal Food as a Moral Duty*, which, in turn, influenced Percy Bysshe Shelley.[8] Cowper was an important precursor of the Romantic poets. They developed his representation of animals as sentient individuals, his pitting of rural sports against reflection, and his connection between cruelty to animals and cruelty to humans. We see an example of Cowper's influence in William Wordsworth's "Hart-Leap Well."[9]

Wordsworth's "Hart-Leap Well" emphasizes animal sentience and generates sympathy for the hart's "toil along the mountain side" (29), its "desperate race" lasting "thirteen hours" (141), and the "last deep groan his breath had fetched" (43): "What thoughts must through the creature's brain have passed!" (137). The poem's speaker, listening to the shepherd's story, observes that "This beast not unobserved by Nature fell" (159) and gleans the "lesson": "Never to blend our pleasure or our pride / With sorrow of the meanest thing that feels" (175–76). For Perkins, the poem "presents a development of, or into, a state of higher moral sensitivity": "the modern poet, more reflective, sensitive, and aware than Sir Walter, has no wish to hunt, because his insight and feeling connect him more sympathetically with nature" (*Romanticism and Animal Rights* 84). In that sense, "Hart-Leap Well" is similar to Coleridge's "The Rime of the Ancient Mariner." The mariner's moral that "He prayeth well, who loveth well / Both man and bird and beast. / He prayeth best, who loveth best / All things both great and small" (7.612–15) has been seen as too obvious to be taken seriously. Surely the shooting of the bird must be a symbol of something more important, but Kenyon-Jones reminds us that in a nineteenth-century cultural context, the poem's "power ... should not be underestimated ... to preach effectively the simple moral of kindness to animals": "as late as 1881 Frederick Thrupp, lithograph illustrator of Coleridge's work, was interpreting the poem in this straightforward spirit in his essay decrying blood sports, 'The Antient [sic] Mariner and the Modern Sportsman'" (72). Oerlemans argues convincingly that "the strangeness of the poem, its deliberate supernaturalness, can in part be taken as a strategy for making unfamiliar—and thereby allowing us to reconsider—a moral that would be found merely childish by the majority of its readers" (86). Both Wordsworth and Coleridge portray hunting as cruel and "egoistic self-assertion" (Perkins, *Romanticism and Animal Rights* 84). Following

---

[8]   Thomas Young also quoted *The Task* in support (36, 85, 91), as did George Nicholson in *On the Primeval Diet of Man; Arguments in Favour of Vegetable Food; On Man's Conduct to Animals* (65–67). This is not to elide significant differences among these writers. For example, Shelley and Ritson were vegetarian, while Cowper was not and his *Task* maintains an anthropocentric view of the world: "The sum is this.—If man's convenience, health, / Or safety interfere, his rights and claims / Are paramount, and must extinguish their's" (*Task* 6.581–83).

[9]   Rachel Trickett explores the influence of Cowper on William Wordsworth. She does not examine hunting or the ecological implications of both poets, but provides useful parallels between the two poets' descriptions of animals.

Cowper's opposition between hunting and "contemplation," Wordsworth and Coleridge show reflection as leading to sympathy for animals. Similarly, in *Don Juan*, Byron depicts rural sports as an index of intellectual vacuity:

> The gentlemen got up betimes to shoot,
>   Or hunt: the young, because they liked the sport—
> The first thing boys like after play and fruit;
>   The middle-aged, to make the day more short;
> For *ennui* is a growth of English root,
>   Though nameless in our language:—we retort
> The fact for words, and let the French translate
> That awful yawn which sleep can not abate. (13.101)

Byron's two-couplet "To These Fox Hunters in a Long Frost" (1806–07) succinctly summarizes this view: "Of unlearned men Lord Falkland did say / 'I pity em much on a long rainy day.' / Ye Fox-hunters too are quite as much lost / When winter the ground has clothed in frost."

The Romantics connected the hunter's hierarchical relationship with nature to other social hierarchies. Sir Walter in Wordsworth's "Hart-Leap Well" is a knight who has at his disposal not only nature but also "vassals" who carry out the commands he "crie[s] out" at them (3–4).[10] Byron in *Don Juan* draws attention to the way rural sport reifies class division:

> The mellow Autumn came, and with it came
>   The promised party, to enjoy its sweets.
> The corn is cut, the manor full of game;
>   The pointer ranges, and the sportsman beats
> In russet jacket:—lynx-like in his aim,
>   Full grows his bag, and wonder*ful* his feats.
> Ah, nutbrown Partridges! Ah, brilliant Pheasants!
> And ah, ye Poachers!—'Tis no sport for peasants. (13.75)

In canto 16, "There were two poachers caught in a steel trap / Ready for gaol, their place of convalescence" (16.61). Similarly, P.B. Shelley considered the game laws "despotism" and an "insult and outrage of the rights of … fellow-man" and condemned the "barbarous and bloody sport from which every enlightened and amiable mind shrinks in abhorrence and disgust" ("On the Game Laws" 280, 281).

Reading Austen in the context of Cowper and the Romantic writers allows us to recognize her participation in the rural sport controversy. She, too, casts rural

---

[10]   Peter Mortensen examines "Hart-Leap Well" as a rewriting of Gottfried August Bürger's "Der Wilde Jäger": in the latter the focus "is not that [the Knight] treats animals poorly, but rather that he treats the poor like animals" (302), whereas in Wordsworth's poem, "the hart's suffering is a subject of ethical interest in itself" (303). For a full discussion of animals in Wordsworth's poetry, see Kenyon-Jones (141–64), Oerlemans (88–97), Schotland, and Fosso.

sport as the opposite of contemplation and emphasizes rural sport's reification of social hierarchies. The comparison to Cowper and the Romantics also makes visible Austen's feminist development of the anti-sport argument. Deuchar notes the "implied connection between sport and sex" as "a logical development of sport's ancient claim to be the epitome of manliness" (130), and Donald similarly points out that "the analogy with sexual pursuit was woven into hunting culture, and informed its imagery at every level" (243). If we return to Wordsworth's "Hart-Leap Well," we see this implied connection between the hunt and sexual conquest. As Perkins points out, Wordsworth gestures towards the erotic associations of the hunt and the "pleasure house" built in its commemoration as a "traveller's shed, the pilgrim's cot, / A place of love for damsels that are coy" (59–60). The house is also associated with trickery: Sir Walter will employ "a cunning Artist … to frame / A bason for that fountain in the dell" (61–62). And since the house commemorates the killing of a deer (obviously not a willing participant in the chase), we ought to be suspicious of Sir Walter's "place of love for damsels that are coy" (60). The narrator's description of the hart as "stone-dead / With breathless nostrils stretched above the spring" (77–78) counterpoints Sir Walter's chivalric language: given Sir Walter's interpretation of a hart fighting for its life as "gallant," his definition of "coy damsels" might similarly be self-serving and elide resistance, rewriting rape as "pleasure." Wordsworth does not develop the pleasure-house as a monument to both kinds of hunting, but in Austen's work, this parallel is central.

Austen shifts the focus to female subordination in the sexual game. For example, in *Mansfield Park*, Henry Crawford sadistically speaks of "mak[ing] a small hole in Fanny Price's heart" (267). Austen pointedly associates the sportsman's so-called virility with cruelty. Ecofeminist theory suggests that masculinity is defined "in opposition to the natural world" (Kheel 110) and, as argued by Matt Cartmill, the "importance of hunting lies in its symbolism" (28), its "armed confrontation between humanness and wilderness, between culture and nature" (30) extending to a "symbolic attack on women" (240). Similarly, Carol J. Adams sees the language of the hunt as "a variation of rape" (*Sexual Politics* 74).[11] In Mary Wollstonecraft's *The Wrongs of Woman*, both Maria and Jemima describe themselves as hunted animals (1:110, 112, 160, 165, 168, 179). Austen's novels consistently develop the connections between women and animals as objects of prey. This chapter takes its epigraph from *Northanger Abbey*; General Tilney's remark that "It was such a dead time of year, no wild-fowl, no game, and the Lady Frasers were not in the country" (215) is telling, the grammar of the list revealing the parallel position of women and animals. And the sentence's irony plays with the differing perspectives of hunter and prey: it may be a "dead time" for the hunter, but surely not for the animals!

The topic of sport in Austen has received little attention. David Selwyn claims in *Jane Austen and Leisure* that "there is … nothing either unusual or blameworthy in

---

[11] For environmentalist defenses of hunting, consult Holmes Rolston III and Theodore Vitali.

a young man shooting" (98) and "such activities are made little of" (91). In contrast, in her introduction to the Oxford edition, Margaret Anne Doody notes that *Sense and Sensibility* sets up hunters in "antithesis" and "antagonism" to mothers (xxix), and Alison Sulloway remarks that Willoughby "hunted both women and animals" (127). Patricia Jo Kulisheck offers the only detailed examination of hunting. She observes that "hunting is associated with characters who behave improperly" (23), but limits this analysis to the "minor characters" of Reginald de Courcy in "Lady Susan," Lord Osborne and Tom Musgrave in "The Watsons," John Thorpe in *Northanger Abbey*, and Sir John Middleton in *Sense and Sensibility*. "Only three main characters hunt": Henry Crawford, John Willoughby, and Edmund Bertram, who "seems to take no more interest in the sport than is suitable to his station" (23). This point, as we will see, is questionable, given Edmund's chosen profession. Rural sport is pervasive in Austen: William Price, Mr. Bingley, Captain Wentworth, and Charles Musgrove, to name just a few, are all hunters. Nor is Austen's critique of rural sport limited to villains or secondary characters; it is more far-reaching and includes the heroes of *Mansfield Park* and *Persuasion*.

In *Northanger Abbey*, Austen clearly draws on the hunting debate in her characterization of John Thorpe. His character belies the notion that hunting "strengthen[s] the mind, intellectually and morally, as well as the body," as defenders of the sport claimed it did (Itzkowitz 21). John Thorpe is first introduced to us as a "most knowing-looking coachman" driving along "with all the vehemence that could most fitly endanger the lives of himself, his companion, and his horse" (38). He boasts to Catherine that he "never read[s] novels; I have something else to do" (43):

> He told her of horses which he had bought for a trifle and sold for incredible sums; of racing matches, … of shooting parties, in which he had killed more birds (though without having one good shot) than all his companions together; and described to her some famous day's sport, with the foxhounds, in which his foresight and skill in directing the dogs had repaired the mistakes of the most experienced huntsman, and in which the boldness of his riding, though it had never endangered his own life for a moment, had been constantly leading others in difficulties, which he calmly concluded had broken the necks of many. (63)

Catherine "could not entirely repress a doubt" of John Thorpe "being altogether completely agreeable" (63). Throughout *Northanger Abbey*, Thorpe is satirized. The physical prowess boasted by the hunting ideal is undercut: Thorpe "was a stout young man of middling height" with "a plain face and ungraceful form" (39). The intellectual benefit of hunting also is thrown into doubt. He is fond of drinking— "There is not the hundredth part of the wine consumed in this kingdom, that there ought to be. Our foggy climate wants help" (60)—and, his oratory skills sadly lacking, he relies on "exclamations, amounting almost to oaths" (61) and frequent use of "Oh! d——" (40). And, of course, he is a prolific boaster. Catherine has to bear "the effusions of his endless conceit" (63): "she readily echoed whatever he chose to assert, and it was finally settled between them without any difficulty, that his equipage was altogether the most complete of its kind in England, his carriage the neatest, his horse the best goer, and himself the best coachman" (61). Thorpe's boasts about his riding are about dominance; he assures Catherine that his horse "will soon know his master" (58).

It is telling that Thorpe's first appearance is associated with his cruelty towards animals: encountering his sister and Catherine on the street, the "horse was immediately checked with a violence which almost threw him on his haunches" (39). Catherine is more sensitive to his horse than he is. When he asks her if she "did ... ever see an animal so made for speed," Catherine responds, "He *does* look very hot to be sure" (40). Perhaps Austen here drew on Cowper's portrait of the rider who "clamorous in praise / Of the poor brute, seems wisely to suppose / The honours of his matchless horse his own" (*Task* 6.436–38). When Thorpe promptly suggests another outing after an already extensive excursion, Catherine objects, "but will not your horse want rest?" to which he replies, "Rest! ... all nonsense, nothing ruins horses so much as rest; nothing knocks them up so soon" (42).[12] His boasts objectify his horse: "Such true blood ... . Look at his forehand; look at his loins; only see how he moves; that horse *cannot* go less than ten miles an hour: tie his legs and he will get on" (40). The implied sadism in the latter comment sheds a troubling light on his treatment of women.[13] Thorpe would like to master Catherine the way he does his horse. When Catherine wants to honor her engagement with the Tilneys, Thorpe deceives her and prevents her leaving the carriage: he "only lashed his horse into a brisker trot" (85) and "smacked his whip," leaving Catherine with "no power of getting away, [and] obliged to ... submit" (86). It is significant that Austen frames this assault on Catherine as a carriage ride, drawing attention to the reins, which similarly restrict women and animals. Both Catherine and the horse are at John Thorpe's mercy. That the parallel exists in his mind is evident when Catherine, in another instance, resisting the attempt to constrain her person, "broke away and hurried off": "'She is as obstinate as—.' Thorpe never finished the simile, for it could hardly have been a proper one" (101). Just as his objectifying gaze dismembers horses—"look at his loins" (40)—he cuts up women, calling his sister's ankles "thick" (119) and looking at women as "faces" that he can "condemn" or "praise" in "short decisive sentences" (42). Both women and animals are commodities for Thorpe. He objectifies Catherine as a trophy, bragging to General Tilney about his conquest, and keeping her waiting "in a very

---

[12] Such passages are particularly important, given that the treatment of horses occupied premier significance in debates about animal cruelty. See Chapter 6 ("Prosperity and Adversity: The Life of the Horse") in Donald.

[13] Also see the chapter on *Northanger Abbey* in Jill Heydt-Stevenson's *Austen's Unbecoming Conjunctions: Subversive Laughter, Embodied History*: "Thorpe, playing the role of the hypermasculine man's man, relishes the exchange of horses between men and savors brutalizing his animals and the women they symbolize" (20). Heydt-Stevenson draws attention to Thorpe's misogyny and his possessive, abusive treatment of animals as "sodomitical stereotypes" employed by Austen to "deconstruct sexual identities" (123). See pp. 117–24 in particular.

easy manner": after securing Catherine as a dance partner, he tellingly abandons her to arrange for "an exchange of terriers," leaving our heroine in "mortification" (50) and not at liberty to accept Mr. Tilney's offer.

In a text which vindicates the novel genre and its audience, Thorpe's preference of hunting to reading hardly recommends the sport. Moreover, given that *Northanger Abbey*'s vindication of novel reading is gendered, defending women writers and women readers, John Thorpe's avowed disdain for reading Frances Burney's *Camilla* also reveals his misogyny. The novel's hero is delineated in sharp contrast to Thorpe. Henry Tilney confidently asserts that "the person, be it gentleman or lady, who has not pleasure in a good novel, must be intolerably stupid" (107). When riding in a curricle under his direction, Catherine is pleasantly surprised: "Henry drove so well,—so quietly—without making any disturbance, without parading to her, or swearing at … [the horses]; so different from the only gentleman-coachman whom it was in her power to compare him with" (160). The fact that he does not curse the horses distinguishes Henry from Thorpe in his treatment of animals: Henry is not associated with cruelty towards animals. At Woodston, a "large Newfoundland puppy and two or three terriers" are "the friends of his solitude" (219). While the text does imply that Henry hunts, he does not make it a topic of conversation and "weary" (74) Catherine, nor is he shown as actively engaging in rural sports. The only textual reference to his hunting is a description of his room as "strewed with his litter of books, guns, and great coats" (188). In *Persuasion*, the opposition between reading and sporting is treated more consistently than in this early work, but John Thorpe, defined by his passion for hunting and his ignorance of books, is an early example of a type present in many of Austen's novels. *Sense and Sensibility* continues the satire of the sportsman in its delineation of Sir John Middleton.

Sir John Middleton is characterized by his love for hunting on the one hand, and a "total want of talent and taste" (38) on the other. During Marianne's musical performance, he "was loud in his admiration at the end of every song, and as loud in his conversation with the others while every song lasted" (41). If the hunting ideal emphasizes hospitality and generosity, Sir John possesses these qualities with a vengeance; Austen makes clear that there is a self-serving motive underlying his generosity: a family party is to be avoided at all costs. It is not long before the Dashwood women experience his hospitality as oppressive: as Marianne puts it, "The rent of this cottage is said to be low; but we have it on very hard terms, if we are to dine at the park whenever any one is staying either with them, or with us" (126). While he may be infinitely generous with his company, there are limits when it comes to the more material. He does charge rent to his impoverished female relatives, and is possessive of his hunting grounds:

> In shewing kindness to his cousins therefore he had the real satisfaction of a good heart; and in settling a family of females only in his cottage, he had all the satisfaction of a sportsman; for a sportsman, though he esteems only those of his sex who are sportsmen likewise, is not often desirous of encouraging their taste by admitting them to residence within his own manor. (39)

Putting the "satisfaction of a good heart" and "the satisfaction of a sportsman" in opposition to each other, the passage comes close to echoing Cowper's characterization of the hunter as having a "heart ... hard in nature" (*Task* 6.321).

Sir John's marriage completes the satirical picture of the sportsman. Elinor's statement that "perhaps thirty-five and seventeen had better not have anything to do with matrimony together" (45) is relevant to the Middletons. The much younger Lady Middleton ("six or seven and twenty" in contrast to her husband, "about forty") clearly is a trophy wife: "her face was handsome, her figure tall and striking, and her address graceful" (36). There is no suggestion of mutual affection or even respect between them; constant diversion is "necessary to the happiness of both": "They were scarcely ever without some friends staying with them in the house, and they kept more company of every kind than any other family in the neighbourhood" (38). While Lady Middleton enjoys social visits— they "gave exercise to [her] good breeding" (38), the novel also notes that Sir John's hunger for company sets the agenda. When, unbeknownst to her, Sir John invites the Steele sisters for an extended visit to Barton Park, Lady Middleton's unease is registered and she retaliates by nagging: she "resigned herself to the idea of it, with all the philosophy of a well bred woman, contenting herself with merely giving her husband a gentle reprimand on the subject five or six times every day" (137). Tara Goshal Wallace is right to point out the lack of "sensitivity and sense of a man who would so casually foist house-guests on his wife" (152).[14] If Sir John fails as a husband, he also fails as a father. The Middleton offspring, certainly the least flattering portrait of children in Austen, are "noisy" and entertain themselves by tearing their mother's clothes (41). When the Steele sisters are at Barton, they are at the receiving end of similar attention, "their sashes untied, their hair pulled about their ears, their work-bags searched, and their knives and scissors stolen away" (139). The sportsman, then, is an inadequate model of domestic affection, a theme repeated in the portrait of Charles Musgrove in *Persuasion*.

If Sir John Middleton is a satire of the hunting ideal, Willoughby, who enters the novel as "a gentleman carrying a gun, with two pointers playing round him" (50), initially appears to be its celebration. He is handsome, eloquent, and warm; he is interested in books and music; and his rescue of Marianne shows he is a man of action: he "offered his services, and perceiving that her modesty declined what her situation rendered necessary, took her up in his arms without farther delay, and carried her down the hill" (50) and "then departed, to make himself still more interesting, in the midst of an heavy rain" (51). But Austen carefully reveals that he is too good to be true and that his virtues are partly the product of Marianne's "busy" imagination:

> His person and air were equal to what her fancy had ever drawn for the hero of
> a favourite story; and in his carrying her into the house with so little previous

---

[14]   Wallace, however, goes on to argue that Austen shifts the attention from Sir John's lack of sensitivity to Lady Middleton's coldness as an example of the novel's anti-feminism.

formality, there was a rapidity of thought which particularly recommended the action to her. Every circumstance belonging to him was interesting. His name was good, his residence was in their favourite village, and she soon found out that of all manly dresses a shooting jacket was the most becoming. (51)

Willoughby's literary taste, in particular, is suspect and subject to the novel's irony:

> [Marianne] proceeded to question him on the subject of books; her favourite authors were brought forward and dwelt upon with so rapturous a delight, that any young man of five and twenty must have been insensible indeed, not to become an immediate convert to the excellence of such works, however disregarded before. Their taste was strikingly alike. The same books, the same passages were idolized by each—or if any difference appeared, any objection arose, it lasted no longer than till the force of her arguments and the brightness of her eyes could be displayed. He acquiesced in all her decisions, caught all her enthusiasm. (56)

Clearly, Willoughby is more sensible to female charms than literary ones. *Mansfield Park*'s Henry Crawford is similarly a gifted actor; he reads well, but always with a female audience in mind. Willoughby's admiration of Cowper (57) particularly rings false given the poet's stance on rural sport. It is interesting that in an earlier passage, Marianne Dashwood is disappointed by Edward's "spiritless" and "tame" reading: "if he is not to be animated by Cowper!" (20). Jane Austen does not specify the particular passage in question. Ang Lee's film adaptation shows Edward reading from Cowper's "The Cast-Away," and Doody suggests possible allusions to the "critique of slavery," the "praise of liberty," or the "sense of the divine in nature" found in *The Task* (xvii). It is also possible that Austen had in mind an anti-sport passage, especially since, later on in the novel, it is Edward Ferrars who comments that "every body does not hunt" (106) and, in the same conversation, points to Marianne's love of "Thomson, Cowper, Scott" (107). Willoughby initially conforms to the hunting ideal, but he (and the hunting ideal) are eventually discredited.

Margaret thinks of Willoughby as "Marianne's preserver," but Austen undercuts this glamorized view as "more elegan[t] than precis[e]" (55) and, as the novel progresses, Willoughby comes close to being Marianne's destroyer. Austen's orchestration of their first meeting is telling: Willoughby, clearly out on sport, runs into the injured Marianne. His dalliance with Marianne is framed as a form of sport. While Elinor initially cannot "believ[e] him so unprincipled as to have been *sporting* with the affections of her sister from the first" (203; emphasis mine), after listening to Willoughby's confession at Cleveland, she accurately concludes that "It was selfishness which first made him *sport* with … [Marianne's] affections" (398; emphasis mine). In Willoughby's own words, he had been "Careless of her happiness, thinking only of my own amusement" (362). The fate of the first Eliza makes Willoughby's predatory nature explicit, and his conduct towards women is repeatedly described in terms of "cruelty" (209, 215, 216, 363, 365). No wonder that "his seduction and desertion of Miss Williams, the misery of that poor girl, and the doubt of what his designs might *once* have been on herself, preyed … on … [Marianne's] spirits" (241).

Marianne's love of Cowper is stated three times and ironically undercuts her relationship with Willoughby, whose sporting activities are emphasized throughout the novel. Even during Marianne's "season of happiness" (64), Willoughby's mornings are dedicated to sport, while "the rest of the day was spent by himself at the side of Marianne, and by his favourite pointer at her feet" (84). Marianne misreads her place in this tableau and fails to recognize that she is merely a diversion, another form of prey. Moreover, as Doody points out, "Marianne begins dangerously to collude with the hunters" (xxix) and "becomes greedy and predatory" (xxx) when visiting Allenham: "She would sweep away all trace of the former mistress … without a qualm. She bears in this instance a horrid likeness to her half-brother" (xxxi). Marianne's "collusion" with Willoughby not only endangers her but also makes her thoughtless of others.

While Willoughby feels "a pang" for Marianne, "he lived to exert, and frequently to enjoy himself" and "in his breed of horses and dogs, and in sporting of every kind, he found no inconsiderable degree of domestic felicity" (430). His "sporting of every kind" insinuates that he will continue his pursuit of women alongside that of animals. The fact that Marianne is "his secret standard of perfection in woman; and many a rising beauty would be slighted by him in after-days as bearing no comparison with Mrs. Brandon" (430–31) suggests that he will continue to seek "amusement" (362). Sir John's assessment of Willoughby turns out to be not that incomplete after all: Willoughby is "a very decent shot" (52).

Mansfield Park's Mr. Rushworth is another satirical portrait of the sportsman in the style of Sir John and John Thorpe. He is no great reader. "An inferior young man, as ignorant in business as in books" (233), he struggles with his "two and forty speeches" (164) in the rehearsing of *Lovers' Vows*, and instead, focuses on his fine costumes: "I … come in first with a blue dress, and a pink satin cloak, and afterwards am to have another fine fancy suit by way of a shooting dress" (163). The reference to the "shooting dress" links Rushworth's literary ignorance, personal vanity, and sporting as objects of the text's satire. Game books, rather than plays or novels, likely are more his speed.[15] Rushworth falls far short of being the steward of land and community imagined in the idealizing portraits of the hunting gentleman. Maria is "doomed to the repeated details of his day's sport, good or bad, his boast of his dogs, his jealousy of his neighbours, his doubts of their qualification, and his zeal after poachers" (135). Neither does Tom Bertram live up to the hunting ideal. His hunting and horse-racing incur debts which damage the family fortune. At the beginning of Chapter 12 we are told that "Sir Thomas was to return [from Antigua] in November, and his eldest son had duties to call

---

[15]   Game books "began in their modern form in the mid-eighteenth century, and by the nineteenth all those participating in hunting and shooting were encouraged to keep one … . They were primarily a record of visitors, numbers of guns, and the quantity of game shot on each day of the season" (MacKenzie 34).

him earlier home. The approach of September brought tidings of Mr. Bertram *first in a letter to the gamekeeper*, and then in a letter to Edmund; and by the end of August, he arrived himself" (134; emphasis mine). Tom's priorities in letter writing underscore his failure as a responsible and affectionate oldest son and brother.

Like Tom Bertram, Henry Crawford plans his arrivals and departures according to the hunting calendar: "The season and duties which brought Mr. Bertram back to Mansfield, took Mr. Crawford into Norfolk. Everingham could not do without him in the beginning of September" (134–35). The female characters, in particular Fanny, of course, do not enjoy such mobility. Henry's hunting trip to Everingham is associated with his "thoughtless and selfish" conduct towards Julia and Maria: "a fortnight of sufficient leisure in the intervals of shooting and sleeping" should "have convinced the gentleman that he ought to keep longer away, had he been more in the habit of examining his own motives, and of reflecting to what the indulgence of his vanity was tending" (135). Time away to pursue rural sport does not lead to contemplation; Crawford returns to renew his pursuit of the Bertram sisters. Like Willoughby in *Sense and Sensibility*, Henry Crawford targets women and animals alike. The perceptive Fanny understands this: "I cannot think well of a man who sports with any woman's feelings" (419).

Crawford pursues Fanny as sport; indeed, he synchronizes his dalliance with his hunting: "And how do you think I mean to amuse myself … on the days that I do not hunt? … I have a plan for the intermediate days … . My plan is to make Fanny Price in love with me" (267). He aims to "mak[e] a small hole in Fanny Price's heart" (267) in the course of his two-week stay. When Mary objects that "she is as good a little creature as ever lived, and has a great deal of feeling," Henry glibly replies, "if a fortnight can kill her, she must have a constitution which nothing could save" (269). The passage indicts Henry's cruelty and dishonesty, for obviously any puncture of the heart, no matter how "small," will kill. That Fanny is no easy target increases her appeal: "A little difficulty to be overcome, was no evil to Henry Crawford. He rather derived spirits from it … . His situation was new and animating" (377). That Fanny's love was "withheld" makes Henry "determined … to have the glory, as well as the felicity, of forcing her to love him" (376). Ruth Yeazell is right to note the "sadistic excitement that the narrator registers here" (145). Mary Crawford may advise Fanny to enjoy the "glory of fixing one who has been shot at by so many" (419) and Henry may claim to have been "caught" (338) by Fanny, but it is clear that Fanny is the one preyed upon. She suffers severe consequences for her refusal of Henry; Sir Thomas "exile[s]" (455) Fanny to Portsmouth and intends her "being starved, both mind and body, into a much juster value for Mr. Crawford's good company and good fortune" (479). The narrator dryly remarks that had Sir Thomas seen the effects of his "medicinal project" (425), "he would probably have feared to push his experiment farther, lest she might die under the cure" (479).

While the treatment of sport in *Sense and Sensibility* and *Northanger Abbey* focuses on the novels' buffoons and villains, sport in *Mansfield Park* binds all the men together. Even Fanny's beloved brother William eagerly pursues rural sports. Biographer David Nokes suggests that Austen resented sport's associated privileges and its "convenient means of self-promotion" (107). Hunting marks the world of opportunities and independence and women's exclusion from it. William's promotion is helped along during his outings with Henry Crawford, as is the latter's pursuit of Fanny: he "fully intended" that his lending of a horse to William for the foxhunt "produce" obligation on Fanny's part (276). The hunting of the fox and Fanny are in tandem. It is also significant that on his last day of visiting Mansfield, William "determined to make this ... a day of thorough enjoyment, was out snipe shooting" (310), rather than spending the day with his sister. This is a detail which puts sport in opposition to domestic affection; in contrast to William, Fanny is anxious not to lose a moment with her brother. Against her uncle's advice, she insists on getting up early after the ball to share breakfast: "It will be the last time you know, the last morning" (325).

Fanny manages to escape Henry, but the novel's likening of courtship to a sport which objectifies and harms women implicates the central marriage plot. Edmund is not outside the world of hunters. When Edmund and Fanny are invited to dinner with the Grants and the Crawfords at the Parsonage, "there is ... much between the two men about hunting" (260). We are told earlier about Edmund shooting with his brother (212), and of hunting with Crawford (280). The participation of the clergy in rural sport was of some controversy during Austen's time and "there were those who, while willing to accept hunting as a sport for laymen, saw it as an unfit occupation for the clergy" (Itzkowitz 37). Cowper condemns the "cassock'd huntsman" (111) in "The Progress of Error."[16] Since Fanny quotes *The Task* on the cutting of trees, she presumably also recalls Cowper's denunciation of hunting in the same poem. During Fanny's most severe trial—Sir Thomas's coercion to accept Henry Crawford's proposal—Edmund, motivated by his own interest in the Crawfords, fails her: he is "entirely on his father's side of the question" (387). The choreography of the following scene casts Henry's pursuit of Fanny as a form of hunting and makes Edmund complicit in the "attack":

> as Edmund perceived, by his [Henry's] drawing in a chair, and sitting down close by her, that it was to be a very thorough attack, that looks and undertones were to be well tried, he sank as quietly as possible into a corner, turned his back, and took up a newspaper, very sincerely wishing that dear little Fanny might be persuaded into explaining away that shake of the head to the satisfaction of her ardent lover; and as earnestly trying to bury every sound of the business from himself in murmurs of his own, over the various advertisements of 'a most desirable estate in South Wales'—'To Parents and Guardians'—and a 'Capital season'd Hunter.' (395)

---

[16] William Gilpin also denounces clergymen's hunting in *On the Amusements of Clergymen*; see Itzkovitz (37). Austen was familiar with Gilpin's writings on the picturesque.

That Fanny marries a sportsman is one of the novel's final ironies and contributes to the "parodic elements of [the] denouement" (Johnson 114):

> I purposely abstain from dates on this occasion, that every one may be at liberty to fix their own, aware that the cure of unconquerable passions, and the transfer of unchanging attachments, must vary much as to time in different people.—I only intreat every body to believe that exactly at the time when it was quite natural that it should be so, and not a week earlier, Edmund did cease to care about Miss Crawford, and became as anxious to marry Fanny, as Fanny herself could desire. (544)

In *Sense and Sensibility* and *Northanger Abbey* the structural parallels between the hunting of animals and of women are developed in subplots which cast shadows over the main marriage plots, but in *Mansfield Park* the parallels are on center stage. Moreover, in this novel, Austen connects the ideology of sport to imperialism. John M. MacKenzie argues in *The Empire of Nature: Hunting, Conservation and British Imperialism* that hunting was an "expression of global dominance" (50).

When William tells stories about his navy experiences in the West Indies, Henry's and Edmund's thoughts turn to hunting; Henry "longed to have been at sea, and seen and done and suffered as much":

> His heart was warmed, his fancy fired, and he felt the highest respect for a lad who, before he was twenty, had gone through such bodily hardships, and given such proofs of mind. The glory of heroism, of usefulness, of exertion, of endurance, made his own habits of selfish indulgence appear in shameful contrast; and he wished he had been a William Price … . The wish was rather eager than lasting. He was roused from the reverie of retrospection … by some inquiry from Edmund as to his plans for the next day's hunting; and he found it was well to be a man of fortune at once with horses and grooms at his command. (275–76)

Contrasting William's naval service to the gentlemen's idleness, the passage undercuts the hunting ideal. Henry may long to have "suffered as much" but he clearly has not, and so, far from leading to patriotic action, as defenders of the sport claimed, sport is put in opposition to it. The passage arguably is an early treatment of the contrast between Captain Wentworth and the gentry in *Persuasion*. But William, too, is keen to participate in the hunt, and his eagerness links all male characters. One might argue, then, that the turn in conversation from the West Indies to hunting establishes a connection between the two. The mastery of nature which underpins the sporting paradigm also implies the mastery of those associated with nature (children, women, the poor, colonial others, and slaves); it is in this sense that Matt Cartmill sees hunting as "a symbol of the whole imperial enterprise" (135). Chapter 4 explores in more detail the connections made in *Mansfield Park* between the mastery of nature and the mastery of humans.

The structural parallels between the positions of women and animals struck Austen at an early age. In *Personal Aspects of Jane Austen*, Mary Augusta Austen-Leigh imagines a young Austen's longing to join her brothers' sport:

> Jane when five or six must often have gazed with admiring, if not envious, eyes at her next oldest brother, Frank, setting off for the hunting field at the ripe age of seven, on his bright chestnut pony squirrel (bought by himself for £1 12s.), dressed in the suit of scarlet cloth made for him from a riding habit which had formed part of his mother's wedding outfit. (57)

A look at the juvenilia, however, suggests that Austen's feelings diverge rather sharply from admiration and envy. In "Sir William Mountague" the eponymous hero, at age 17, inherits "a handsome fortune, an ancient House and a Park well stocked with Deer" (*J* 47). The early fragment, dedicated by Austen to her brother Charles, plays with the idea that avid hunters are cavalier with the affections of women. In the space of merely two pages, Sir William falls in love with seven women, becomes engaged to two of them, and then marries a third one, but, forced to choose between a wedding and the opening of the shooting season, opts for the latter:

> Sir William was a Shot and could not support the idea of losing such a Day, even for such Cause … . Lady Percival was enraged … . Sir William was sorry to lose her, but as he knew that he should have been much more greived by the Loss of the 1st of September, his Sorrow was not without a mixture of Happiness, and his Affliction was considerably lessened by his Joy. (*J* 48)

One is reminded of Willoughby, who, at the end of *Sense and Sensibility*, "lived to exert, and frequently to enjoy himself" (430) despite losing Marianne. In "Jack and Alice," written by a teenage Austen, Lucy actively pursues the object of her affections, Charles Adams: "I was determined to make a bold push and therefore wrote him a very kind letter, offering him with great tenderness my hand & heart. To this I received an angry … refusal, but thinking it might be rather the effect of his modesty than anything else, I pressed him again on the subject. But he never answered any more of my Letters and very soon afterwards left the Country." When Lucy pursues Charles to his estate, she "found … [herself] suddenly seized by the leg and … caught in one of the steel traps so common in gentlemen's grounds" (*J* 24). Lucy's fate is a striking image of the sporting world: landed gentlemen protect their right to hunt animals and take on a similarly dominant role in their relationships with women. "Oh! cruel Charles to wound the hearts and legs of all the fair," Alice laments (*J* 25).

Biographer Claire Tomalin suggests that Austen "kept quiet about Cowper's detestation of field sports" (137–38) out of loyalty to her brothers, who did hunt, but, as we have seen, Austen's novels speak loudly about the subject. Austen's correspondence also deserves a closer look. Sulloway notes that Austen's epistolary jokes on the subject of male game-hunting is another example of her implicit contrasts between HIS privileges and *her* deprivations. But her irony on the subject of brothers who relished game-hunting would have cheered … feminists … [who] associated the killing of defenseless game for mere sport with men's legal and social permission to abuse defenseless women. (188)

Austen's letters to her sister take a censorious view of rural sport. For example, in September 1796 Austen writes to Cassandra:

> Edward and Fly [Frank] went out yesterday very early in a couple of Shooting Jackets, and came home like a couple of Bad Shots, for they killed nothing at all. They are out again today, & are not yet returned—Delightful Sport!—They are just come home; Edward with his two Brace, Frank with his Two and a half. What amiable Young Men! (10)

The description rings with irony. The sport is hardly "delightful" to her since she cannot participate in it. Nor does she employ euphemistic language—the sport's success is boldly announced as "killing"—hardly an attribute of "amiable" behavior! Austen's letter to Cassandra dated October 1813 is similarly revealing:

> As I wrote of my nephews with a little bitterness in my last, I think it particularly incumbent on me to do them justice now, & I have great pleasure in saying that they were both at the Sacrament yesterday. After having much praised or much blamed anybody, one is generally sensible of something just the reverse soon afterwards. Now, these two Boys who are out with the Foxhounds will come home & disgust me again by some habit of Luxury or some proof of sporting Mania—unless I keep it off by this prediction.—They amuse themselves very comfortably in the Even^g—by netting; they are each about a rabbit net, & sit as deedily to it, side by side, as any two Uncle Franks could do.—I am looking over Self Control again. (234)

Unfortunately, the letter expressing "bitterness" towards her nephews "was no doubt destroyed by CEA [Cassandra] for this reason" (*Letters* 423, n6). The surviving letter attempts to compensate for the previously expressed "bitter" sentiment with "praise" for the boys, but its attitude "reverse[s]" again to "blame" when reporting their "sporting Mania." Further, it is interesting to note that Austen contrasts the boys' working on their rabbit nets with her reading of Mary Brunton's novel, *Self-Control*.

The novels, I have argued, posit that women and animals are both objects of sport in patriarchy. Austen's letter dated September 1, 1796, from Rowling (the home of Edward Austen Knight prior to inheriting Godmersham Park) takes a similar perspective. Austen writes to Cassandra that she "should be glad to get home by the end of the month" but fears she cannot, for her brother Henry hopes to receive a "leave of absence for three weeks, as he wants very much to have some shooting at Godmersham, whither Edward and Elizabeth are to remove very early in October. If this scheme holds, I shall hardly be at Steventon before the middle of that month" (6). She resigns herself: "I am sorry for it, but what can I do?" (6).

Austen likens her dependence on her brother's travel arrangement to that of the heroine in Frances Burney's *Camilla*: "To-morrow I shall be just like Camilla in Mr. Dubster's summer-house; for my Lionel will have taken away the ladder by which I came here, or at least by which I intended to get away, and here I must stay till his return" (6). Lionel's entrapment of his sisters in the summer-house is one of the many examples of his bullying of his sisters; in this specific case, he abandons them to join "a party of sportsmen ... in defiance of the serious entreaties of his sisters" (282). Trapped in the summerhouse with Mr. Dubster, Camilla and Eugenia are sitting ducks, vulnerable to mockery and unwanted attention. Austen similarly connects her own lack of liberty to her brothers' sporting activities. Further, at the end of the same letter, Austen notes, "We are very busy making Edward's shirts, and I am proud to say that I am the neatest worker of the party. They say that there are a prodigious number of birds hereabouts this year, so that perhaps *I* may kill a few" (7). The letter contrasts the leisure of the brothers' rural sport and her own domestic labor. The italicizing of the "I" highlights Austen's irony: she will be far too busy for the leisure of killing. Her dependence and her labor are framed by the contrasting male privilege which plays itself out in sport.

Austen also undermines the justification of rural sport as promoting "warlike capabilities" and "national loyalty" (Deuchar 155). On August 30, 1805, she writes:

> Next week seems likely to be an unpleasant one to this family on the matter of game. The evil intentions of the Guards are certain, and the gentlemen of the neighbourhood seem unwilling to come forward in any decided or early support of their rights. Edward Bridges has been trying to arouse their spirits, but without success. (112)

She pits sport in opposition to military action, and given that "the danger of invasion was only just past" (*Letters* 384, n2), the gentry's preoccupation with rural sport is depicted as idle.[17] A similar trivialization is evident when Austen mentions an injury with little sympathy: "Mr Heathcote met with a genteel little accident the other day in hunting; he got off to lead his horse over a hedge or a house or a something, & his horse in his haste trod upon his leg, or rather ancle I beleive, & it is not certain whether the small bone is not broke" (56–57).

Austen's reference to rural sport in a letter to her brother Francis is markedly more restrained than the letters to Cassandra:

---

[17] Deirdre Le Faye quotes Chapman's explanation of this passage: "on Friday 30 Aug. (partridge shooting began on the Monday following) the First and Second Grenadier Guards marched from Deal for Chatham, the First Coldstreams and the First Scots Guards from Chatham for Deal. A movement on such a scale might well disturb the birds; and Mr. Edward Bridges may have apprehended that (in spite of the efforts of their officers) some of the men might to a bit of poaching ... . Napoleon's orders for the march from Boulogne to the Danube were not issued until 22 August, and the camp at Boulogne was not finally evacuated until that same fateful 30 August" (*Letters* 384, n2).

Henry has probably sent you his own account of his visit in Scotland. I wish he
had had more time & could have gone farther north, & deviated to the Lakes
in his way back, but what he was able to do seems to have afforded him great
Enjoyment & he met with Scenes of higher Beauty in Roxburgshire than I had
supposed the South of Scotland possessed.—Our nephew's gratification was less
keen than our Brother's.—Edward is no Enthusiast in the beauties of Nature.
His Enthusiasm is for the Sports of the field only.—He is a very promising &
pleasing young Man however upon the whole … & we must forgive his thinking
more of Growse & Partridges than Lakes & Mountains. (230)

Austen does not express any direct criticism of sport here, but she maintains the
opposition between nature and rural sport, an opposition which undoes one of the
sporting world's most cherished ideals.

While some women did participate in the hunt in the eighteenth century,
Austen has sport divide men and women.[18] In "The Watsons," even the 10-year-
old Charles Blake proudly tells Emma "that he … had a horse of his own given
him by Lord Osborne; and that he had been out once already with Lord Osborne's
hounds" (*LM* 99). There are no female hunters in Austen's fiction. The closest we
come to a female hunter is the "captivating" (*LM* 7) Lady Susan, but her targets are
human animals. In Austen's daring "Lady Susan," the heroine's reversal of gender
roles also extends to the terrain of the sexual hunt. When Reginald "accept[s]
Mr. Vernon's invitation to prolong his stay in Sussex that they may have some
hunting together," he also is motivated by "the fascination" with Lady Susan (*LM*
15). Reginald's first letter seems to position him as a Henry Crawford type, and
Lady Susan characterizes his early treatment of her as "a sort of sauciness, of
familiarity" (*LM* 14), yet he soon becomes "captivated" (*LM* 20) by her. To Lady
Susan, Reginald is "a handsome young Man, who promises me some amusement"
(*LM* 14). She revels in her "desire of dominion" (*LM* 19) and for most of the
narrative, achieves this dominion over men (Reginald, Mr. Vernon, Sir James,
and Mr. Manwaring); she is confident in her manipulative skills: "a very few
words from me softened [Reginald] at once into the utmost submission" (*LM* 57).
Lady Susan refers to London as "the fairest field for action" (*LM* 58), suggesting
her approach to flirtation as conquest. Her weapon is her "happy command of
Language … used … to make Black appear White" (*LM* 11–12), and her contempt
for Frederica partly has to do with her "artlessness": "I never saw a girl of her age,
bid fairer to be the sport of Mankind" (*LM* 36). While, as we have seen, Austen
frequently associates sport with a lack of linguistic skill (as in John Thorpe,
Sir John Middleton, and Mr. Rushworth), in Lady Susan's world of "women-

---

[18]   For discussion of women hunters, see Betty Rizzo and Donna Landry. In *The
Invention of the Countryside: Hunting, Walking and Ecology in English Literature, 1671–
1831*, Landry argues that "the exclusion of women from field sports which began in the
eighteenth century coincided with their exclusion from science" (146). Her analysis of sport
in Austen is very different from mine; she suggests "Austen's envy" of her brothers' sport
("Learning to Ride at Mansfield Park" 70).

on-top" (Natalie Zemon Davis, qtd. in Kaplan, "Female Friendship" 163), the heroine's linguistic mastery parallels her metaphoric usurping of the hunter's role. Lady Susan does not express any interest in participating in rural sport but applies its language to her domination of men, reversing sport's gender politics while sidestepping its ritual enactment in the shooting of animals. Lady Susan is an exception, however. Women, in Austen's world, do not hunt; rather they are hunted. The sporting assumption—animals are there for human enjoyment, particularly that of landed gentlemen—extends to the treatment of women: both women and animals are fair game.

Chapter 3
Too Cool about Sporting

Lady Jane Grey ... was ... an amiable young Woman and famous for reading
Greek while other people were hunting. (*J* 180)

We have seen in Chapter 2 that Austen consistently opposes rural sport to
contemplation and reading in *Northanger Abbey*, *Sense and Sensibility*, and
Mansfield Park. While *Persuasion* and *Pride and Prejudice* continue the satire of
the sportsman, both include male characters who prefer books to sport. Captain
Benwick is a lover of poetry, and Darcy's Pemberley is distinctive not only for its
natural beauty but also for its library: Darcy "cannot comprehend the neglect of a
family library" (41). While in her final completed novel, Benwick is a secondary
character who dialogizes the main narrative, undermining its closure, in the earlier
novel Austen places the reading man at the center: Darcy is a bad sport, not only
at odds with Meryton's codes of social politeness but also distanced from the
gentlemen's world of hunting and shooting. Sport and courtship often coincide
in Austen, but in the relationship of Darcy and Elizabeth *Pride and Prejudice*
attempts a utopian challenge to the sporting world and its associated hierarchies.
When we set *Pride and Prejudice* next to *Persuasion*, similarities between Darcy
and Captain Benwick, as well as the novels' depictions of nature, emerge.

Persuasion has long been awarded a special place in the Austen canon on
account of its supposedly new affinity with the Romantic celebration of nature. In
The Common Reader, Virginia Woolf writes that unlike Austen's other novels, in
which "Nature and its beauties" are "approached in a sidelong way of her own"
(140), in *Persuasion* there is "a new sensibility to nature": "She is beginning to
discover that the world is larger, more mysterious, and more romantic than she had
supposed .... She dwells frequently upon the beauty and the melancholy of nature"
(147). While the connections between *Persuasion* and Romanticism have received
ample critical attention, the novel's references to hunting and shooting have not
been examined in this regard. I argue that *Persuasion*'s emphasis on nature and its
depiction of characters as part of natural cycles contribute to the novel's anti-sport
statement. *Persuasion*'s paean to the sea and "the green chasms between romantic
rocks" (103) at Lyme surely casts Charles Musgrove's "cut[ting] off the heads of
nettles" and "hunt[ing] after a weasel" (97) in critical light.

Charles Musgrove, noted for his lack of reading and his selfish pursuit of
pleasure, follows in the footsteps of *Sense and Sensibility*'s Sir John Middleton.
Anne never regrets her refusal of his marriage offer: "he did nothing with much
zeal, but sport; and his time was otherwise trifled away, without benefit from
books, or any thing else" (47). Without sport, he is at a loss; he accompanies
Captain Harville, who has "business" in Bath, "by way of doing something, as

shooting was over" (235). Austen highlights Charles's failure as husband and
father, and explicitly opposes rural sport to domestic affection. When Anne
first arrives at Uppercross, she finds her sister alone and unwell: "Charles is out
shooting. I have not seen him since seven o'clock. He would go, though I told him
how ill I was. He said he should not stay out long; but he has never come back, and
now it is almost one" (40). Since Mary's "ailments lessened by having a constant
companion" (50) in Anne, it follows that Charles plays a key role in producing his
wife's hypochondria. Moreover, even when his son is seriously injured, he is out
shooting the next day: "what was there for a father to do? This was quite a female
case, and it would be highly absurd in him, who could be of no use at home, to
shut himself up" (59). And on the walk back from Winthrop, Charles abandons
both Mary and Anne, who "was tired enough to be very glad of Charles's ... arm"
(96), to "cut off the heads of some nettles in the hedge with his switch" and "to
hunt after a weasel which he had a momentary glance of" (97). As Roger Sales
dryly comments, Charles's "fondness for hunting weasels and rats is not meant to
endear him" (196). Partnered with the petulant beheading of nettles, the killing of
animals is depicted as pointless; moreover, the fact that he hunts weasels because
he is "out of temper with his wife" (96) suggests a displaced violence. The last we
see of Charles Musgrove is when he takes his leave of Anne and Wentworth for the
"sight of a capital gun" (261).

Persuasion also includes male characters who, in contrast to Charles Musgrove,
occupy an ambiguous position in relation to rural sport. Charles Hayter is a "scholar
and gentleman" (80) who will not "value" the hunting privileges of his new living
as a curate "as he ought": he "is too cool about sporting" (236), says his cousin,
Charles Musgrove. Captain Benwick is characterized by an admiration for the
"richness of the present age" (108) of poetry on the one hand, and a lack of interest
in rural sport on the other, the first perhaps leading to the latter. Benwick's pursuits
are "sedentary" (104): "Give him a book, and he will read all day long" (143). The
description of Benwick as a "reading man" (199) is emphasized and clearly meant to
distinguish him; Anne correctly surmises that "his usual companions had probably
no concern" (108) in books: "Captain Harville was no reader" (106). Benwick's
abstinence from sport causes considerable anxiety amongst the Musgroves and
Admiral Croft. In the social world *Persuasion* depicts, rural sport demarcates
separate spheres: "The Mr. Musgroves had their own game to guard, and to destroy;
their own horses, dogs, and newspapers to engage them; and the females were fully
occupied in all the other common subjects of house-keeping, neighbours, dress,
dancing, and music" (46). Wentworth and Charles are "shooting together," while
"the sisters in the Cottage were sitting quietly at work" (89). For women, hunting
is strictly a spectator activity: the only sporting Louisa and Henrietta do is the
"hunting of the Laconia" (72) in the navy lists. Given the gendered nature of sport,
Benwick is indeed a "very odd young man"; as Mary puts it,

> I do not know what he would be at. We asked him to come home with us for a
> day or two; Charles undertook to give him some shooting, and he seemed quite

delighted, and for my part, I thought it was all settled; when behold! on Tuesday night, he made a very awkward sort of excuse; "he never shot" and he had "been quite misunderstood." (141)

As hunting marks the mastery of nature, Captain Benwick's lack of interest in sport puts his masculinity into question. Admiral Croft feels that his "soft sort of manner does not do him justice" and finds his manner "rather too piano for me" (186). Anne attempts to defend Benwick by "oppos[ing] the too-common idea of spirit and gentleness being incompatible with each other" (187). At the end of the novel, we do hear of Benwick "rat-hunting" at Uppercross from Charles: "We had a famous set-to at rat-hunting all the morning, in my father's great barns; and he played his part so well, that I have liked him the better ever since" (237). The choice of words here is suggestive. Benwick "plays his part"; sport is a performance, a ritual enactment, of masculinity. Benwick's "play[ing] his part" also might suggest that his participation is half-hearted.[1]

While the Musgroves and Admiral Croft find Benwick "odd," his love for books unites him with the novel's heroine. Not a hunter, he also takes on a more egalitarian role in his relationship with women. Anne and Benwick's conversations about literature are an exchange. Their first conversation is "a brief comparison of opinion as to the first-rate poets, trying to ascertain whether *Marmion* or *The Lady of the Lake* were to be preferred, and how ranked the *Giaour* and *The Bride of Abydos*" (108). In contrast to the ironic description of Marianne and Willoughby's reading in *Sense and Sensibility* ("the same passages were idolized by each" [56]), Anne and Benwick are not in perfect harmony; Anne interrupts Benwick's rhapsodies: "she ventured to hope he did not always read only poetry; and to say, that she thought it was the misfortune of poetry, to be seldom safely enjoyed by those who enjoyed it completely" (108). Anne, "feeling in herself the right of seniority of mind" (108), gives advice to Benwick, and he "noted down the names of those she recommended, and promised to procure and read them" (109). Their conversation about books is developed on two further occasions. On the second day of the Lyme visit, Anne and Benwick again "walked together some time, talking as before of Mr. Scott and Lord Byron, and still as unable, as before, and as unable as any other two readers, to think exactly alike of the merits of either" (116), and in the final walk along the cobb later that day, their conversation again turns to Byron.

These conversations are especially resonant given that, from its very opening sentence, *Persuasion* sets up reading as a touchstone of character. The novel's first sentence establishes Sir Walter's vanity and stupidity through the paucity of his reading: "Sir Walter Elliot ... was a man who, for his own amusement, never took up any book but the Baronetage; there he found occupation for an idle hour, and consolation in a distressed one; there his faculties were roused into admiration and

---

[1]   Further, there is a significant difference between rural sport and the farm management in which Benwick is said to have participated.

respect" (3). His eldest daughter, Elizabeth, only "pretend[s]" to have read books lent to her by Lady Russell: "I really cannot be plaguing myself for ever with all the new poems and states of the nation that come out" (233). Mary, his youngest daughter, also is not much of a reader: she "had no resources for solitude" (39), and her visits to the Lyme library are primarily social outings: "There had been so much going on every day, there had been so many walks between their lodgings and the Harvilles, and she had got books from the library and changed them so often" (141). In contrast to her family, Anne Elliot turns to books as a "resource for solitude": during the walk to Winthrop, for example, she "repeat[s] to herself some few of the thousand poetical descriptions extant of autumn, that season of peculiar and inexhaustible influence on the mind of taste and tenderness, that season which has drawn from every poet, worthy of being read, some attempt at description, or some lines of feeling" (90). Anne's conversations with Captain Benwick establish her literary knowledge as authoritative.

Books are not the only thing that Anne and Benwick have in common. They also share the role of nurse, as is clear in Austen's choreography of the fall at the cobb: when the shocked Henrietta faints, she "would have fallen on the steps, but for Captain Benwick and Anne, who caught and supported her between them" (118). Both are instrumental to Louisa's recovery. Benwick is often seen as Austen's parody of the Romantic poet; he claims to be forever lost in grief over the death of his first beloved, but recovers quickly to marry Louisa. Deresiewicz astutely points out that "this view ignores Anne's own response to her fellow mourner": "she later joins Captain Harville in deploring the rapidity with which Benwick gets reengaged, but she not only recognizes the genuineness of his grief, she had encouraged him to overcome it." Anne "recognizes that it is the very strength of Benwick's passion ... not its superficiality, that insures that he will soon fall in love again" (*Romantic Poets* 134). Further, it is significant that Benwick's recovery from grief coincides with Louisa's recovery from physical and emotional suffering. Benwick heals *and* so does Louisa. Charles Musgrove's description of the "altered" Louisa as a startled animal is striking in the context of Benwick's anti-sport position: "there is no running or jumping about ... . If one happens only to shut the door a little hard, she starts and wriggles like a young dab chick in the water" (237). While Wentworth is notably absent from Louisa's sickroom, Captain Benwick brings her back to life, "sit[ting] at her elbow, reading verses, or whispering to her, all day long" (237). Benwick nurses life, rather than hunting it.

Austen's opposition of rural sport to domestic affection and nature is particularly resonant in *Persuasion*, with its emphasis on healing and recovery. Trauma abounds in this autumnal novel: the death of Anne's mother; the loss of Kellynch Hall; the broken engagement between Wentworth and Anne; Louisa's fall from the cobb; the death of Fanny Harville; the injury of Captain Harville; Mrs. Smith's loss of her health and fortune; even Mary Musgrove's hypochondria. Deresiewicz writes that "Widowhood ... becomes the central metaphor for a great array of losses, bereavement and mourning the template for the process of loss and recovery as such" (*Romantic Poets* 143). He argues that the farmer, "meaning to have spring again" (91), who is observed by Anne during the Uppercross walk, is the "novel's archetype of the healthy response to loss" (*Romantic Poets* 143). Anne and Benwick are associated with this process of healing both for themselves—Anne's "bloom" (112) returns—and for others. Their role as healers is counterpointed by the role of sport and its wilful destruction of life. Moreover, this pointed contrast is set on a national stage. In *Mothers of the Nation*, Anne K. Mellor suggests that "Austen urges an alternative political model, the model of a family politic, a well-managed national household governed by a loving mother who is attentive to the needs of all her dependents" (138). Anne's role is paramount: she is "the exemplar of excellent domestic management—both in public and at home" (Mellor, *Mothers of the Nation* 132). Similarly, Knox-Shaw argues that *Persuasion* is "directly concerned with the effects of war" (220) and

> effectively provides (with a patriotism modified by the end of hostilities) ... a corrective to the values that have imperceptibly gained ground in wartime Britain. These values, borne of national militancy, and ingrained in the texture of everyday life, are viewed from a feminine standpoint, and set against a celebration of the strength of women. (222)

In her arranging help for Louisa, her nursing of her injured nephew, her comforting of her invalid friend Mrs. Smith, and her counseling of Captain Benwick, Anne restores physical and emotional life rather than destroying it. Anne's role as healer presents an alternative to rural sport, which the novel connects to militarism.

Why, then, does our heroine marry a sportsman? The novel's closure is not exempt from the rigors of Austen's satirical examination of marriage. The novel holds up a narrative of romantic fulfillment, but also subjects it to irony: Anne's "prett[y] musings of high-wrought love and eternal constancy ... along the streets of Bath" were "almost enough to spread purification and perfume all the way" (208). Almost. Wentworth is a compromised hero. His sporting aligns him with Charles Musgrove; after meeting each other for the first time, they "seemed all to know each other perfectly, and he was coming the very next morning to shoot with Charles" (63). Given that Charles Musgrove comes in for a fair amount of the novel's satire, and if we are judged by the company we keep, then the friendship between Wentworth and Charles should give us pause. While clearly Wentworth is not satirized in the same way that Charles is, Austen pointedly undermines one of the primary justifications of the sport. Louisa's fall from the cobb leaves Wentworth "in an agony of silence" (118). If ever there is a moment to valorize the hunter as a man of action, Austen passes it up. When he does speak, "the first words which burst from ... [him], in a tone of despair, and as if all his own strength were gone" are "Is there no one to help me?" (118). It is Anne who responds and takes charge of the situation and, as we have seen, Captain Benwick who joins her efforts.

It is easy to idealize Wentworth in the context of Austen's satire on the landed gentry, and his rise to prominence in the navy has long been celebrated as the triumph of the "self-made man." Yet, there are some similarities between Sir Walter and Wentworth. The latter had been lucky in his profession, but spending freely, what had come freely, had realized nothing. But, he was confident that he should soon be rich;—full of life and ardour, he knew that he should soon have a ship, and soon be on a station that would lead to every thing he wanted. He had always been lucky; he knew he should be so still. (29)

Both men "spend ... freely," and coincidence, rather than merit, figures in both of their financial fates—Sir Walter inherits his money, and Wentworth makes his by "luck." While Lady Russell's objection to Wentworth as a suitable husband for Anne is often put down to class snobbery, Southam's *Jane Austen and the Navy* sheds a more sympathetic light on Lady Russell's objections to Wentworth. Watching her brothers' naval careers, Austen would have been very aware that advancement in the navy was not just a matter of merit. Austen does not detail how Wentworth made his fortune, but Admiral Croft's anger at Admiral Brand and his brother hints at the less savory side of success: "Shabby fellows, both of them! ... They played me a pitiful trick once—got away some of my best men" (184). And while Sir Walter Elliot certainly proves himself unworthy of inherited wealth, we do well to "remember that Wentworth earns his fortune by theft: he literally steals or captures ships ... in acts of war—or equally accurately, in state-licensed piracy. Moreover, he is cavalier about the loss of life that such risk-taking acts of military piracy might incur" (Mellor, *Mothers of the Nation* 125). This "cavalier" approach transfers to his courtships. As Southam points out, "the traits which make Wentworth appear so 'dangerous' to Lady Russell are the very qualities of character which won British Captains mastery of the seas" (*Navy* 272). Admiral Croft's choice of naval metaphor for courtship is appropriate: "I wish Frederick would spread a little more canvas, and bring us home one of these young ladies to Kellynch" (99). Wentworth makes his "handsome fortune" by "successive captures" (32), and once his hunting on the high seas has paid off, he is ready to catch a wife: "it was now his object to marry" (66). In his flirtation with Louisa, Henrietta, and the Hayter girls, who also "were apparently admitted to the honour of being in love with him" (77), he bears an unflattering resemblance to Henry Crawford. Anne's assessment that he was "wrong in accepting (for accepting must be the word) of two young women at once" (88) is a conservative estimate. Moreover, his toying with the Musgrove sisters plays havoc with Charles Hayter's relationship with Henrietta. Knox-Shaw observes the "string of military metaphors [which] underlines [Charles Hayter's] haplessness in this contest":

> Anne is pleased to note that Wentworth is aware of "no triumph, no pitiful triumph" in stealing her young cousin's affections, and Charles after leaving her dangerously "unguarded" is forced "after a short struggle to quit the field," and then finds it necessary to "withdraw" from that position also. (Knox-Shaw 227)

Louisa quickly learns from Wentworth that all is fair in love and war. The description of Louisa at Lyme being "now armed with the idea of merit in maintaining her own way" (101) is, as Knox-Shaw points out, "suggestive" of "a distinct male slant to the lessons that Louisa receives" (229). Anne's assessment that the two Musgrove sisters "were not decided rivals" (71) does not hold up. During the walk at Uppercross, Louisa is all too eager for Henrietta to visit (and reconcile) with Charles Hayter: "Louisa seemed the principal arranger of the plan" (92). As she explains it simply to Wentworth, "I made her go" (93). Clearly Louisa benefits from her sister's reunion with Hayter: "Every thing now marked out Louisa for Captain Wentworth" (96). Deresiewicz relates the topography of the Uppercross walk (its ups and downs) to the novel's theme of loss and healing (*Romantic Poets* 141). The topography also foregrounds the theme of competition: for Louisa to win Wentworth, Henrietta must lose him. Competition is so embedded in the scene that it is reflected even in the following detail of Mary's dissatisfaction:

> Mary was happy no longer; she quarreled with her own seat,—was sure Louisa had got a much better somewhere,—and nothing could prevent her from going to look for a better also … . Anne found a nice one for her … . Mary sat down for a moment, but it would not do; she was sure Louisa had found a better seat somewhere else, and she would go on, till she overtook her. (93)

The theme culminates in Wentworth's famous hazelnut image: "This nut … while so many of its brethren have fallen and been trodden under foot, is still in possession of all the happiness that a hazel-nut can be supposed capable of" (94). Wentworth's language of brotherhood is ironic here; the image speaks of competition and conquest, not solidarity. It is significant, then, that the context of the walk is a failed hunting expedition, for "just as" Anne, Mary, and the Musgrove girls "were setting off, the gentlemen returned. They had taken out a young dog, who had spoilt their sport, and sent them back early. Their time and strength, and spirits, were, therefore, exactly ready for this walk, and they entered into it with pleasure" (90). The dynamics of sport are transferred to the walk and produce social discord. Rather than offering Anne the expected solace and rejuvenation, the outing "tire[s]" (97) her.

Wentworth claims to value "firmness of mind" in women, but his view of women is "riddled with contradiction":

> On the one hand, he upholds the virtues of daring and resolution that he so handsomely exemplifies himself; on the other hand, he insists on the essential passivity of the fair sex. The paradox is well brought home in the run-up to his parable-like speech on the nut when he lets slip that the worst thing about a yielding disposition is that "you are never sure of a good impression being durable" (88)—from which it appears that impressibility is what he is really after. (Knox-Shaw 229)

No wonder, then, that Wentworth is pleased by Louisa's cheerfully co-dependent "If I loved a man … I would be always with him … and I would rather be overturned by him, than driven safely by anybody else" (91). That Wentworth values passivity in women is confirmed by the much-quoted exchange with his sister, Mrs. Croft. When he states that "women and children have no *right* to be comfortable on board," Mrs. Croft objects in a Wollstonecraftian vein, "I hate to hear you talking so, like a fine gentleman, and as if women were all fine ladies, instead of rational creatures" (75).[2] The passivity which Wentworth holds up as a feminine ideal is given a morbid shading in the scene at the cobb:

> the report of the accident had spread among the workmen and boatmen about the Cobb, and many were collected near them, to be useful if wanted, at any rate, to enjoy the sight of a dead young lady, nay, two dead young ladies, for it proved twice as fine as the first report. To some of the best-looking of these good people Henrietta was consigned, for, though partially revived, she was quite helpless. (120)

That Henrietta's helplessness is a source of eroticism for the male spectators offers a pointed comment on the sexual subordination of women.

Given the thematic significance of books, it is worth noting that when we see Captain Wentworth reading, it is only the Navy Lists with the Miss Musgroves in a scene of decided flirtation. This scene of reading is reminiscent of Sir Walter's reading of the Baronetage; as Adela Pinch notes, "both Sir Walter Elliot and Captain Wentworth find pleasure and consolation in reading books that mark their own place in national history" (157). Wentworth does not allude to books; instead he "was very fond of music" (195), but does not make it a topic of conversation. When hero and heroine find themselves at a concert in Bath, music is very much in the background, and the scene is dominated by stock comic misunderstandings between hero and heroine and social satire: "The room filled again, benches were reclaimed and re-possessed, and another hour of pleasure or of penance was to set out, another hour of music was to give delight or the gapes, as real or affected taste for it prevailed" (206). Deresiewicz argues that "In a novel in which the social fabric is so clearly fraying, and in which the heroine in particular is largely isolated from the social world, characters are repeatedly set against the kind of monumental natural backdrops—vast meadows, the sea—that mark them as natural creatures rather than social actors" (*Romantic Poets* 137). While this is true of Anne and Benwick, Austen plants Wentworth and Anne in a social context. The pivotal scene of Wentworth's writing the letter of declaration takes place in a crowded room, at an inn called "The White Hart," perhaps Austen's hint that this courtship is not outside the hunting world. Anne's response to the letter does take place on a walk, once Charles leaves the lovers alone in order to shop for guns, but the walk is an urban one, and the lovers are not alone: "sauntering politicians, bustling house-keepers, flirting girls, ... nursery-maids and children" share that "comparatively quiet and retired gravel-walk" (261–62). After this walk, their next meeting is at the crowded evening party at Camden Place, where they can snatch only moments

---

[2]   Southam explains that Mrs. Croft's advocacy of women's active role is not in keeping with naval practice: "Strictly speaking, it was against regulations to carry women on board ship unless on Admiralty orders, or, after 1806, on orders either from the Admiralty or a Captain's 'Superior Office'" (*Navy* 282).

of conversation while pretending to be "occupied in admiring a fine display of green-house plants" (267). It is striking that in a novel seen as sympathetic to the Romantic ideal of nature, Austen would choose to set her lovers inside. The detail of the greenhouse plants furthers the sense that the relationship of Anne and Wentworth is bound by social conventions, rather than transgressing them. The "indoor" nature of their relationship is in marked contrast to the friendship between Anne and Benwick, and the central relationship between Elizabeth and Darcy in *Pride and Prejudice*.

The sardonic description of Charles and Mary's marriage—"upon the whole … they might pass for a happy couple" (47)—has a broader application in the novel. Joseph Kestner argues, "Neither Jane Austen nor her contemporaries believed marriage terminated the condition of 'things as they are'" ("English Romantic Novel" 308). One part of Austen's social critique of "things as they are" is that the laws of sport also apply to marriage. Anne and Wentworth's marriage does not exist outside the world of rural sport, a world which opposes all the positive values in the novel: nature, books, healing, and domestic affection. If *Persuasion* is Austen's depiction of "things as they are," *Pride and Prejudice* is her imagining of things as they could be. The relationship between Darcy and Elizabeth is outside of the world of hunting and shooting, and the male and female roles this world demarcates.

Like Captain Benwick, Darcy is depicted as a reader and, as we will see, is distanced from hunting and shooting. At Netherfield, Darcy declines cards and instead "took up a book" (60). Miss Bingley chooses "the second volume of his" and her "attention was quite as much engaged in watching Mr. Darcy's progress through *his* book, as in reading her own; and she was perpetually either making some inquiry, or looking at his page." Unable to "win him … to any conversation," she becomes "quite exhausted by the attempt to be amused with her own book," "yawned," and finally "threw aside her book" (60). The importance of Darcy's reading is further underscored by Mr. Hurst, who "had … nothing to do, but to stretch himself on one of the sophas and go to sleep," and Mrs. Hurst "principally occupied in playing with her bracelets and rings" (60). Bingley admits to not being a great reader: "I am an idle fellow, and though I have not many, I have more [books] than I ever look into" (41). While he "protest[ed] that he never read novels" (76), there is little evidence of Mr. Collins reading much of anything else. Like Miss Bingley, he reads for show only: in Mr. Bennet's library he is "nominally engaged with one of the largest folios in the collection, but really talking to Mr. Bennet, with little cessation, of his house and garden at Hunsford" (79–80). And Lydia's visits to the Brighton library revolve around officers and "such beautiful ornaments as made her quite wild" (264).

In contrast, Pemberley's extensive library reflects "the work of many generations" and Darcy's continuing influence: "you have added so much to it yourself, you are always buying books" (41), says Mr. Bingley. When Miss Bingley's list of accomplishments omits reading, Darcy quickly points out the oversight: "she must yet add something more substantial, in the improvement of her mind by extensive reading" (43). He alludes to *Twelfth Night* in his repartee with Elizabeth, whose quick comeback about sonnets suggests that she gets the Shakespearean reference:

> "I wonder who first discovered the efficacy of poetry in driving away love!"

> "I have been used to consider poetry as the food of love," said Darcy.

> "Of a fine, stout, healthy love it may. Every thing nourishes what is strong already. But if it be only a slight, thin sort of inclination, I am convinced that one good sonnet will starve it entirely away." (49)

Attempting to engage Elizabeth further in conversation at the Netherfield ball, he again raises the topic of books, and when Elizabeth rebuffs his attempt to do so with "I am sure we never read the same, or not with the same feelings," he replies, "I am sorry you think so; but if that be the case, there can at least be no want of subject.—We may compare our different opinions" (104). This exchange offers an interesting parallel to Anne and Benwick, whose conversations about books are debates, as they are "unable as any other two readers, to think exactly alike" (*P* 116). Moreover, we see here Deresiewicz's point that Darcy understands "the difference between an 'argument' and a 'dispute,'… between rational disagreement and personal enmity" ("Community and Cognition" 523), while Elizabeth, at this stage of the novel, does not. This is not surprising, given that her father, while a great reader, tends to not admit others into his library.

In keeping with the emphasis on Darcy's reading, Austen distances him from rural sport. Charlotte Lucas's young brother fantasizes that if he "were as rich as Mr. Darcy," he "would keep a pack of foxhounds, and drink a bottle of wine every day" (22), but this is not the Darcy we see. In fact, he does not live up to the social expectation of sport. When Darcy visits Charlotte and Elizabeth at Hunsford, they mistakenly speculate that his "visit … proceed[ed] from the difficulty of finding any thing to do … . All field sports were over" (202). Similarly, near the end of the novel, Mrs. Bennet misses the point of Darcy's visits: "What can he mean by being so tiresome as to be always coming here? I had no notion but he would go a shooting, or something or other" (415). The only hunting that Darcy does is "hunting for" Wickham and Lydia in London (356). Apart from one indirect mention of Darcy and Bingley sporting—they arrive at the Longbourne dinner "to the credit of their punctuality as sportsmen" (376)—Austen chooses not to focus on Darcy as a hunter. Instead, the references to hunting and shooting cluster around Mr. Bingley. His purchase of an estate is delayed, since his rental of Netherfield included "the liberty of a manor" (17), the right to shoot game. In volume 3, Bingley returns to Netherfield "to shoot there for several weeks" (366), and, presumably, renew his pursuit of Jane. Mrs. Bennet, delirious at the prospect of Mr. Bingley's "four or five thousand a year" (4), enthusiastically offers, "When you have killed all your own birds, Mr. Bingley … I beg you will come here, and shoot as many as you please, on Mr. Bennet's manor. I am sure he will be vastly happy to oblige you, and will save all the best of the covies for you" (373). Indeed, to help secure the connection, "An engagement was formed, chiefly through his own and Mrs. Bennet's means, for his coming next morning to shoot with her husband" (383). Bingley shoots with Mr. Bennet in the morning and that evening proposes to Jane in the drawing room. That Bingley's courtship of Jane is cojoined with his sport suggests the conventionality of their marriage, opposed to Austen's re-envisioning of male-female relationships in Darcy and Elizabeth.

I have argued so far that the dichotomy of the heroes' rural sport and the heroines' appreciation of nature casts a shadow on the novels' concluding marriages. *Pride and Prejudice* is distinctive in the Austen canon in its linking of *both* heroine and hero with nature. Darcy, writes Alison Sulloway, is a "green-world lover" (206) and "really more comfortable outdoors" (207). Similarly, Beth Lau argues that he "is associated with nature rather than society": "one could … compare Darcy … to most of the speakers and characters in Wordsworth's poetry, who dislike cities and social gatherings and prefer the company of nature and a few like-minded intimates" ("Placing Jane Austen in the Romantic Period" 259). A number of readers have noted Elizabeth's association with nature throughout the novel.[3] Her solitary hike to Netherfield—"crossing field after field at a quick pace, jumping over stiles and springing over puddles with impatient activity" (36)— leaves her looking "almost wild" (39), according to Miss Bingley. She also returns "tanned" (299) from her travels with the Gardiners. While Elizabeth is able to appreciate the cultivated beauty even at Rosings—"Every park has its beauty and its prospects; and Elizabeth saw much to be pleased with" (182)—she longs to see the wildness of the Lake District:

> "My dear, dear aunt," she rapturously cried, "what delight! What felicity! You give me fresh life and vigour. Adieu to disappointment and spleen. What are men to rocks and mountains? Oh! what hours of transport we shall spend! And when we *do* return, it shall not be like other travellers, without being able to give one accurate idea of anything. We *will* know where we have gone—we *will* recollect what we have seen. Lakes, mountains, and rivers shall not be jumbled together in our imaginations." (175)

---

3   Robert Kern notes Elizabeth's and the narrator's "identification" with nature, which "sets [them] apart from just about every other character in the novel" (13). Mary Jane Curry compares the nature scenes in *Pride and Prejudice* to those in Wordsworth and Cowper: the novel "attribute[s] the protagonist's self-understanding to a calming freedom produced by viewing the non-human physical world" ("Solitary Walk" 177) and invests the connection to nature with moral weight ("Solitary Walk" 183). Similarly, Lisa Altomari writes that Austen "creates a heroine who has a desire for and a bond with the outdoors and all that nature represents: freedom, space, autonomy" and "sets up a polemic between nature and 'social' space" (50). William Snyder also argues that Elizabeth "resist[s] the machinations and delusions of society" and is "shown to have an intimacy with Nature" (149).

While this passage is often interpreted as Austen's satire on travel writing and Romanticism,[4] Elizabeth is fond of escaping into nature throughout the novel. At Hunsford, "not a day went by without a solitary walk" (235), her "favourite" being "a nice sheltered path, which no one seemed to value but herself, and where she felt beyond the reach of Lady Catherine's curiosity" (191). Elizabeth's "tour to the Lakes was … the object of her happiest thoughts; it was her best consolation for all the uncomfortable hours, which the discontentedness of her mother and Kitty made inevitable" (263). Elizabeth never makes it to the North, but not because the novel "deliberately swerves away from an engagement with nature" as Deresiewicz claims (*Romantic Poets* 20). Rather, like the case of Emma, who, despite her economic standing, has never seen the ocean, Elizabeth's failed trip to the Lake District is a comment on female dependence: "it was her business to be satisfied" (265). As part of the utopian resolution of the novel, Pemberley becomes a symbolic substitution for the Lake District.

Pemberley's natural beauty is distinguished from that of Rosings and the other great houses in Austen. It is not "merely a fine house richly furnished." Its "delightful" (267) grounds are the focus:

> It was a large, handsome, stone building, standing well on rising ground, and backed by a ridge of high woody hills;—and in front, a stream of some natural importance was swelled into greater, but without any artificial appearance. Its banks were neither formal, nor falsely adorned. Elizabeth was delighted. She had never seen a place for which nature had done more, or where natural beauty had been so little counteracted by an awkward taste. (271)

Austen, as William Snyder suggests, depicts Pemberley "as built into its setting, and not imposed upon it" (149), thus reflecting not only "mutuality of human and natural" but also "masculine and feminine" elements (161). Darcy's sensitivity to nature is emphasized. He pauses in a walk through the grounds to observe a "water plant" (283), a significant moment which signals that he views nature in non-instrumental terms. Pemberley's natural beauty is linked to the novel's ethical landscape.[5]

---

[4]   Vivien Jones, for example, suggests that "Elizabeth's outburst in favour of nature rather than humanity is, perhaps, a relic of *First Impressions*, which might have been a more explicitly satirical novel along the lines of *Northanger Abbey*" (329, n2).

[5]   For contrasting views, see Penny Gay, who argues that Pemberley is "the embodiment of the Augustan ideal" ("Changing View" 54): "'nature' is at its best when subtly ordered by human 'taste'" ("Changing View" 55). Deresiewicz sees Pemberley as antithetical to Romantic views of nature: it is "a socioeconomic unit whose condition bears witness to its master's character. He has formed Pemberley, in other words; Pemberley has not formed him" (*Romantic Poets* 24). Kern argues that at Pemberley, the "environment, through a sort of acculturation, has been thoroughly appropriated for human purposes, with the result that there is, in effect, little difference between the natural phenomena outside the house and the room and furniture within it" (15).

Not tyrannical over landscape, Mr. Darcy also is "a liberal man" who "did much good among the poor" (292). The housekeeper, Mrs. Reynolds, asserts that he is "The best landlord, and the best master ... not like the wild young men now-a-days, who think of nothing but themselves. There is not one of his tenants or servants but what will give him a good name" (276). Even as a boy he was "generous-hearted" (275). Elizabeth knows how to value this commendation: "What praise is more valuable than the praise of an intelligent servant?" (277). It is at Pemberley that we hear of Darcy as a fisher. He is the only Austen hero associated with fishing. This is significant, for fishing, as Deuchar explains, "had become established as the gentlest and most contemplative of all sports—and it was developing a character far removed from that of ... hunting and racing" (44–45); it was seen as "a quiet game of patience, calmly pursued beside still brooks by those of a particularly sensitive and scholarly bent" (45), and "was scarcely an object of controversy at all" (94).[6] It is important that Austen distances Darcy from sports embroiled in the cruelty question. Moreover, Darcy's fishing is contextualized as an act of hospitality to Mr. Gardiner, who "though seldom able to indulge the taste, was very fond of fishing" (281). Darcy's "civility" gestures towards a bridging of the class distinctions inscribed in rural sport: Elizabeth "heard Mr. Darcy invite him, with the greatest civility, to fish there as often as he chose, while he continued in the neighborhood, offering at the same time to supply him with fishing tackle, and pointing out those parts of the stream where there was usually most sport" (282). That the sport still perpetuates gender privilege is something that Austen does not forget: Mr. Gardiner left his wife and niece "soon after breakfast" (294). Significantly, Darcy leaves the gentlemen's fishing party "on learning that the ladies of the family intended a visit to Georgiana that morning" (297). Austen distinguishes Darcy by distancing him from the pursuits that occupy the landed gentlemen in her other novels. Austen links all three elements of Pemberley: the natural landscape, the fishing scene, and the civility of "guardianship" (277). Pemberley is Austen's compensatory attempt to imagine an ideal community where the relationship to nature does not inscribe social hierarchies. Penny Gay notes that Pemberley "is something of a Utopia, or prelapsarian Eden, eliminating class barriers, as the novel's last paragraph reminds us by insisting on the Gardiners as 'the means of uniting them'" (*Austen and Theatre* 88). The pun on Gardiners is underscored when, as Gay notes, the Gardiners "are accompanied by a real 'gardener'" (*Austen and Theatre* 87) on the tour of the grounds. At Darcy's estate, a nonviolent relationship to nature is

---

[6]   It should be noted that there were arguments against fishing based on its cruelty. George Nicholson speaks of fishing as "torture" (*On the Primeval Diet* 199). Byron did not distinguish fishing from hunting; he saw both activities as cruel. He indicts fishing as "that solitary vice, / Whatever Isaak Walton sings or says: / The quaint, old, cruel coxcomb, in his gullet / Should have a hook, and a small trout to pull it" (*Don Juan* 13.106). See Kenyon-Jones, p. 35.

emphasized. The visit to Pemberley substitutes for the trip to the Lake District and unites Darcy and Elizabeth in their love of nature.

It is fitting, then, that the novel's denouement is orchestrated as lengthy conversations during two walks shared by hero and heroine. Deresiewicz describes these exchanges as "arguments" which allow "complementary interplay" ("Community and Cognition" 527) and which "combine" Elizabeth's and Darcy's "individual perspectives" (529). This conversational give-and-take has been described as a "duet" which "represents equality in speech" (151) by Marylea Meyersohn and a model of "reciprocity" by Susan Kneedler (159). The cultural context of pedestrianism further underscores the theme of equality: "Choosing pedestrian travel represented a democratizing gesture with regard to those who could afford no other form of transport, and a refusal of even the appearance of sporting privileges. There was a democratizing of human relations with the animal world as well as a leveling of class privilege" (Landry, *Invention of the Countryside* 127).[7] The "democratizing" nature of walking is important in the light of Elizabeth and Darcy's earlier disagreement about distance; Darcy casually states that "It must be very agreeable" to Charlotte "to be settled within so easy a distance of her own family and friends," but Elizabeth rebuts, "I should never have said Mrs. Collins was settled *near* her family … . Where there is fortune to make the expense of traveling unimportant, distance becomes no evil. But that is not the case *here*" (201). Elizabeth walks to Netherfield partly out of necessity: she "was determined to go … though the carriage was not to be had; and as she was no horse-woman, walking was her only alternative" (35). Elizabeth and Darcy's joint walks thus signal the shared ideal of equality between the two lovers.

Austen's heroines, on the whole, do not ride; even the "handsome, clever, and rich" (*E* 3) Emma Woodhouse is no "horse-woman" (*E* 206). Maria Bertram prides herself on her "good horsemanship," since it "has a great deal to do with the mind" (*MP* 81), but Austen suggests it has more to do with social power. In *Sense and Sensibility*, Marianne cannot afford to accept Willoughby's gift of a horse. We see Austen satirize the social hierarchies inscribed by riding in the early "Tour through Wales—in a Letter from a young Lady":

> We travelled on horseback by preference. My Mother rode upon our little poney and Fanny and I walked by her side or rather ran, for my Mother is so fond of riding fast that She galloped all the way. You may be sure that we were in a fine perspiration when we came to our place of resting. Fanny has taken a great Many Drawings of the Country, which are very beautiful, tho' perhaps not such exact resemblances as might be wished, from their being taken as she ran along. (*J* 224)

In "The Watsons," Lord Osborne "wonder[s] every lady does not" ride, since "a woman never looks better than on horseback" (*LM* 115), but Emma Watson

---

[7]   Robin Jarvis examines the rise of pedestrian culture at the end of the eighteenth century and its "levelling" (34) politics in Romantic writing.

quickly "silence[s]" (*LM* 116) him: "every woman may not have the inclination, or the means" (*LM* 115).

Cowper described rural sport as owing "its pleasure to another's pain" (*Task* 3.327). The selfishness that Cowper sees as paradigmatic is reflected in Austen's characterization of sportsmen. For example, John Thorpe's "conversation, or rather talk, began and ended with himself and his own concern" (*NA* 63). And Henry Crawford is "thoughtless and selfish" (*MP* 135). In contrast, in *Pride and Prejudice* both hero and heroine are distinguished by their strong ethical sense—their recognition, rather than denial, of the subjectivity of others—and their relationship evolves into equality and reciprocity. Throughout, Elizabeth is distinguished by her caring nature: "self, though it would intrude, could not engross her" (307). When Elizabeth hears of Lydia's situation, she "was wild to be at home—to hear, to see, to be upon the spot, to share with Jane in the cares that must now fall wholly upon her, in a family so deranged" (309). In an earlier passage, we see Elizabeth's "anxiety" for her sister, "which drew off her attention even from Wickham" (130). This, of course, marks her in sharp contrast to the majority of the novel's characters, who are driven almost entirely by self (such as Lydia, Miss Bingley, and Mr. Bennet), and instead aligns her with her aunt and uncle. The Gardiners, who take on a surrogate parental role towards Elizabeth and Jane, exemplify active concern for others. Both are crucial during the Lydia crisis: Mr. Gardiner travels to London to find Lydia, while Mrs. Gardiner stays at Longbourne, for "her presence might be serviceable to her nieces. She shared in the attendance on Mrs. Bennet, and was a great comfort to them, in their hours of freedom" (324).

In Elizabeth's initial rejection of Darcy, his perceived "selfish disdain of the feelings of others" (215) and his "unfeeling manner" and "cruelty" (260) figure large; her feelings towards Darcy change when she observes his care for others at Pemberley and, of course, in his rescue of Lydia. The second proposal continues the emphasis on "the feelings of others." Darcy's renewed declaration is precipitated by Elizabeth's wanting to thank him for his "generous compassion": "Mr. Darcy, I am a very selfish creature; and, for the sake of giving relief to my own feelings, care not how much I may be wounding your's. I can no longer help thanking you for your unexampled kindness to my poor sister" (405). Darcy introduces his proposal with a compliment—"you are too generous to trifle with me"—and gives her the opportunity to "silence [him] for ever with one word" (406). His self-reflection continues the theme: "I have been a selfish being all my life, in practice, though not in principle ... . Unfortunately an only son (for many years an only *child*) I was spoiled by my parents, who though good themselves ... allowed, encouraged, almost taught me to be selfish and overbearing, to care for none beyond my own family circle" (409). The extension of care "beyond" one's "own family circle" is at the heart of the ethics proposed in the novel.[8] The

---

8   Also see Anne K. Mellor, who argues in "Why Women Didn't Like Romanticism" that Austen, like Mary Shelley, was a proponent of the "education of the rational woman and the ethic of care" (285), and thus, for Mellor, in opposition to male Romantic writers.

most generous acts are committed outside the narrow confines of the immediate family, and at the end of the novel, community is not defined along bloodlines. The novel's final sentence foregrounds the Gardiners, rather than the heroine's or hero's immediate family: "With the Gardiners, they were always on the most intimate terms. Darcy, as well as Elizabeth, really loved them; and they were both ever sensible of the warmest gratitude towards the persons who, by bringing her into Derbyshire, had been the means of uniting them" (431). Beth Lau connects Pemberley to the "utopian communities" found in "other Romantic texts, in which a perfectly matched couple and a handful of like-minded friends create an ideal society" ("Placing Jane Austen in the Romantic Period" 264). Austen's Pemberley re-imagines the relationship between men and women as well as the relationship between humans and nature.

Both "Catherine, or the Bower" and "The Watsons" have been seen as early drafts of *Pride and Prejudice*. If John Halperin is correct in suggesting that the character of Edward Stanley in "Catherine, or the Bower" is a precursor of Darcy (*Life* 46), there is a significant difference between them. Edward Stanley is depicted as a sportsman. He first arrives on the scene because of the death of his "favourite Hunter" (*J* 275), but his feelings do not run deep: "it is a most confounded shocking affair, and makes me miserable to think of it; ... Oh! Do you know that I met the prettiest little waiting maid in the World, when I came here?" (*J* 270).[9] The easy switch from horse to maid suggests that women and animals occupy similar positions in his mind. Like *Sense and Sensibility*'s Willoughby, Edward Stanley toys with Catherine's affections just because he can. And his "sport" (*J* 290) includes taking "infinite pleasure in alarming the jealous fears of her Aunt by his attention to her" (*J* 283). Alluding to Alexander Pope's *The Rape of the Lock* in the "powder and pomatum" (*J* 271) of Edward's toilette, Austen underscores Edward's predatory nature. Like the Baron who "the bright locks admired, / He saw, he wished, and to the prize aspired" (Pope, *Rape of the Lock* 2.29–30), Edward "possessed an opinion of his own Consequence, and a perseverance in his own schemes which were not to be damped by the conduct of others" (*J* 275). Lord Osborne in "The Watsons" also has been seen as a version of Darcy. Again, unlike Darcy, however, Lord Osborne is associated with the bravado of the sportsman. In a draft of "The Watsons," he enthuses, "Nobody can be indifferent to the glorious sounds (Everybody allows that there is not so fine a sight in the world) as a pack

---

[9]   There is a similar scene in *Mansfield Park*. Tom Bertram gives Fanny "an account of the present state of a sick horse, and the opinion of the groom, from whom he had just parted," but no indication is given that Tom is in any way concerned. He quickly turns to reading the newspaper and the context of the scene further highlights his lack of feeling about the horse. He offers "in a languid way" to dance with Fanny in a manner that she cannot accept—"If you want to dance, Fanny, I will stand up with you" (139)—and then jumps at the chance to dance in order to get out of playing cards with Mrs. Norris, Mrs. Rushworth, and Dr. Grant. Tom's focus is on himself, not his horse or anyone else.

of Hounds in full cry" (*LM* 340).[10] Lord Osborne invites Emma to be a spectator at the next hunt, an invitation met with "astonishment" and silence (*LM* 117). A look at the male characters in "The Watsons" and "Catherine" further underscores the deliberate significance of Darcy's coolness about sport. *Pride and Prejudice* reworks the male suitor so as not to divide the heroine and hero along the lines demarcated by sport. As we have seen, rural sport is integral to Austen's work and her feminist analysis of the human-nature dualism. This critical focus continues in the representation of pets and tree-cutting in *Mansfield Park* and *Sense and Sensibility*, and is developed in the interconnections between the domination of nature, animals, women, and colonial others.

---

[10]   While Austen did not include this particular sentence in her final manuscript version, the characterization of Lord Osborne as an enthusiastic hunter remains.

Chapter 4
Evergreen

Mr. Tilson admired the trees very much, but greived that they should not be
turned into money. (*Letters* 193)

In the fourth chapter of the second volume of *Mansfield Park*, Fanny Price admires
the trees at the Grants' Parsonage:

> I am so glad to see the evergreens thrive! ... My uncle's gardener always says the
> soil here is better than his own, and so it appears from the growth of the laurels
> and evergreens in general.—The evergreen!—How beautiful, how welcome,
> how wonderful the evergreen!—When one thinks of it, how astonishing a
> variety of nature!—In some countries we know the tree that sheds its leaf is the
> variety, but that does not make it less amazing, that the same soil and the same
> sun should nurture plants differing in the first rule and law of their existence.
> You will think me rhapsodizing; but when I am out of doors, especially when I
> am sitting out of doors, I am very apt to get into this sort of wondering strain.
> One cannot fix one's eyes on the commonest natural production without finding
> food for a rambling fancy.

Mary Crawford replies: "To say the truth ... I am something like the famous Doge
at the court of Lewis XIV, and may declare that I see no wonder in this shrubbery
equal to seeing myself in it" (244).

This passage is often cited as evidence of the contrast between Fanny's
sensitivity and Mary Crawford's selfishness. Recent postcolonial criticism has
read the passage as nationalistic celebration of green England. Jon Mee argues
that "Fanny has a feeling for what she thinks of as the distinctive beauties of
the English countryside, such as the evergreens which she praises in comparison
to the flora of other countries" (81). However, Fanny specifically compares the
shrubberies at the Parsonage with those at Mansfield Park, not England and other
nations. It is difficult to find textual support for the claim that Fanny identifies "the
distinctive beauties of the English countryside," since she appears to be struck
by precisely the opposite—the lack of a distinctive uniformity in English flora:
she finds it "amazing, that the *same* soil and the *same* sun should nurture plants
differing in the first rule and law of their existence" (244; emphasis mine). Fanny
does mention "other countries ... where the tree that sheds its leaf is the variety,"
but her "rambling fancy" does not assert a hierarchical value of one over the other:
rather, she marvels at "how astonishing a variety of nature." Furthermore, Mee's
argument does not account for numerous other passages which show Fanny's
interest in nature. Her reverie on the stars seems particularly difficult to attribute
to nationalist enthusiasm. This chapter takes postcolonial readings of *Mansfield*

Park as a point of departure.¹ Building on feminist arguments that the novel
explores the connections between imperialism abroad and patriarchy at home, I
expand the scope of Austen's critique by including nature. While the dependent
and disadvantaged Fanny, indeed, is treated like a slave by the Bertrams, she is
also, at times, treated as an animal.

Erin O'Connor's "Preface for a Post-Postcolonial Criticism" contends that
"the postcolonial narrative of literary history has largely overwritten the Victorian
novel, that it has ignored—even at times denied—the genre's thematic subtleties,
structural indeterminacies, and genuine intellectual rigor in order to make the
novel into the means of establishing broadly applicable theoretical paradigms"
(220). While O'Connor's focus is the legacy of Gayatri Spivak's "Three Women's
Texts and a Critique of Imperialism" and the "Victorian novel as postcolonial
theory's favorite stomping ground—the genre it loves to hate" (219), she identifies
a similar trait in Austen Studies: Edward Said "do[es] unto *Mansfield Park* ... what
Spivak did unto *Jane Eyre*" (225). In *Culture and Imperialism*, Said argues that
"Jane Austen sees the legitimacy of Sir Thomas Bertram's overseas properties as a
natural extension of the calm, the order, the beauties of Mansfield Park, one central
estate validating the economically supportive role of the peripheral other" (79).²
Susan Fraiman, in one of the early responses to Said, points out the "failure to
consider Austen's gender" (808) and the "potential ... radical overlap of outrage"
(813) at the similarity of the position of slaves and women in Austen's work.³ While
Fraiman states explicitly that "it is not [her] intention to pick up the pieces of a
shattered idol" (821), her essay since has been read in precisely these terms. Mee,
seeing Fraiman as representative of the "liberal critic seeking to save Austen's
humanist reputation" (86), instead argues that the "conservative" (83) Austen
capitalizes on the potential for female agency in patriotic discourse. Similarly,
Clara Tuite writes that "Austen's satire is not engaged in an outright denunciation

---

¹   Also see the gloss on the "evergreen" passage in essays by Clara Tuite and Donna
Landry in *The Postcolonial Jane Austen*. Tuite reads the green curtain used for the theatricals
as "metonymiz[ing] the estate in Antigua, and the colony exploited for its natural resources
behind the scenes": "The relationship between estate and colony can be figured through
the correlation of the green curtain (as Antigua) with the avenue of trees. The green curtain
as the green chain of islands that include Antigua works to rejuvenate the green avenue of
trees of England, to keep Fanny's 'wonderful evergreen!' ... evergreen, dependent upon
the proceeds of the green islands" (109). *Mansfield Park* is a "country-house romance" in
which "landed privilege and a kind of Tory feminism of upward bourgeois female mobility
are mutually vindicating" (96).
²   See Margaret Kirkham, Meenakshi Mukherjee, and Patrick Brantlinger for
discussions of the novel's imperialist context prior to Said.
³   Gabrielle White offers a full-length rebuttal of Said's position, and argues for an
abolitionist, subversive Austen. George E. Boulukos claims that postcolonial criticism has
reduced the complexities of the early nineteenth-century slavery debate to "pro" and "con"
stances without looking at the politics of amelioration, and demonstrates its relevance to
Mansfield Park.

of these institutions of empire and aristocracy (as Fraiman's account would seem to suggest) but is an attempt to renovate them" (97). The debate has come full circle: Said's implication of Austen in imperialist ideology was challenged by feminist arguments positing Austen as an incisive critic of empire, which, in turn, have been charged with "engag(ing) a somewhat idealized category of gender" (Tuite 94). It is in this context that John Wiltshire calls for a "Decolonising" of *Mansfield Park*, the title of an article published in 2003: "Austen knew about slavery in the West Indies but it did not preoccupy her, nor was it referred to in her fiction in anything but the most marginal way; it simply represented a fact in the background of English life" (317).[4] His introduction to the Cambridge edition of *Mansfield Park* reflects his disagreement with postcolonial readings: "'the slave trade,' emerging *only* in Fanny's question to her uncle, recedes again into obscurity" (lxxxiii; emphasis mine). Given the scholarly reputation of Cambridge editions, Wiltshire's polemical stance might well prove influential in redirecting readings of the novel. My interpretation is not meant to "decolonise *Mansfield Park*" in Wiltshire's sense, but rather is an attempt at what O'Connor terms a "Post-Postcolonial Criticism" with a focus on nature and animals.

Fanny Price's appreciation of nature is consistently emphasized in the novel. Traveling to Sotherton, she takes pleasure "in observing the appearance of the country, the bearings of the roads, the difference of soil, the state of the harvest, the cottages, the cattle, the children" (94). At Sotherton, she contemplates the "sweet wood" (109) and laments the "cut[ting] down an avenue!"(66). Part of her suffering in Portsmouth is the loss of "all the pleasure of spring": "She had not known before, how much the beginnings and progress of vegetation had delighted her" (500). Only when walking along the Portsmouth ramparts does she feel joy: "every thing looked so beautiful under the influence of such a sky, the effects of the shadows pursuing each other … the ever-varying hues of the sea now at high water, dancing in its glee and dashing against the ramparts with so fine a sound" (474). When finally returning to Mansfield Park, "her perceptions and her pleasure were of the keenest sort … . Her eye fell every where on lawns and plantations of the freshest green" (515). The most concentrated examples of Fanny's responsiveness to nature occur in the context of her stay at Portsmouth. Having refused a legitimate offer of marriage, thus disobliging Sir Thomas, she

---

[4]   Wiltshire argues that postcolonial criticism has exaggerated the financial dependence of the Bertrams on Antigua, that it has "overdetermined" (306) the references to abolition in the title of the novel and Mrs. Norris's name (305–6), and that parallels between the slave economy and the domestic one simply do not hold: "It is difficult to understand … how a modern reader of even a few of the genuine narratives by slaves, or the diaries of their masters, could possibly think there is any but the loosest relation between the state of slavery and the condition of a genteel young English woman as depicted in the novel" (308). While in his 1992 *Jane Austen and the Body*, Wiltshire wrote that "The use both aunts make of Fanny, 'standing and stooping in the hot sun,' might call to mind the use Sir Thomas, now in Antigua, makes of his slaves" (72), he clearly has had a change of mind about the novel.

is sent to Portsmouth as punishment, yet she continues her "wilful and perverse" (367) ways. This problematizes the claim that Fanny's appreciation of nature marks her Englishness as well as her conventional femininity (Landry, "Learning to Ride"). Further, Fanny's response to nature is worth pursuing, since it is in pointed contrast to that of the other characters.

While Fanny reflects on "the sweets of ... autumn" and admires the "growth and beauty" of the shrubbery at the Parsonage, her companion, Mary Crawford, "untouched and inattentive, had nothing to say" (243): she "saw nature, inanimate nature, with little observation; her attention was all for men and women" (94). Mrs. Grant talks about Everingham only in terms of "timber!" (71), and Dr. Grant has a similarly instrumental view of nature: he "never pass[es]" the apricot tree "without regretting that the fruit should be so little worth the trouble of gathering," even though, according to Mrs. Norris, "it cost seven shillings" (64). It is important that Fanny's attentiveness to nature has an ethical dimension. Looking at "the brilliancy of an unclouded night, and the contrast of the deep shade of the woods," Fanny "feel[s] as if there could be neither wickedness nor sorrow in the world; and there certainly would be less of both if the sublimity of Nature were more attended to, and people were carried out of themselves by contemplating such a scene" (132). Deresiewicz is right to link the meditation's ethical dimension explicitly to the Romantic poets: "the morally healing power of immersion in nature is precisely Coleridge's theme in 'The Dungeon,' Wordsworth's in 'The Convict,' and ... 'Tintern Abbey'" (*Romantic Poets* 21). At this point in the novel Fanny has had direct personal experience with "wickedness" and "sorrow," such as the loss of her family and her ongoing humiliation at the hands of Mrs. Norris. She also has observed Henry Crawford's unscrupulously selfish dalliance with the Bertram sisters, now divided by envy and jealousy. And, immediately preceding Fanny's comment is a conversation between Mary Crawford, Edmund, and herself about Dr. Grant's temper and the resultant domestic unhappiness, and the announcement of Sir Thomas's return from Antigua. All of these could be the specific examples of "wickedness" Fanny has in mind. Fanny's observation of nature is linked not to social conformity but to social critique, and leads her to think about others.

The visit to Sotherton highlights the pointed contrast between Fanny's observation of nature and the other characters' neglect of it. Mrs. Norris's admiration of Sotherton takes the form of "spunging": "a beautiful little heath ... cream cheese ... [and] pheasant's eggs" (123). With the exception of Fanny, everyone looks at the grounds as a commodity, as territory to be "improved" or an opportunity to indulge in behavior at the expense of others. Maria's lament that the "iron gate ... give[s] me a feeling of restraint and hardship. I cannot get out, as the starling said" (115–16) is rhetorical only, for Maria at no point identifies with nature. She sees Sotherton's trees only in monetary terms: "the park ... is not ugly, you see, at this end; there is some fine timber" (96). If, as Carl Plasa argues, the Sotherton visit is a "rehearsal of a colonial paradigm" (43), it is important that the paradigm plays itself out in the human interaction with nature.

The connections Austen draws between the subordination of Fanny as a dependent woman and the oppression of slaves have been well charted in readings by Fraiman and Moira Ferguson, among others.[5] Austen not only examines the connections between the status of women and the status of slaves, but also links their subjugation to that of nature and animals. As a number of studies have pointed out, in eighteenth-century culture women, slaves, and the lower classes were seen as closer to the position of the animal in the chain of being than white upper-class men. Marjorie Spiegel's *The Dreaded Comparison* is a vivid exploration of the interdependence of racism and speciesism in the slavery system. Conversely, texts which protested animal cruelty also protested slavery, as Keith Thomas has established (44–45, 184–87). "The *white* man ... can have no right ... to enslave and tyrannize over a *black* man," writes Humphrey Primatt in *A Dissertation on the Duty of Mercy and Sin of Cruelty to Brute Animals* (11), and similar arguments were advanced by Oswald's *The Cry of Nature* and Ritson's *An Essay on Abstinence from Animal Food as a Moral Duty.* Laura Brown posits that "Animals helped Europeans imagine Africans, Native Americans, and themselves":

> the fable of the nonhuman being served as a powerful and common resource for structuring the encounter with cultural difference. This fable repeatedly raises questions about the nature of the human, just as it also repeatedly implicates itself with the unprecedented forms of "ruthless exploitation" that mark modern Europe's engagement with the peoples of the world. (*Fables of Modernity* 262)

Austen uses Fanny's encounter with animals to comment critically on the colonial one.

In their anxiety about social hierarchy, the Bertrams continually remind Fanny of her lower status, at times treating her like an animal. The novel not only demonstrates the interconnectedness of the ideologies which objectify women, slaves, and animals, but also directly challenges these ideologies by clearly establishing Fanny as the most feeling being in the novel. The physiological and psychological effects of Fanny's inferior status at Mansfield Park are vividly documented in the novel, as John Wiltshire's *Jane Austen and the Body* illuminates. Over and over it is made explicit that the justification of her treatment, such as Lady Bertram's "It can make little difference to you, whether you are in one house or the other" (28), is patently untrue. Fanny suffers emotionally and physically. When arriving at Mansfield Park at 10 years old, she is "afraid of every body, ashamed of herself, and longing for the home she had left" (14) and "sob[s] herself to sleep" (16). Her exertions in the hot sun fatigue her and make her ill with headache (84). While Fanny has not won popularity contests among readers, it is virtually impossible to not see her as the most reflective character in the novel. These two factors—her sentience and her intellect—serve to indict those who treat her as "the lowest and last" (258), and vindicate the rights of the heroine and, by association, women, slaves, and animals. Furthermore, the novel draws attention to the ways in which the heroine views nature and animals differently

---

[5]   Plasa points to "the potential narrative line ... which places ... William [Price] in the position of slave" (36).

than the other characters. *Mansfield Park* draws ideological connections between the mistreatment of women and animals, and positions the recognition of a connectedness to nature and animals as an alternative ethical system. Fanny's belief that "there could be neither wickedness nor sorrow in the world" or, at least, "less of both if the sublimity of nature were more attended to" (132) grounds human conduct in a connectedness to nature, rather than an androcentric domination of it. Fanny is animalized in two ways: the Bertrams and Mrs. Norris treat Fanny as an animal to subjugate her, and the novel challenges the human-animal hierarchy (and other social hierarchies thus enabled) by attaching positive associations to Fanny's closeness to the animal world.

    Mansfield Park is the only Austen novel which includes pets in its cast. In *Northanger Abbey*, when Catherine, General Tilney, and Elinor visit Woodston, Henry Tilney meets them at the door with "the friends of his solitude, a large Newfoundland puppy and two or three terriers" (219), and part of the afternoon is spent in the stables in "a charming game of play with a litter of puppies just able to roll about" (221).[6] But these references are isolated. Catherine, in keeping with Austen's parody of conduct-book advice, had little interest in practicing maternity with pets: she "was fond of all boys' plays, and greatly preferred cricket not merely to dolls, but to the more heroic enjoyments of infancy, nursing a dormouse, feeding a canary-bird, or watering a rose-bush" (5–6). *Mansfield Park*'s representation of pets is significant because the novel is intimately concerned with "the distinction proper to be made" (11–12) between Fanny and her cousins. This "distinction"— who has the benefit of fire and who does not, who rides for "pleasure" versus who rides for "health," and so on—extends outward from the domestic world to its larger context: the distinction between Mansfield Park and Portsmouth, England and Antigua. Austen uses the figure of the pet to destabilize these social boundaries. Marc Shell argues that pet owners "experience a relationship ever present in political ideology: the relationship between the distinction of which beings are our familial kin from which are not kin and the distinction of which beings are our species kind from which are not our kind" (121). The pet is situated at the boundary between those animals we love and those we use. The pet also crosses (and draws into question) the human-animal boundary. As Erica Fudge writes, "we could say that pets are animals out of place, and that in that 'out-of-placedness' they disturb the hygiene of the boundaries that give us certainty about who we are" (19). The precariousness and potential transgression of the pet is pivotal to the novel's examination of slavery. There are four pets in the novel: Lady Bertram's dog, Fanny's pony, her mare, and, I argue, at times Fanny herself.

    In eighteenth-century literature and culture, lapdogs, as Markman Ellis demonstrates, frequently "emblematize the malevolent, spiteful, and hypocritical quality of their female owners, who demonstrate an 'unfeeling' nature" (101)

---

[6]   Kenyon-Jones points out that the Newfoundland dog "was perceived as a notably masculine animal, with sturdy, dependable characteristics" (48) and "could be adopted as particularly British and patriotic" (49).

towards their human dependents. In Frances Burney's *The Wanderer* (1814) we find one such example: Mrs. Ireton's Bijou is "fat, round, well furred, and over-fed ... accustomed to snarl, scratch, stretch, and roll himself about at his pleasure" (536), while the servants are tryannized; the heroine recognizes that her mistress uses her lapdog to degrade her human dependents. Louise Robbins argues that criticisms of pets as luxury "melded with broader criticisms that castigated women for being superficial, frivolous, and flighty" (140). In keeping with this theme, Lady Bertram "think[s] more of her pug than her children" (22) and her exertion to welcome Fanny to Mansfield Park is limited to "smil[ing] and mak[ing] her sit on the sofa with herself and pug" (14). Lady Bertram showers her pug with attention, but is oblivious to her niece's dread of having to live with Mrs. Norris (28). Similarly, she is inattentive to Fanny's physical suffering due to "standing and stooping in the hot sun" (85) to gather roses; Lady Bertram's concerns are only for herself and her pug: "the heat was enough to kill any body. It was as much as I could bear myself. Sitting and calling to Pug, and trying to keep him from the flower-beds, was almost too much for me" (86). And just as Lady Bertram is blind to Fanny's suffering, so is she to the suffering under the hot sun of Antigua. As McKenzie-Stearns points out, pugs, originating in China, are "an imperial commodity" (450) and "the lapdog's symbolism is ... the silent presence of imperialism in British family life" (451).

A recurrent concern reflected in the eighteenth-century trope of the lapdog is the blurring of the human-animal hierarchy. Palmer argues that Austen "uses Lady Bertram's treatment of the pug to give a moral lesson in how dogs should *not* be treated": "Austen accords with the traditional Christian view, based on the Great Chain of Being, of mankind's superiority to brutes" (par. 6). Austen's representation of the lapdog, however, is more complex: the pug is not simply living in the lap of luxury. Humans' interactions with pets are characterized simultaneously by "dominance and affection," to borrow the title of Yi-Fu Tuan's history of pet-keeping: pets may be loved, but they are also utterly dependent on their masters. Pet-keeping was viewed as cruel by some in the eighteenth century,[7] and it seems that Austen's view was ambivalent. The dog has some discomforts of his own. When Sir Thomas and Mrs. Norris discuss the adoption of Fanny, Lady Bertram is concerned that Fanny might "tease my poor pug ... . I have but just got Julia to leave it alone" (11). Given that understatement is somewhat of an art at Mansfield Park (Sir Thomas describes the systemic abuse of Fanny as "little privations and restrictions" [361]), we can imagine that Julia's "teasing" of the dog might well have a cruel edge. This is perhaps why Lady Bertram, on the prospect of Fanny's marriage to Henry Crawford, promises a pet only to Fanny, not her daughters: "I will tell you what, Fanny—which is more than I did for Maria—the next time pug has a litter you shall have a puppy" (385). Jodi Wyett argues that Fanny would not "accept" such a gift because of "the indignity of a lapdog living in luxury made possible by the unspoken sufferings of human slaves on West

---

[7]   See Ingrid H. Tague (295).

Indian soil" (292). Had Austen meant pug only to function as a trope for female error, surely she would have accessorized Julia and Maria accordingly. My point here is that the pet cannot be reduced to one meaning in the text, and that Austen, by acknowledging the dog's discomforts (restraint and "teasing"), also points to the dog's subjectivity.

The fact that Lady Bertram does not name her dog, simply identifying him by his breed, undercuts her claim to feel affection for the dog. Richard Nash relates the emerging practice of naming companionate animals in the eighteenth century to growing recognition and consideration of animal subjectivity. Calling the dog by his generic breed indicates that the dog is valued primarily as a commodity (in the case of pugs, a breed connected to imperial trade) and as "a symbol of the human ascendancy over nature" (Ritvo, "Emergence" 27). Not only does Lady Bertram not name her dog, she also is clueless about the dog's sex, alternately calling the dog male (86), female (385), and "it" (11). John Sutherland reads the shifts in the pug's sex as a "tiny error" (34) on Austen's part, as does Tony Tanner ("Cop"), but Austen's narrator is consistent; a pronoun indicating sex is used only in one instance: pug barks in "his mistress's arms" (94). All other references simply are to "pug" with no indication of sex (14, 22, 210). The error is Lady Bertram's. This, of course, can be interpreted in general terms as an instance of Lady Bertram's vacuity of mind, but we can also see it as revealing her attitude towards her pug and animals. She appears to know very little about her dog, and referring to him as an "it" is in keeping with not naming the animal, thus denying the dog individuality and subjectivity. Given the animalizing of slaves in eighteenth-century culture, Lady Bertram's view of her pug also implicitly tells us about her acquiescent role in the "dead silence" (231) following Fanny's question about the slave trade. Austen's focus is not on the excess of affection showered on the pug, as Palmer claims, but rather the *pretense* of affection. This reading is further supported by the examples of Mrs. Norris, whose claims to "feel" for animals are transparently self-interested, and the contrasting example of Fanny, who does feel for animals, as we shall see.

There are three instances in which Mrs. Norris claims affection for animals to gain her own ends. At Sotherton she thinly disguises her "spunging" by insisting it was all "quite force[d] upon" her. She will nurture "those beautiful pheasant's eggs" and keep them as pets: Mrs. Whitaker, the Sotherton housekeeper, "said it must be such an amusement to me, as she understood I lived quite alone, to have a few living creatures of that sort; and to be sure it will … be a great delight in my lonely hours to attend to them" (123–24). The likelihood of the pheasants being eaten effectively negates Mrs. Norris's claims to love animals for their own sake. Trying to sidestep Sir Thomas's questions about her failure to dissuade her charges from the theatricals, she shifts the topic to the Sotherton visit she had engineered and speaks at length of her compassion—"You know how I always feel for the horses":

> And when we got to the bottom of Sandcroft Hill, what do you think I did? You will laugh at me—but I got out and walked up … . It might not be saving

them much, but it was something, and I could not bear to sit at my ease, and be dragged up at the expense of those noble animals. I caught a dreadful cold, but *that* I did not regard. (222)

The scene's context makes it very clear that these professions are empty. Mrs. Norris again pretends concern for the horses when returning from dinner with the Grants at the Parsonage: "Come, Fanny, Fanny, what are you about? … . Quick, quick. I cannot bear to keep good old Wilcox waiting. You should always remember the coachman and horses" (292). Mrs. Norris uses the discourse of kindness to servants and animals to harass Fanny who, in her mind, is lower than both.

In contrast to Lady Bertram's ownership of her dog and Mrs. Norris's pretended affection for animals, Fanny's relationship with her pony is described in affective terms. The "dear old grey pony" is "her valued friend" whose death affects Fanny: "for some time she was in danger of feeling the loss in her health as well as in her affections" (41). Fanny's emotional connection with the pony challenges the instrumental view of animals. It is telling when we compare Austen's treatment of Fanny's grief for her pony to a poem written by Austen's brother, James, for his son in January 1811: "To Edward on the Death of His First Pony." The poem's speaker is sympathetic to the boy's loss and commends him for not "abus[ing]" (57) his power over the pony: "no Quadrupede / A kinder milder master knew / Than Pony ever found in you" (69–71). But the poem quickly moves away from "not … blam[ing]" Edward's "tears" to urging him to "check" his "grief" (52):

> Let reason come to your relief
> ....
> Check the deep sigh, & flowing tear,
> And from this loss your mind prepare,
> More serious ills of life to bear.
> (53, 74–76)

The pony's death is a "light woe" (101) that should "teach … this salutary truth":

> That every sorrow will be light,
> When all within our breasts is right;
> That a well regulated mind
> In such distress will comfort find,
> And, unreproving Conscience still
> Provide a cure for every ill. (102–8)

This poem, then, subscribes to a traditional hierarchy of beings in which humanity, on the basis of possessing reason, is clearly superior to and distinct from animals. Jane Austen, in contrast, moves beyond the moral of "kindness to animals" and the paternalism it implies. Fanny's "feeling the loss" is neither minimized by placing it in a hierarchy of legitimate grief nor treated didactically. Furthermore, Fanny consistently empathizes with animals. When Mary Crawford borrows Fanny's horse for an especially long ride, Fanny "began to think it rather hard upon the mare to have such double duty; if she were forgotten the poor mare should be remembered" (79). Fanny believes in the shared sentience of human and nonhuman animals, for she, like Catherine Morland, who asks John Thorpe if his horse needs rest, can imagine the mare's physical exhaustion. Wiltshire reads Fanny's pity for the mare as "a comically desperate last resort" (*Jane Austen and the Body* 69) at self-deception, and Landry claims it is merely "displaced self-pity" ("Learning to Ride" 65). But the point is that Fanny is thinking about herself *and* the horse. She identifies with the "poor mare" in part because of her own marginal status within Mansfield Park. Like Fanny, who is a servant and family at the same time, the horse occupies an ambiguous position within Mansfield Park.

Fanny's emotional connection with her pony suggests the pony is a pet, but given the pony's utility function, it is also distinct from the category of pets who are usually defined by the companionship they offer as opposed to utility (food, transportation, or labor).[8] Fanny's pony is not a pet in the same sense that Lady Bertram's pug is. This is partly a reflection of Fanny's own social position, since the ability to own a pet is a class privilege. Pugs, in particular, had aristocratic and royal associations (Wyett 278). Similarly, when Edmund arranges for Fanny's horseback riding, he does so for her "health," while the Bertrams and the Crawfords ride for "pleasure" (80), an important contrast. Moreover, the horse "continued in name as well as fact, the property of Edmund," and that is the only way "Mrs. Norris could tolerate its being for Fanny's use" (43). Ownership is a privilege which would place her dangerously close to the status of her cousins. The horse which Edmund lends her is his third horse, "a useful road-horse" (42). The "mare" is the equine counterpart to Fanny, who is also valued for her use.

The pony's and mare's ambiguous status mirrors Fanny's own. She is a member of the family, but there has to be "a difference" (21): she "cannot be equal" (12). Fanny is both inside and outside the Bertram circle. Mary Crawford's question— "Is she out, or is she not" (56)—has a more general application than the one she intends. Shell argues that the pet is a "crossing-over point":

> Insofar as we conceive the pet, as both human and nonhuman, it stands at the intersection between species (it is my kind and another kind as well). Similarly, insofar as we conceive the pet as being both familial and nonfamiliar it stands at the intersection between families (it is my kin and not my kin). (137)

---

[8]   See the definition by Keith Thomas (112–15) and Tague: "they live in the domestic space, and their primary purpose for humans is entertainment and emotional companionship" (290). Harriet Ritvo demonstrates that the "widespread pet ownership among members of the middle classes can be dated from the late eighteenth and early nineteenth centuries. This period saw a series of radical changes in the general relationship of human beings (at least European human beings) to the natural world. Whereas at the beginning of the eighteenth century natural forces had been perceived as largely out of human control, by the end of the century science and engineering had begun to make much of nature more manageable" ("Emergence" 20). See also Tuan.

The pet's status, then, is mirrored in Fanny's. Mrs. Norris's injunction to remember "who and what she is" (172) captures this perfectly. Fanny is and is not a member of the Bertram family; a "who" and a "what," she is and is not human. Fanny's almost perpetual "gratitude" is somewhat akin to the unconditional loyalty human owners expect from their pets, and it is telling that her gratitude is often mixed with "pain" (93). As both Wyett and Braunschneider point out, lapdogs were valued for their malleability. In a parallel way, Fanny's supposed lack of "independence of spirit" (367) endears her to Sir Thomas. Mary Crawford remarks that Fanny is "as good a little creature as ever lived, and has a great deal of feeling" (269). Like a pet, Fanny lives under the duality of "dominance and affection." For Fanny to receive her uncle's affection, she must submit to his domination. When Fanny refuses Henry Crawford's proposal, she earns Sir Thomas's "displeasure" (364, 366), "cold sternness" (367), and "anger" (370), and she is removed from the "elegancies and luxuries of Mansfield Park" to bring her "mind into a sober state" (425). Sir Thomas's anger fills her with guilt, and her choice of words is telling: "I must be a brute indeed, if I can be really ungrateful" (372).

The novel consistently aligns Fanny and nature to explore the ideological connections between the position of nature and animals and that of women and the lower classes. Fanny's room, significantly, is her "nest of comforts" (179); formerly inhabited by the governess, then abandoned, it is a room that "nobody else wanted" (177). Among Fanny's "comforts" are mementos, books, plants, and "her works of charity and ingenuity" (178), giving the room both ethical and creative dimensions. Commenting on the Wordsworthian echoes in Fanny's room, Deresiewicz perceptively points out that the room is a green space: "with its houseplants, [it] is also verdant, or makes a gesture towards the verdant—a silly idea, this would be, were these not the only houseplants in all of Austen, appearing just here, of all places" (*Romantic Poets* 58). Further, the lack of a fire (one of the privations marking Fanny's second-class status) situates the room between inside and outside, for Fanny's residence there is dependent on the seasons and weather: "even without a fire it was habitable in many an early spring, and late autumn morning, to such a willing mind as Fanny's, and while there was a gleam of sunshine, she hoped not to be driven from it entirely, even when winter came" (177–78). This description situates Fanny on the threshold of inside and outside. No wonder Sir Thomas thinks of Fanny's adoption as "her transplantation" (321). When Fanny first arrives at Mansfield Park, Julia and Maria marvel that she "cannot put the map of Europe together," "cannot tell the principal rivers in Russia," and has "never heard of Asia Minor" (20). Mee reads this scene as an example of Fanny's "unworldliness," which "confirms her essential Englishness" (81): "Part of Fanny's symbolic virtue is precisely that she is ignorant of the wider world" (86). However, Jacqueline Pearson demonstrates that geography was "widely recommended to women readers" (55) precisely because it emphasized England's national superiority as well as valorizing patriarchal values of conquest. Surely, then, Austen is making a point about Fanny's educational and economic disadvantage in comparison to her cousins. The connection between class privilege and the domination of nature is implicit in the mapping of the natural world, and it is not surprising that Fanny cannot put the world together; she is associated with the nature that is controlled and made to be useful.

Fanny's room as a nest is an example of metaphoric associations that run throughout the novel, linking the heroine to animals. The pedagogical plan of raising Fanny with "the distinction proper to be made between the girls as they grow up" (11–12)—"they cannot be equals" (12)—is a form of "breed[ing]" (7), as Mrs. Norris puts it. The repeated references to Fanny as "creeping" through the house reveal her status in the hierarchy as always less-than, barely even human. In the early days at Mansfield Park, Fanny "crept about in constant terror of something or other" (16). During the rehearsals of *Lovers' Vows*, "it was a pleasure to *her* to creep into the theatre" (193), and Tom attempts to persuade Fanny to take on the part of the Cottager's wife by telling her "you may be as creepmouse as you like": "it is a nothing of a part, a mere nothing, not above half a dozen speeches altogether, and it will not much signify if nobody hears a word you say" (171). And after being ordered by Sir Thomas to leave the ball early—"'Advise' was his word, but it was the advice of absolute power"—Fanny "creep[s] slowly up the principal staircase" (326). Given the imperative to "consider ... who and what she is" (172), it is no wonder that Fanny internalizes feeling less than human. As we have seen, not all animals are equal. Some are pets and some are brutes without feeling.

Not surprisingly, Fanny internalizes that she is a thing.[9] During the holidays, "Fanny had no share in festivities of the season; but she enjoyed being avowedly useful as her aunt's companion, when they called away the rest of the family; and as Miss Lee had left Mansfield, she naturally became every *thing* to Lady Bertram during the night of a ball or a party" (40; emphasis mine). During the theatricals, Fanny's "spirits sank ... and she felt herself becoming too nearly *nothing*" (199; emphasis mine): "She might go or stay, she might be in the midst of their noise, or retreat from it to the solitude of the East room, without being seen or missed" (187). For Mary, "intimacy" with Fanny meets her "desire for *something* new" (242; emphasis mine). Hoping that Fanny will reconsider Henry's proposal, Sir Thomas's "object" was that Henry "should be missed": "She had tasted of consequence in its most flattering form; and he did hope that the loss of it, the sinking again into *nothing*, would awaken very wholesome regrets in her mind" (422; emphasis mine). Sir Thomas and Lady Bertram value Fanny for her usefulness to them: "I am very glad we took Fanny as we did, for now the others are away, we feel the good of it" (331), says Lady Bertram of Fanny as a replacement child. And at end of the novel, Fanny again is Sir Thomas's pet: she "was indeed the daughter that he wanted. His charitable kindness had been rearing a prime comfort for himself. His liberality had a rich repayment" (546).

---

9   In "The Thing about Fanny Price," Mark Raymond Blackwell examines Fanny's treatment as an object. Blackwell's study of It-Narratives (see his edited collection, *The Secret Life of Things: Animals, Objects, and It-Narratives in Eighteenth-Century England* [2007]) provides a provocative context for *Mansfield Park*.

Susan Fraiman's point that Said's argument is weakened by its sole focus on *Mansfield Park* equally applies to other postcolonial readings. When we place *Mansfield Park* in the comparative context of *Sense and Sensibility*, we see that both heroines admire nature as well as the poetry of William Cowper. We have already traced the importance of Cowper to Fanny Price; *Sense and Sensibility*'s Marianne is associated with Cowper on three occasions (20, 57, 107), establishing him as also one of "her favourite authors" (56). And like Fanny, Marianne is characterized in part by her love of trees. While Fanny's reverie on the "evergreen" is written off by postcolonial critics as nationalist enthusiasm for the England the trees supposedly represent, Marianne Dashwood's love for the Norland trees is dismissed by many as Austen's parody of sensibility.[10] The striking similarities between the heroines suggest that we consider their love of trees in a different light and consider the continuity of Austen's representations of nature. Marianne's appreciation of nature is undercut by Elinor, most famously in her acerbic "It is not everyone … who has your passion for dead leaves" (101), but Elinor is not Austen.

Marianne's emotional leave-taking of Norland Park includes its trees:

> Dear, dear Norland … when shall I cease to regret you!—when learn to feel a home elsewhere!—Oh! happy house, could you know what I suffer in now viewing you from this spot, from whence perhaps I may view you no more!— And you, ye well-known trees!—but you will continue the same.—No leaf will decay because we are removed, nor any branch become motionless although we can observe you no longer!—No; you will continue the same; unconscious of the pleasure or the regret you occasion, and insensible of any change in those who walk under your shade!—But who will remain to enjoy you? (32)

Marianne's reflection on Norland is left on its own to conclude volume one's Chapter 5, the final chapter set at the family estate: Marianne gets the last word. The narrator, in fact, says nothing. Critics have rushed in to fill this silence. Bodenheimer states that "Marianne is hardly invoking unity with nature; she is really berating the house and trees for not caring, and asserting the strength of her suffering … in a world full of non-suffering, non-appreciative objects" (609). Gay agrees that the passage reveals only Marianne's "egoism" ("Changing View" 51), and Jonathan Bate argues that "she is taking something for herself from [nature], using it as a source of nourishment for the spirit, just as the man who encloses land does so in order to increase its yield of nourishment for the body" (132). Bate compares Marianne's appreciation of nature to contemporary popular environmentalism that protects certain natural sites and animal species deemed beautiful and valuable from an androcentric perspective. But Marianne's reflection recognizes the alterity of nature, that the trees exist outside of human demands— whether utilitarian or aesthetic. Rather than narcissistically projecting her feelings

---

[10]   For example, Deresiewicz, placing the novel in Austen's Augustan phase, states that "in both *Sense and Sensibility* and *Northanger Abbey*, characters' observation of nature serves only to exhibit and ridicule stereotyped modes of response" (*Romantic Poets* 19).

onto the landscape, Marianne acknowledges that the trees "will continue the same" (32) with or without her. Moreover, Marianne's grief includes her mother and sisters, for she speaks of their common loss of the trees: "we can observe you no longer" (32). The timing of Marianne's reflection also is surely important: she "wandered alone around the house, on the last evening of their being there" (32). Marianne has just lost her father and is about to lose the home in which she grew up. The novel's first and second chapters clearly set out for the reader the injustice of the Dashwood women's displacement and, as Claudia L. Johnson has argued so compellingly, the patent falseness of Burkean ideals: "the family, far from being the mainspring for all moral and social affections, is the mainspring instead for the love of money, the principal vice in *Sense and Sensibility*, and in so much progressive fiction" (53). Given that the novel presents the Dashwood women's disenfranchisement in feminist terms, "methodically examin[ing] the lot of women who have become marginalized due to the death or simple absence of male protectors" (Johnson 52), it appears unlikely that the narrator shows Marianne's grief only to laugh at it. In fact, the narrator does not subject the moment to the kind of irony leveled at Marianne's grief for Willoughby: "Marianne would have thought herself very inexcusable had she been able to sleep at all the first night after parting from Willoughby" (96).

The second main passage characterizing Marianne through her connection to the natural environment occurs in Chapter 16 of the first volume, when Edward visits Barton:

> "Have you been lately in Sussex?" said Elinor.
>
> "I was at Norland about a month ago."
>
> "And how does dear, dear Norland look?" cried Marianne.
>
> "Dear, dear Norland," said Elinor, "probably looks much as it always does at this time of year. The woods and walks thickly covered with dead leaves."
>
> "Oh!" cried Marianne, "with what transporting sensations have I formerly seen them fall! How have I delighted, as I walked, to see them driven in showers about me by the wind! What feelings have they, the season, the air altogether inspired! Now there is no one to regard them. They are seen only as a nuisance, swept hastily off, and driven as much as possible from the sight."
>
> "It is not everyone," said Elinor, "who has your passion for dead leaves."
>
> "No, my feelings are not often shared, not often understood. But *sometimes* they are." (101)

Again, it is important to register the distance between Elinor and the author. Marianne has a point here. Her feelings, indeed, are not often understood, certainly not by her current social circle: Sir John Middleton, Lady Middleton, and Mrs. Jennings. And she is right that the new owners of Norland Park do not appreciate the trees. Like Mr. Rushworth in *Mansfield Park*, Mr. and Mrs. John Dashwood are keen to improve the landscape and, like the Sotherton trees, the Norland trees face cutting: John Dashwood tells Elinor that the "old walnut trees are all come down to make room" for a hothouse (257). Further, it is significant that when Elinor hears of this, she feels "provocation" and "censure" (257). Elinor attempts to distance herself from feelings of loss by deflecting them onto Marianne, especially in front of an audience (Edward, after all, is brother to Mrs. John Dashwood). Marianne's respect for trees, in fact, is shared by Elinor.

In contrast to Marianne, Edward Ferrars "do[es] not like crooked, twisted, blasted trees": "I admire them much more if they are tall, straight and flourishing ... . I am not fond of nettles, or thistles, or heath blossoms" (113). Barton "exactly answers [his] idea of a fine country because it unites beauty with utility" (112). Bate explains that Edward "is an embodiment of Enlightenment man, who regards nature as something that must be tamed, ordered and made serviceable to the community" (131). This view is often seen as "endorse[d]" by the novel as a whole (Gay, "Changing View" 52).[11] But before taking Edward's mockery of Marianne at face value and equating Edward with Austen, we should consider the fact that his view of nature is not far from that of Mr. John Dashwood's appraisal of Delaford: "And his woods! I have not seen such timber anywhere in Dorsetshire as there is now standing in Delaford Hanger!" (425). The use of the present tense suggests Mr. Dashwood's plans: trees stand to be cut. Further, Edward's dig at Marianne for reading "every book that tells her how to admire an old twisted tree" (107) fails to work, for she readily acknowledges that the "admiration of landscape scenery is become a mere jargon ... . I detest jargon of every kind, and sometimes I have kept my feelings to myself, because I could find no language to describe them in but what was worn and hackneyed out of all sense and meaning" (112–13). Marianne's view of nature cannot simply be reduced to parody. The novel's sympathetic treatment of Marianne's feelings for nature is further underscored by the contrast of Mrs. Palmer. Upon her return to Cleveland,

> the loss of her favourite plants, unwarily exposed, and nipped by the lingering frost, raised the laughter of Charlotte,—and in visiting her poultry-yard, where, in the disappointed hopes of her dairy-maid, by hens forsaking their nests, or being stolen by a fox, or in the rapid decease of a promising young brood, she found fresh sources of merriment. (343–44)

It is also significant that Edward's favoring of nature with utility value is extended to humans. His preference for "a troop of tidy, happy villagers" to "the finest banditti in the world" (113), while intended as parodic, is reiterated without the comic valence a few moments later: "very fine country" includes "rich meadows

---

Edward Ferrars "clearly represents Austen's approved way of evaluating a rural scene at that point in her career": "beauty understood in terms of utility, of the health and prosperity of a country's human inhabitants" (Deresiewicz, *Romantic Poets* 20).

and several neat farm houses" (112). This is important because in *Sense and Sensibility* women are prized for their market value.

John Dashwood's view of nature as being only about money is extended to his view of women. Speaking to Elinor, he praises Mrs. Jennings as a "most valuable woman indeed":

> Her house, her style of living, all bespeak an exceeding good income; and it is an acquaintance that has not only been of great use to you hitherto, but in the end may prove materially advantageous.—Her inviting you to town is certainly a vast thing in your favour; and indeed, it speaks altogether so great a regard for you, that in all probability when she dies you will not be forgotten.—She must have a great deal to leave. (257)

Elinor's stock on the marriage market has gone up in her stepbrother's estimation, given the "destr[uction]" of Marianne's "bloom": "Her's has been a very short one! She was as handsome a girl last September, as any I ever saw, and as likely to attract the men" (258). John Dashwood's commodification of nature is linked by Austen to the ways in which the Dashwood women are discarded both in the family and in courtship systems. Margaret Anne Doody's suggestion that the "Dashwoods seem to bear an autumnal name, to be leaves dashed from the wood" (xl) is apt, pointing to the parallel between the ideologies which objectify nature and women.

It is, then, telling that Mr. and Mrs. John Dashwood take their son Harry "to see the wild beasts at Exeter Exchange" (252). Visits to animal exhibits were part of fashionable eighteenth-century consumer society (Plumb, "Acceptance of Modernity" 323). Exhibitions included humans from colonized parts of the world alongside animals, and, hence, in very concrete terms asserted not only human dominion over animals, but also English dominion over colonized peoples, naturalizing the latter by equating it with the former. Bob Mullan and Garry Marvin argue that zoos historically are "institutions of power" (160) which "separate ... the animal and human worlds" (68).[12] Further, the zoo "acts as both a model of empire (where humanity holds dominion over lesser species arrayed for our pleasure, our betterment, our *use*) and simultaneously as a metaphor for the larger, more important imperial enterprises in the sociopolitical hierarchy amid which it flourishes" (Malamud 59).[13] That the greedy and cruel Mr. and Mrs. John Dashwood, rather than our heroines, are credited with the visit to Exeter implies Austen's criticism of animal exhibitions. This is further underscored by the context for the reference to Exeter. Alongside visiting the "wild beasts," Mr. Dashwood mentions his role in the enclosure of Norland common, the purchasing of farms

---

[12]   MacKenzie demonstrates the "connections between hunting, hunters and natural history displays": "Classification meant killing, and the collection of specimens for scholarly examination and public display involved killing on a large scale" (36).

[13]   See Mathew Senior's "The Ménagerie and the Labyrinthe: Animals at Versailles, 1662–1792" and Louise Robbins's *Elephant Slaves and Pampered Parrots*.

adjacent to Norland Park, and the cutting of trees to make room for a hotho
all the while lamenting his so-called "poverty" in order to "do away the necessity
of buying a pair of ear-rings for each of his sisters" (257), never mind heeding
his father's deathbed request that he look after his sisters. Austen takes care to
situate the visit to Exeter in a context that connects the domination of animals to
patriarchy, class, and imperialism.

Austen turns the Mr. Tilson who "admired the trees very much, but greived
that they should not be turned into money" (*Letters* 193) into a character type.
Mansfield Park and *Sense and Sensibility* juxtapose their heroines' connectedness
to nature with those who view nature simply as a resource, and both novels connect
androcentrism to patriarchal and imperialist ideologies. When Marianne takes
her farewell of the Norland trees, she is speaking from a position of exclusion.
The context of her soliloquy is her eviction from Norland. Those who inherit
Norland Park are indifferent to the fate of the widowed and orphaned Dashwood
women and, as Marianne correctly anticipates, indifferent to nature, too: the
trees come down to make room for a hothouse. Placing Marianne Dashwood
next to Fanny Price, who also laments the cutting down of trees, demonstrates
the continuity of Austen's treatment of nature. When Fanny self-consciously
qualifies her admiration of the evergreen—"You will think me rhapsodizing"
(244), she anticipates critical responses to Marianne's reverie on nature. But in
both cases, the heroines' admiration of nature as a living presence with its own
value, regardless of utility to humans, is important. Those who objectify nature
also objectify women and colonial others who become part of a lifeless landscape,
there to be exploited. A post-postcolonial approach accounts for the ways in which
Austen connects the domination of slaves, women, animals, and nature. By taking
seriously Marianne's mourning of the trees, Fanny's admiration of the evergreen,
and her friendship with animals, we can trace Austen's green politics.

Chapter 5
Legacies and Diets

A large income is the best recipe for happiness I ever heard of. It certainly may secure all the myrtle and turkey part of it. (*MP* 226)

While Laura in "Love and Freindship" rises above the "mean and indelicate employment of Eating and Drinking" (*J* 111), her author did not. Jane Austen's enjoyment of food is evident in her correspondence. For example, responding to her brother Francis's letter from Sweden, she writes that "Rostock Market makes one's mouth water" (229), and, "very glad the new Cook begins so well," she writes to Cassandra: "Good apple pies are a considerable part of our domestic happiness" (291). Maggie Lane explains that while the Austen family always employed a cook, meal planning was part of the housekeeping duties that fell to Mrs. Austen and her daughters, Cassandra and Jane. Since housekeeping was part of women's education for married life and since the Austen family at Steventon were almost entirely self-sufficient in food supply, Jane Austen grew up familiar with the production of food.[1] The nature of the letters as family correspondence partly explains Austen's reporting on the food supply: "We have one dead lamb" (38); "I am likewise to tell you that one of [the] Leicestershire sheep, sold to the butcher last week, weighed 27 lb. and 1/4 per quarter" (20). The *Letters* also relate gifts of food: "two hampers of apples" (152), "4 brace of Birds" (140), "two Pheasants" (142), "Ham" (264), "a Hare & 4 Rabbits" (301). When Austen is away from home, she gives her sister details of her meals en route ("we had Asparagus & a Lobster which made me wish for you, & some cheesecakes" [39]), and she inquires about the food stores at home: "Does Butcher's meat keep up at the same prize? & is not Bread lower than 2/6?" (239). The *Letters* do more than simply record food, however; they offer critical commentary on food as a demarcation of social hierarchy and on women's role in food production. Noting "a fall in Bread" (249) and "a rise in tea" (259) alongside family news, the *Letters* document Austen's understanding that food was not simply a matter of unmediated taste. Reporting to Cassandra on a recent party, Austen describes a Miss P.T. neglected by Mr. P. She sits with "an empty plate," "even" forced to "ask … him to give her some Mutton without being attended to for some time." Austen jokes to her sister: "There might be Design in this, to be sure, on his side;—he might think an empty Stomach the most favourable for love" (199). The maxim is treated less comically in Austen's novels. Women are dependent on men for their survival, and not all plates are filled equally. Her fiction elaborates the unequal power relations pervading the production, distribution, and consumption of food.

---

[1]   For detailing of Austen's housekeeping role, see Lane's *Jane Austen and Food* (17).

Lane observes that Austen "was always highly conscious of the difference between households like their own, where economy had to be observed, and others of her acquaintance where expense was no object" (*Jane Austen and Food* 20). We see this clearly in those letters sent from Godmersham Park, the estate of her brother Edward Knight: "I have no occasion to think of the price of Bread or of Meat where I am now;—let me shake off vulgar cares & conform to the happy Indifference of East Kent wealth" (229). The letters to Cassandra also reveal some anxiety on Austen's part about this "happy Indifference": "It seems odd to me to have such a great place [the yellow bedroom] all to myself, and to be at Godmersham without you is also odd" (125). Food at her brother's estate is mentioned in the comparative context of Steventon or, later, Chawton. She asks Cassandra, "Have you any Tomatas? Fanny & I regale on them every day" (235) and "I want to hear of your gathering Strawberries, we have had them three times here" (131). She assures Cassandra, "I find time in the midst of Port & Madeira to think of the 14 Bottles of Mead very often" (246) and "I am happy to hear of the Honey.—I was thinking of it the other day.—Let me know when you begin the new Tea—& the new white wine.—My present Elegancies have not yet made me indifferent to such Matters" (225).

A stay at Godmersham Park meant not only more expensive food but also freedom from housekeeping:

> In another week I shall be at home—& then, my having been at Godmersham will seem like a Dream … . The Orange Wine will want our Care soon.—But in the meantime for Elegance & Ease & Luxury … . I shall eat Ice & drink French wine, & be above Vulgar Economy. (139)

Interestingly, as Deirdre Le Faye notes, the manuscript letter indicates that Austen "first wrote 'Vulgar Economy & Cares,' then cancelled the last two words" (391, n11). The self-editing betrays an anxiety about being "above" the domestic labor, the "care," she shares with her sister. This is further suggested by the sentence Austen added "below [the] address panel" after having composed the rest of the letter: "Luckily the pleasures of Friendship, of unreserved Conversation, of similarity of Taste & Opinions, will make good amends for Orange Wine" (139). At Godmersham, rather than serving, Austen is served: "I did not mean to eat, but Mr. Johncock [the butler] has brought in the Tray, so I must.—I am all alone. Edward is gone into his Woods.—At this present time I have five Tables, Eight & Twenty Chairs & two fires all to myself" (249). The passage records not only Edward Austen Knight's wealth (his woods, his furniture, his butler) but also some discomfort on Austen's part: there is a sense of coercion in that she "must" eat the served food to conform to Godmersham Park's power relations, but the food, like the number of tables and chairs, seems excessive to her.

Lane's *Jane Austen and Food* is the only sustained study of food in the novels.[2] Lane presents a case for "Jane Austen's own distaste, as narrator and on behalf of

---

[2]   For a brief overview, see Peggy Hickman, and for an introduction to the historical background to food in Austen, see Eileen Sutherland.

her most esteemed characters, for discussing food at all" (xii): "To take an interest in food in a Jane Austen novel is to be almost certainly condemned as frivolous, selfish or gross" (78). The heroines (with the noted exceptions of Marianne Dashwood, Fanny Price, and Jane Fairfax) and all the heroes share the attitude of "indifference" (86) towards food. Austen "refuses to fall into either an excess of refinement on the one hand, or preoccupation with bodily satisfaction on the other. The two are always kept in play together. In matters of eating, as in other aspects of life, she is concerned with achieving balance" (78). This is in sharp contrast to the depiction of food in the early writings and in the correspondence, for which Lane accounts by speculating that "the young Jane Austen was not mentally editing out the mundane as in work intended for publication (the same applies to her letters)" (78). Unlike Lane, I see a continuity between the early and personal writing and the mature works prepared for publication: there is a consistent focus on unequal power relations. Lane rightly argues that Austen "attacks the excesses of patriarchy" by "showing how those to whom much is given are liable—and able—to demand more" (93). For example, in *Sense and Sensibility*, Elinor Dashwood characterizes Mr. Palmer by his "epicurism, his selfishness, and his conceit" (264) and generalizes that his "traits" are not "at all unusual in his sex and time of life": he was "nice in his eating, uncertain in his hours," and "idled away the mornings at billiards, which ought to have been devoted to business" (263). My point, as distinguished from Lane, is that the excessive consumption of the likes of Mr. Palmer spills over into the novels as a whole. The ability to command food is linked to social hierarchy and to the domination of nature and women. In Austen food does not create community—it creates division.

Austen made connections between food and social hierarchies already in her early compositions. In Act II of "The Visit," the comedy depends on the reader's recognition of the disparity between its genteel cast of characters and their very plain fare: "fried Cowheel and Onion ... red herrings ... Tripe ... Liver and Crow ... [and] Suet pudding" (*J* 66). Austen also drew attention to food's demarcation of a gendered hierarchy. In "Evelyn," composed at age 17, Austen experimented with a character type to which she would return in her fiction. In his travels Mr. Gower stumbles upon the village of Evelyn, admires it, and makes a "wish for a house in this sweet village" (*J* 231). Mr. and Mrs. Webb are happy to vacate their own home—within the "half hour" so "politely" offered by Mr. Gower (*J* 233)— and even throw in their "eldest daughter in marriage with a handsome portion" (*J* 234). The only son of 14 children, Mr. Gower appears perfectly nonplussed by such treatment. Britton Wenner comments, "Mr. Gower sees his future wife as just part of the landscape, which, he assumes, belongs to him" (64–65). Austen's satire of patriarchal privilege comes to its comic apotheosis in the parade of food called up for Mr. Gower:

> Bring up some Chocolate immediately; Spread a Cloth in the dining Parlour, and carry in the venison pasty—. In the mean time let the Gentleman have some sandwiches, and bring in a Basket of Fruit—Send up some Ices and a bason of Soup, and do not forget some Jellies and Cakes ... . The Chocolate,

> The Sandwiches, the Jellies, the Cakes, the Ice, and the Soup soon made their appearance, and Mr Gower having tasted something of all, and pocketted the rest, was conducted into the dining parlour, where he eat a most excellent Dinner and partook of the most exquisite Wines, while Mr and Mrs Webb stood by him still pressing him to eat and drink a little more. (*J* 232–33)

House, wife, and food are all served to Mr. Gower on a platter. The juvenilia, often satirizing social norms by way of exaggeration, also delights in the reversal of the gendered nature of food consumption. In "The Visit," the female characters are in control of both food and marriage. Sir Arthur Hampton does not utter a single word; his domineering wife quickly rejects all offers of food and drink to her husband, and then proceeds to enjoy them herself. Austen delights in her female characters "toss[ing] off a bumper" (*J* 66) and taking the lead in courtship. Willoughby shows no matrimonial interest, but at the conclusion of the play, he finds himself the passive and silent recipient of Miss Fitzgerald's marriage proposal: "Since you are the only one left, I cannot refuse your earnest solicitations—There is my Hand" (*J* 68). In the juvenilia, female characters who eat with gusto also want the associated masculine privileges of mobility, adventure, and liberty. In "The Beautifull Cassandra," the eponymous heroine's journey includes a visit to the pastry-cooks, where she "devoured six ices, refused to pay for them, knocked down the Pastry Cook and walked away" (*J* 54). And in "Frederic and Elfrida," Charlotte, after having accepted two marriage proposals in one day, "sat down to Supper on a young Leveret, a brace of Partridges, a leash of Pheasants and a Dozen of Pigeons" (*J* 9).

To be able to command food that others cannot inscribes social hierarchy. In *Pride and Prejudice* food is one of the weapons in Lady Catherine's arsenal of intimidation. Before their first dinner at Rosings, Mr. Collins "instruct[ed]" Elizabeth and Charlotte's father and sister "in what they were to expect, that the sight of ... so splendid a dinner might not wholly overpower them" (181). Once there, Mr. Collins "carved, and ate, and praised with delighted alacrity; and every dish was commended, first by him, and then by Sir William, who was now enough recovered to echo whatever his son in law said" (184). Lady Catherine "seemed gratified by their excessive admiration ... especially when any dish on the table proved a novelty to them" (184). Similarly, *Northanger Abbey*'s General Tilney, with his chocolate, tea, and pineapples, would be pleased to hear that John Thorpe fantasizes about his "famous dinners": "I should like to dine with him" (95)! Robert Hopkins places the novel in the historical context of food shortages:

> The serious grain shortage of 1795 combined with inflationary grain prices led to riots and parliamentary action. The poor suffered the most. General Tilney's hot-houses producing a hundred pineapples while, to Catherine's eyes, a 'whole parish' seems to be at work, suggest a callous lack of concern for the commonweal. (216)

Furthermore, as Lane argues, the fact that the Abbey has a heated room specifically for supper (the meal at the very end of the day, after dinner and tea) is "the height

... of conspicuous consumption" (*Jane Austen and Food* 53). Food is linked to not only social status but also tyranny in *Northanger Abbey*, for only in the General's absence is "every meal a scene of ease and good-humour" (227). At a local inn, the General's "discontent at whatever the inn afforded, and his angry impatience at the waiters, made Catherine grow every moment more in awe of him" (159). Henry's anxiety about his father's visit to Woodston is telling, as is his expression of "frightening my old housekeeper out of her wits" to "prepare a dinner" (217).

Mansfield Park makes a similar link between food and dominance. Deresiewicz rightly calls *Mansfield Park* a "novel of eaters" in which food, like everything else, is divvied up according to a "pecking order" (*Romantic Poets* 67). Mrs. Norris polices food consumption. She fears that the size of the new dinner table at the Parsonage reflects the Grants' attempt to "step out of their proper sphere" (257). She "faults" Mrs. Grant for giving "her cook as high wages as they did at Mansfield Park" and "could not speak with any temper of ... the quantity of butter and eggs that were regularly consumed in the house" (35). Mrs. Norris protests that she is incapable of "neglecting" Fanny, but when she asks, "could I bear to see her want, while I had a bit of bread to give her?" (8), the reader is inclined to answer in the affirmative. Proud of foiling 10-year-old Dick Jackson's attempt to sit in on dinner at the servants' quarters, she is indeed "well-named" (Hardy 185): "This false nurturer's name derives from the French 'nourrice' and English 'norris'" (Harris 147). Henry Crawford's visit to Fanny in Portsmouth emphasizes the connection of food to social hierarchy: "*He* went to while away the next three hours as he could, with his other acquaintance, till the best dinner that a capital inn afforded, was ready for their enjoyment, and *she* turned in to her more simple one immediately" (478). Austen's emphasis on the "he" and "she" is significant, reminding us that Fanny Price's "being starved, both mind and body" (479) reflects her gender as well as her class.

In Austen's novels, unequal power relations are manifest not only in the distribution and consumption but also in the production of food. Food is linked to masculine dominance, as women are expected to cater to men. It is interesting that in Austen's final fiction, the unfinished "Sanditon," Arthur Parker is an epicurean, but of a different kind than Dr. Grant or General Tilney or Mr. Elton. Arthur Parker's passion for cocoa ("Oh! Arthur, you get your cocoa stronger and stronger every evening" [*LM* 197], cry his sisters) is not associated with dominance. While in the other works the male epicureans feel they deserve more and are given it without question, Arthur's sisters, Susan and Diana, attempt to control how much he eats: "he is only too much disposed for food. We are often obliged to check him" (*LM* 191). Arthur has to sneak his buttery toast when he can: "Charlotte could hardly contain herself as she saw him watching his sisters, while he scrupulously scraped off as much butter as he put on, and then seize an odd moment for adding a great dab just before it went into his mouth" (*LM* 198). Moreover, Arthur is actively involved in food preparation; he attends the "toils" of "coddling and cooking [cocoa] to his own satisfaction and toasting some slices of bread" (*LM* 196–97) and, not immune to a "fine young woman" (*LM* 195) such as Charlotte, even stirs himself to prepare *her* food. These reversals in food consumption and preparation are significant in light of the absence of a marriage plot in "Sanditon," which will be discussed in the next chapter.

Austen's correspondence registers some resentment on the duty of hospitality. A letter to Cassandra, dated September 8, 1816, expresses relief at the conclusion of her brother's visit:

> I enjoyed Edward's company very much, as I said before, & yet I was not sorry when friday came. It had been a busy week, & I wanted a few days quiet, & exemption from the Thought & contrivances which any sort of company gives. I often wonder how *you* can find time for what you do, in addition to the care of the House;—And how good Mrs West c^d have written such Books & collected so many hard words, with all her family cares, is still more a matter of astonishment! Composition seems to me Impossible, with a head full of joints of mutton & doses of rhubarb. (321)

The female labor associated with food takes time away from the "collection" of "words."[3] An earlier letter to Cassandra (January 7, 1807) similarly rejoices at the prospect of the departure of her brother, sister-in-law, and baby niece: "When you receive this, our guests will be all gone or going; and I shall be left to the comfortable disposal of my time, to ease of mind from the torments of rice puddings and apple dumplings, and probably to regret that I did not take more pains to please them all" (114). Austen evidently performed her hosting duties somewhat grudgingly, for they, as she confesses to her sister, interfered with her writing. A letter composed when Austen was 23 years old shares in the reversals characteristic of the juvenilia:

> My mother desires me to tell you that I am a very good housekeeper, which I have no reluctance in doing, because I really think it my peculiar excellence, and for this reason—I always take care to provide such things as please my own appetite, which I consider as the chief merit in housekeeping. I have had some ragout veal, and I mean to have some haricot mutton tomorrow. We are to kill a pig soon. (20)

Austen, of course, knew that the role of housekeeping was to provide for the appetites of others, primarily the man of the house, and she delights in turning social norms upside down. The prominence of meat in the conjured menus is also important.

In her letters, Austen joked about the primacy of meat: "We made our grand Meal, and then with admiring astonishment perceived in what a magnificent manner our support had been provided for—We could not with the utmost exertion

---

[3]   For a different interpretation of the letter, see Tristram Stuart's comment that "for all [Austen's] mockery" of Mr. Woodhouse's diet in *Emma*, "she was not immune to dietary doctrines herself when, for example, she betrays her assumption that full meals clog the brain" (193).

consume above the twentieth part of the beef" (81). And she writes to Cassandra, "liv[ing] upon Pheasants [is] no bad Life!" (299). In the Western hierarchy of food, as Julia Twigg and Nick Fiddes have demonstrated, meat occupies top status. This is the case in Austen's day and continues to be so in our own. Meat "historically ... has acted as a signifier of social class: the more meat one could afford to eat, the wealthier one was" (Lupton 28). This is precisely the point made in late eighteenth- and early nineteenth-century tracts on vegetarianism.[4] John Oswald writes that "animal food is a luxury, which the major part of mankind cannot reach" (15), and P.B. Shelley, in "A Vindication of Natural Diet," argues that meat "directly militates with th[e] equality of the rights of man" (15) since "the peasant cannot gratify these fashionable cravings" (15): "It is only the wealthy that can, to any great degree, even now, indulge the unnatural craving for dead flesh" (13).[5] No wonder, then, that Lady Catherine finds Mrs. Collins's "joints of meat ... too large for her family" (*P&P* 190) and that Mrs. Bennet, at the prospect of Mr. Bingley's visit, worries, "good lord! How unlucky! there is not a bit of fish to be got to-day" (*P&P* 68). While there is a steady supply of "a turkey or a goose, or a leg of mutton" (*MP* 252) at Mansfield Park and the Grants' Parsonage, Mrs. Price complains, "It is very inconvenient to have no butcher in the street" (*MP* 437). General Tilney boasts to Catherine of his gifts of game to the neighborhood's "set of very worthy men": they "have half a buck from Northanger twice a year" (*NA* 216). As Deuchar points out, "Game itself ... became a useable symbol of social status, a symbol which could assert a social relationship: a gift of game by a 'qualified' gentleman to one 'unqualified' was an act of benevolence, of patronage, and one which naturally carried all the associated connotations of immutable hierarchy" (79). At Woodston, Catherine "could not but observe" that despite "the abundance of the dinner, General Tilney was still "looking at the side-table for cold meat which was not there" (*NA* 221). When Austen quips to her sister, in a letter from Godmersham dated October 12, 1813, "I dined upon Goose yesterday—which I hope will secure a good sale of my 2[d] Edition" (235) of *Sense and Sensibility*, she is adapting the proverb that "That who eats Goose on Michael's Day, / Shan't Money lack, his Debts to pay" and playing on her culture's valuing of meat above other foods and its association with power.

The primacy of meat is directly connected to human supremacy over nature. Food is one of the most direct ways in which humans interact with nature. Meat, as Fiddes argues, "tangibly represents human control of the natural world" (2) and

---

[4]   For accounts of the history of vegetarianism see Michael Allen Fox, Jon Gregerson, and Tristram Stuart. For vegetarian discourses in the eighteenth and nineteenth centuries, see Timothy Morton (*Shelley and the Revolution in Taste*) and Anita Guerrini. Not all vegetarian discourses focused on animals; some arguments were primarily driven by health or religious concerns. My study focuses on those texts which put the treatment of animals and the implications thereof at the center of their arguments.

[5]   See Morton's *Shelley and the Revolution in Taste*, Onno Oerlemans, and Lisbeth Chapin for detailed discussion of Shelley's vegetarianism.

"power over nature" (45): its "signification ... principally relates to environmental control, and it has long held an unrivalled status amongst major foods on account of this meaning" (45). Meat also represents control over the social groups associated with nature. Ecofeminist theory suggests that the objectification of nature and "the logic of domination" (Warren 144) which underpins the turning of animals into meat is extended to social groups associated with animals. Carol J. Adams's *The Sexual Politics of Meat* proposes a "Feminist-Vegetarian Critical Theory," and argues that patriarchy objectifies both women and animals. Meat's sexual politics—meat as female and the consumption of meat as male—reinforces other hierarchies. Lupton and Fiddes also demonstrate the gendering of meat-eating as male. We already have seen that Austen's representations of rural sport parallel the objectification of animals and women. A similar argument is at work in the representation of food and, in some cases, critiques of sport and food are linked. Henry Crawford, an avid sportsman, was brought up "in a school of luxury and epicurism" (*MP* 472) and is a connoisseur of both food and women. We are reminded of P.B. Shelley's question: "Is it to be believed that a being of gentle feelings, rising from his meal of roots, would take delight in sports of blood?" ("Vindication" 11).[6]

In *Emma*, when the inhabitants of Highbury are eagerly planning the Crown Inn ball, the narrator notes, "A private dance, without sitting down to supper, was pronounced an infamous fraud upon the rights of men and women" (273). Austen was aware of the politics of food. She drew on late eighteenth- and early nineteenth-century writings on diet, including vegetarianism, which often intersected with other claims for social justice in the argument that a meatless diet advances egalitarianism and fosters nonviolence. In his Preface to *The Cry of Nature; Or, An Appeal to Mercy and to Justice, on Behalf of the Persecuted Animals* (1791), John Oswald includes vegetarianism among other revolutionary causes:

> when he [the author] considers the natural bias of the human heart to the side of mercy, and observes on all hands the barbarous governments of Europe giving way to a better system of things, he is inclined to hope that the day is beginning to approach when the growing sentiment of peace and good-will towards men will also embrace, in a wide circle of benevolence, the lower orders of life. (ii)

Joseph Ritson's *An Essay on Abstinence from Animal Food as a Moral Duty* posits that "animal food [is] the cause of cruelty and ferocity" (86) such as the "slave-trade, that abominable violation of the rights of nature ... as well as a variety of violent acts, both national and personal" (89). Similarly, Shelley argues that the production of meat necessitates desensitization and, hence, normalizes other forms of violence. Meat leads to "hatred, murder and rapine, wars, massacres and revolutions" ("Vegetable System" 337): "Who that is accustomed to the

---

[6]   Not all writers opposed to rural sport extended the argument to vegetarianism. Primatt, for example, did not oppose the eating of animals provided they were killed quickly; he considered the eating of lobsters cruel because they are boiled while alive.

sight of wounds and anguish will scruple to inflict them, when he shall deem it expedient?" ("Vegetable System" 343). Catharine Macaulay also addressed the ethics of vegetarianism in *Letters on Education*. Catherine Gardner notes that "Macaulay's advice on the healthfulness of a mainly vegetarian diet for children is not directed solely at the physical health of the child; the eating of meat and the moral development of the child seem inextricably linked" (123).[7] Nor is the advocacy of vegetarianism limited to children. For Macaulay, meat is a "habit" (278): "I can from my own experience affirm with Rousseau, that the taste of flesh is not natural to the human palate, when not vitiated by carnivorous habits" (38). To disrupt the social practice of meat-eating is to call into question social hierarchies. Macaulay's *Letters on Education* connects meat consumption, which is "to inflict that fate on other beings which would be terrible to ourselves" (38), to a dulling of sympathy, and it is sympathy which is "the best guard against the abuse of the extensive power with which [Nature] has entrusted" man (39). While consistently denaturalizing meat consumption, she speaks of the importance of making methods of slaughter as painless as possible and that slaughterhouses should be "sequestered from the haunts of men" (278) so that humans do not become accustomed to killing. Her argument about capital punishment runs along similar lines: "all executions should be performed in private" (279). In this, she differs from her contemporaries. Oswald argued that "On the carcase we feed, without remorse, because the dying struggles of the butchered creature are secluded from our sight" (30), a point shared by many twenty-first-century writers on meat production, such as Jonathan Safran Foer.

While Austen did not adopt a vegetarian diet, there is considerable ambivalence towards meat in her writings. References to meat are accompanied by a critical awareness of the social dominance meat demarcates. Further, at times, the parallels between women and animals extend to criticism of meat from a feminist perspective. It is important to point out, as Oerlemans does, that "there seem to have been very few committed vegetarians around while [the vegetarian debate] was taking place" in the early nineteenth century: discussions of vegetarianism "reflect" in part "the much larger and more obvious concern … about the place of humankind in nature" (103). Austen's investigation into the "place of humankind in nature," as we have seen, is directly connected to her feminist critique; the treatment of nature impinges directly on the treatment of women and other subordinate social groups. Significantly, Austen draws attention to meat in her pictures of domestic tyranny.

In *Mansfield Park*, Mary Crawford describes Dr. Grant as an "indolent selfish bon vivant, who must have his palate consulted in every thing" and "if the cook makes a blunder, is out of humour with his excellent wife … . Henry and I were partly driven out this very evening, by a disappointment about a green goose, which he could not get the better of. My poor sister was forced to stay and bear it"

---

[7]   "Milk, fruit, eggs, and almost every kind of vegetable aliment, ought to be the principal part of the nourishment of children" (Macaulay 38).

(130). The equivocal phrasing—does Dr. Grant fail to "get the better of" the goose or the disappointment?—invites us to see the consumption of meat as symbolic of mastery and to see a parallel between the animal's and the wife's subjections. And, later, Mrs. Grant misses one of the rehearsals of *Lovers' Vows*, for "Dr. Grant, professing an indisposition, ... could not spare his wife." As Mary reports with "mock solemnity": "Dr. Grant is ill ... . He has been ill ever since he did not eat any of the pheasant today. He fancied it tough—sent away his plate—and has been suffering ever since" (200–201). Dr. Grant's temper in this instance oppresses not only Mrs. Grant but also Fanny, who consequently faces excruciating pressure to take Mrs. Grant's place in the theatricals: "she must yield" (201). In both cases of Dr. Grant's domestic tyranny, Austen does not leave the food unspecified. Austen sarcastically commented on this kind of tyranny to her sister and inverted its usual male-female power relations: "Our dinner was very good yesterday, & the Chicken boiled perfectly tender; therefore I shall not be obliged to dismiss Nancy on that account" (*Letters* 17).

Austen, at times, also draws the radical connection that both women and animals are meat for men. In "Lesley Castle," Charlotte Lutterel is dismayed at the cancellation of her sister's wedding due to the death of the groom, and she laments, "all my Labour thrown away":

> Imagine how great the Disappointment must be to me, when you consider that after having laboured both by Night and by Day, in order to get the Wedding dinner ready by the time appointed, after having roasted Beef, Broiled Mutton, and Stewed Soup enough to last the new-married Couple through the Honeymoon, I had the mortification of finding that I had been Roasting, Broiling and Stewing both the Meat and Myself to no purpose. (*J* 146)

In the patriarchal economy, she shares the status of animals and becomes meat: she, too, is "roasted." In *Pride and Prejudice*, when Sir William Lucas and Maria return after visiting Charlotte, Lady Lucas "was inquiring of Maria across the table, after the welfare and poultry of her eldest daughter" (245), as if the two were one and the same. Similarly, when Mrs. Bennet boasts of her successful dinner party for Mr. Bingley, she is equally proud of Jane's "great beauty" and the "remarkably well done partridges" and the venison: "everybody said they never saw so fat a haunch" (379).[8] The sexual politics of meat are further highlighted

---

[8]   In contrast, Elizabeth Bennet irreverently animalizes her social superiors. While Maria Lucas is "breathless with agitation" when a Rosings Park phaeton pulls up at the garden gate, Elizabeth maintains her comedic spirit: "And is this all? ... I expected at least that the pigs were got into the garden, and here is nothing but Lady Catherine and her daughter" (179). In a similar vein, Elizabeth declines to walk with Mr. Darcy, Mrs. Hurst, and Miss Bingley at Netherfield: "You are charmingly group'd, and appear to uncommon advantage. The picturesque would be spoilt by admitting a fourth" (58). Referring here to a specific passage in William Gilpin advising that cows be depicted in groups of three, rather than two or four, she deftly lowers her social superiors to the level of animals.

in the male role of carving. Meat, with its association of force and power, is in the hands of men. In *Mansfield Park*, Lady Bertram is "astonished" and relieved to find "how well they did" in Sir Thomas's absence, "how well Edmund could supply his place in carving" (39). The young Austen parodied the association of men and carving in Chloe's song in "The first Act of a Comedy":

> I am going to have my dinner,
> After which I shan't be thinner,
> I wish I had here Strephon
> For he would carve the partridge if it should be a tough one. (*J* 220)

P.B. Shelley, in his "Vindication of a Natural Diet" (1813) and "On the Vegetable System of Diet," pairs alcohol with meat in his analysis of diet. He writes, "the use of animal flesh and fermented liquors, directly militate with th[e] equality of the rights of man" because "the peasant cannot gratify these fashionable cravings" ("Vindication" 15). "Abstinence from animal food and spirituous liquors" ("Vindication" 7), says Shelley, "strike[s] at the root of all evil" ("Vindication" 10). While vegetarian tracts routinely employ the language of "custom" and "habit" (Newton 1) in order to denaturalize the social practice of eating meat, it is striking that Shelley posits meat as an "addict[ive]" ("Vegetable System" 339) substance, like alcohol, which produces "unnatural craving" ("Vindication" 13) and insensitivity to the pain of others. For Shelley, not only do meat and alcohol perpetuate inequality between those who can afford them and those who cannot, but their consumption also creates tyranny and a structure of violence: "Was Nero a man of temperate life?" ("Vindication" 11), he asks.[9] For Shelley, meat-eating by its very nature is intemperate: "the eater of animal flesh ... devour[es] an acre at a meal" ("Vindication" 13).[10] Meat production is wasteful—"the most fertile districts of the habitable globe are now actually cultivated by men for animals, at a delay and waste of aliment absolutely incapable of calculation" ("Vindication" 13)—and is dependent on the empire: "On a natural system of diet, we should require no spices from India ... none of those multitudinous articles of luxury, for which every corner of the globe is rifled" ("Vindication" 14). Furthermore, meat-eating reflects excessive human power over other "sentient being[s]" ("Vegetable System" 344). Shelley proposes dietary temperance as a way to radically alter the structures of society. Temperance—in Shelley's sense—is relevant to Austen.

A link between meat, alcohol, and violence can be found in *Sense and Sensibility*. As Lane points out (*Jane Austen and Food* xi), the only detailed menu we are given in the novel is Willoughby's lunch of beef and porter when he travels

---

[9]   Carol J. Adams and Josephine Donovan point to the "historical alliance" of feminism, vegetarianism, and temperance (Adams 167) in the later nineteenth century based on "the linkage between women and animals as objects of human male domestic violence" (Adams and Donovan 7).

[10]   Also see George Nicholson's *On Food*: "four times the quantity of ground is required to support an ox that is necessary to maintain a man" (43).

to Cleveland from London in one day. When he arrives, Elinor suspects him of being "in liquor," and he confirms, "yes, I am very drunk" (360–361). Willoughby's motivation for coming to Cleveland is far from selfless concern for Marianne: he seeks to make himself "hated one degree less" (361).[11] Elinor "start[s] back with a look of horror at the sight of him" (359), and feels he "force[s]" himself upon her "notice" (361). His morbid fantasy of Marianne is particularly chilling; he speaks of finding solace in remembering "Marianne's sweet face as white as death" when he rejected her at the London Ball: "when I thought of her to-day as really dying, it was a kind of comfort to me to imagine that I knew exactly how she would appear to those, who saw her last in the world. She was before me, constantly before me, as I travelled, in the same look and hue" (371). Willoughby's objectification of Marianne extends to his wanting ownership of her deathbed scene. In his drunken imagination, Marianne's appearance in her final moments is just like her earlier death-like experience at the ball, in which he was the key player.

The language of temperance is used explicitly in *Northanger Abbey*. John Thorpe's speculations about the wealth and leisure of Mr. Allen include the amount of alcohol he consumes: he "has lived very well in his time, I dare say; he is not gouty for nothing. Does he drink his bottle a-day now?" (60). Catherine objects that he "is a very temperate man" and firmly rebuts John Thorpe's opinion that "if every body was to drink their bottle a-day, there would not be half the disorders in the world there are now": "I cannot believe it" (60). When she remarks with disapproval on the "great deal of wine drank in Oxford," he brags,

> Oxford! There is no drinking at Oxford now, I assure you. Nobody drinks there. You would hardly meet with a man who goes beyond his four pints at the utmost. Now, for instance, it was reckoned a remarkable thing at the last party in my rooms, that upon an average we cleared about five pints a head. It was looked upon as something out of the common way. *Mine* is famous good stuff to be sure. You would not often meet with any thing like it in Oxford—and that may account for it. But this will just give you a notion of the general rate of drinking there. (60)

Catherine "was left ... with rather a strengthened belief of there being a great deal of wine drank in Oxford" (61). In Chapter 2, I examined John Thorpe as a satire of the sporting ideal and the prototype of the sportsman who abuses both animals and women. It is significant that Austen includes excessive consumption of alcohol in her characterization of Thorpe and that she notes the heroine's objection. The juvenilia provide an interesting contrast to this gendered pattern. In "Jack and Alice," the red-cheeked Alice "has many rare and charming qualities, but Sobriety is not one of them" (*J* 26). The whole Johnson family is "a little

---

[11] Lane comes to different conclusions about the scene: "Willoughby's choice of good, plain, honest, manly, English fare is ... a mark in his favour ... . Some of the sterling character associated with the roast beef of old England attaches to Willoughby in this, his final appearance in the book" (*Jane Austen and Food* 150).

addicted to the Bottle and the Dice" (*J* 14); they play cards at the masquerade ball "each with a bottle in their hand" (*J* 15). Jack Johnson, the notional "Hero of this Novel," is mentioned in the title only to be killed off, without ever speaking a line, a "natural Consequence" of his "unfortunate propensity to Liquor," while Alice replaces him as "sole inheritress of a very large fortune" (*J* 27) and hero of the piece. "Relish[ing] … Claret" is not the only male role Alice claims for herself. Inebriated, she flies into such a rage that she "almost came to Blows" when Lady Williams dares to suggest that "too red a look" (*J* 20) compromises beauty. Alice also takes on the male role by initiating the marriage proposal to Charles Adams, and when rejected, "she flew to her Bottle and it was soon forgot" (*J* 20). For Alice, alcohol brings liberty from the constraints of gender and romance. In a letter to Cassandra from Godmersham Park, Austen jokes, "as I must leave off being young, I find many Douceurs in being a sort of Chaperon for I am put on the Sofa near the Fire & can drink as much wine as I like" (251). In her fiction, however, alcohol is a male prerogative and Austen includes excessive consumption in her portraits of male tyranny.

In *Mansfield Park*, Mr. Price's first appearance is announced by "his own loud voice preceding him, as with something of the oath kind he kicked away his son's portmanteau, and his daughter's band-box" (438), leaving the heroine's "feelings sadly pained by his language and his smell of spirits" (440). He is consistently associated with drinking and violence. When Mr. Price reads of Maria's running away with Henry Crawford in the newspaper, he insists: "by G— if she belonged to *me*, I'd give her the rope's end as long as I could stand over her" (509). Moreover, the novel's depiction of intemperance cannot be put down to "stereotypes of the urban poor" (Fraiman 810). In Mary Crawford's estimation (which the narrator does not contradict), Dr. Grant "has the best intentions of doing nothing all the rest of his days but eat, drink, and grow fat" (128). The narrator tersely comments that "Mr. Crawford's being [Dr. Grant's] guest was an excuse for drinking claret every day" (55). Tom Bertram's racing and drinking jeopardize the family fortune and bring about his nearly fatal illness: he "had gone from London with a party of young men to Newmarket, where a neglected fall, and a good deal of drinking, had brought on a fever" (494). And even Edmund recalls that "at Oxford I have been a good deal used to have a man lean on me for the length of a street" (110). Thus by the time we meet Mr. Price in Portsmouth, the novel already has established the connection between alcohol and patriarchy—whether manifested in domestic tyranny or the more genteel patriarchal privileges of inheritance and education.

The connection between intemperance and male violence is also made explicit in *Emma* and its heroine's "tête-à-tête drive" with Mr. Elton: "he had been drinking too much of Mr. Weston's good wine, and [Emma] felt sure that he would want to be talking nonsense." Her attempt "to restrain him as much as might be, by her own manners" (139) and conversation fails: "she found her subject cut up—her hand seized—her attention demanded, and Mr. Elton actually making violent love to her. … She tried to stop him; but vainly; he would go on, and say it all." While Emma attributes his behavior to "drunkenness" and "his half and half state" (140), the narrator makes the more devastating point that Mr. Elton "had only drunk wine enough to elevate his spirits, not at all to confuse his intellects. He perfectly knew his own meaning" (141). The wine does not so much alter Mr. Elton's character as bring it out. Like Mr. Collins, Mr. Elton persists even after being refused—"allow me to interpret this interesting silence" (142)—until finally retreating in anger. *Emma*, concluding with the heroine's marriage to a gentleman farmer, is Austen's most developed treatment of legacies and diets.[12]

Having acquired "a taste for dinners" at Maple Grove, Mrs. Elton plans on "soon shew[ing]" Highbury "how every thing ought to be arranged" with "one very superior party" (313). Her daily meals are no less showy: she "should be extremely displeased if Wright were to send us up such a dinner, as could make me regret having asked *more* than Jane Fairfax to partake of it" (306). Mrs. Elton is not alone in her "wild[ness]" for "first circles, spheres, lines, ranks" (390). All of Highbury is concerned with first and second sets (19), "station" (30), and "degree" (32); everyone has her "sphere" (65), "level" (142), and "proper place" (198). Emma dislikes visiting Miss Bates, not only because she is so "tiresome" but also because of "all the horror of being in danger of falling in with the second rate and third rate of Highbury, who were calling on them for ever" (165). Food plays a vital role in demarcating the various "line[s] of life" (450). For example, Emma's offer of "broth from Hartfield" (95) to the poor is directly juxtaposed with Mr. Elton's detailing of his dinner: the "Stilton cheese, the north Wiltshire, the butter, the cellery, the beet-root and all the dessert" (95). The anxieties about rank raised by the Coles' party are soothed by an unequal distribution of food: the first set enjoys dinner, while "the less worthy females were to come in the evening, with Miss Bates, Miss Fairfax, and Miss Smith" (231). Lane argues that in *Emma* the moral theme of "giving and sharing" is "happily embedded in the metaphor of food" (*Jane Austen and Food* 166). The novel, indeed, is stuffed with gifts of food: Mr. Knightley sends the Bates family apples; Mr. Martin woos Harriet with some walnuts; and, to further her son's suit, Mrs. Martin brings Mrs. Goddard a goose. But these gifts of food come with strings attached. They create indebtedness on the part of the receivers, and it is "a great deal better ... to excite gratitude than to feel it" (15). When Emma sends pork to Mrs. and Miss Bates, the latter's language is quite revealing on that score: "My mother desires her very best compliments and regards, and a thousand thanks, and says you really quite oppress her" (186). Mrs. Goddard and Mrs. and Miss Bates are "most come-at-able" (19) and "almost always at the service of an invitation" (20): "Emma found herself very frequently

---

[12]   Lisa Hopkins and Sarah Moss also address the "social attitudes and financial status ... demarcated by food" (Hopkins 63), but our conclusions differ. Both ascribe conservatism to the novel. The "intensely political subtext" is "soothingly mediated through the maternal voice of the narrator, with its emphasis on rebirth and continuity," writes Hopkins (68–69). Similarly, Moss concludes: "As ever in Austen, the way things are is not particularly happy ... but ... virtue consists in seeing, knowing and accepting that love and oppression are often indistinguishable and that ... there is nothing to gain from biting the hand that feeds you" (205–6).

able to collect [them]; and happy was she ... in the power" (21). Miss Bates, always "as grateful as was possible" (241), is so used to being on the indebted side that she considers it "a favour" if Emma accepts her offer to "eat a piece of cake" (166).

Gifts of food enact power relations, and this is one of the reasons why Jane Fairfax, who "had yet her bread to earn" (176), "really eats nothing" (255). Emma may be "tire[d]" of listening to Miss Bates's description of "exactly how little bread and butter [Jane] ate for breakfast, and how small a slice of mutton for dinner" (180), but Jane's refusal of food is an important protest. She rejects food to avoid having to be grateful to her social superiors. Miss Bates reports that "Mr. Perry recommended nourishing food; but every thing they could command (and never had anybody such good neighbours) was distasteful" (425). Emma's gift is sent back: "arrow-root from the Hartfield store-room must have been poison" (439). Arrowroot, originating in the West Indies, reminds Jane of the very trade to which she likens the governess profession: the slave trade, or the "sale ... of human flesh" (325).

Jane Fairfax might have willed herself to starve, and when we hear of thieves "robb[ing]" Mrs. Weston's "poultry-house ... one night of all her turkies" and "other poultry-yards in the neighbourhood" (528), we know that not everyone is served in Highbury. Austen further draws attention to poverty in the gypsy episode. Harriet and Miss Bickerton, on a walk "about half a mile beyond Highbury" (360), find themselves face-to-face with a child begging for money. The ladies immediately respond with fear, rather than charity, and "such an invitation for attack could not be resisted; and Harriet was soon assailed by half a dozen children, headed by a stout woman and a great boy" (361). Frank Churchill rescues Harriet from the "gang," leaving them in "terror" and "completely frightened" (361). As Thomas Hothem points out, Harriet is "a vagrant in the class landscape of the village," making "her encounter with the gypsies poignantly ironic" (56). The gypsies reflect Harriet's own marginality, and their exclusion foreshadows Harriet's from Hartfield at the end of the novel. The vagrants leave Highbury with their needs unaddressed: they "did not wait for the operations of justice; they took themselves off in a hurry" (364). Highbury's justice, then, consists of crime and punishment. Austen directly links the social injustice to the distribution of food, for Mrs. Elton appropriates the gypsies' plight as a theme for her picnic: "I shall wear a large bonnet, and bring one of my little baskets hanging on my arm ... . Nothing can be more simple ... . There is to be no form or parade—a sort of gipsy party" (385). While Mrs. Elton can play at being a gypsy, the vagrant children leave Highbury hungry.

Mr. Knightley's farming has been idealized by critics, and Emma's appreciation of Abbey Mills is seen as an important marker in her progress towards maturity and marriage. Bodenheimer argues that here Emma "finally gets the picture straight, with everyone in his or her appropriate social place" (612). Looking out at Abbey-Mill Farms, Emma sees "rich pastures, spreading flocks, orchard in blossom, and light column of smoke ascending": "a sweet view—sweet to the eye and the mind. English verdure, English culture, English comfort, seen under a sun bright, without being oppressive" (391). Southam argues that Austen's "patriotic intent is undisguised" (*Navy* 260): "No hint of social distress or disorder here, the scene is harmonious and satisfying, a consort of man and nature, a balance of 'prosperity' and 'beauty,' a scene typically, and, in the voice of Jane Austen, empathically 'English'" (*Navy* 259).

But viewed from another perspective, Abbey Mills is less comforting. The fact that Mr. Knightley is a "magistrate" (107) draws our attention to the disciplinary role in his farming activities. With his enthusiasm about "the plan of a drain, the change of a fence, the felling of a tree, and the destination of every acre for wheat, turnips, or spring corn" (107), Mr. Knightley domesticates and controls nature. The focus on profit (258) and records (278, 338) subordinates nature to an accounting system. As Stroup argues, "wilderness is a waste" (160): "to Mr. Knightley nature is inventory: not to be shoddily cared for or neglected, but finally quantifiable and accessible to the rational mind" (160). This, we may add, is as evident in his agricultural business as it is in his collection of "corals" and "shells" (393). While I agree with Stroup's reading of Mr. Knightley's view of nature, I disagree that Austen's is one and the same. Mr. Knightley, according to Stroup, is the "perfect landlord" (159): "We find ourselves confronted, once again, with the deep core of Austen's Tory ideology, proudly embracing a paternal order which many of Austen's readers, at least when outside the spell of her eloquence, find deeply troubling" (158).[13] But this does not take into account the gypsies. The vagrants undermine the so-called "unequivocal" perfection (Stroup 159) of Highbury's social structure, as does the acknowledged poverty at the end of the novel. Mr. Knightley's farming does not feed everyone.

Austen further holds up Mr. Knightley to a critical perspective, as she traces the implications of his view of nature on the treatment of women. Stroup rightly observes that agriculture is "gendered male both in the novel and in the culture at large" (158), and he points to Emma's aversion to the topic. Emma's lack of interest in agriculture is not to be confused with a lack of interest in nature. She eagerly anticipates spring and the "elder ... coming out" (203), and "observes[s] the ... western sun" (473). She seeks relief in the "exquisite sight, smell, sensation of nature, tranquil, warm and brilliant after a storm" (462). While Emma is fond of walking, Mrs. Elton is less so: "you know—in summer there is dust, and in winter there is dirt" (386). Emma's responsiveness to nature is in pointed contrast to Mrs. Elton's love for "exploring" in a "barouche-landau" (295) as well as Mr. Knightley's love of a productive nature. Emma finds agriculture distasteful for the majority of the novel because women are associated with the very nature agriculture seeks to make yield. Mr. Knightley, keen on improving Emma, speaks of marriage in terms of women's submission of will (38). Emma, despite her

---

[13]   Also see Britton Wenner: "In her description of Donwell Abbey, Austen brings together harmonious aspects of English community as expressed by landscape in a way which mirrors Burke's images of preservation and adaptation" (81).

privileged status of being "handsome, clever, and rich" (3), is acutely aware of the systemic domination of women. She reflects on the "duty of woman by woman" (249) and the arbitrariness of women's "destiny" (417): "The world is not their's, nor the world's law" (436). Emma recognizes that Frank Churchill's and Jane Fairfax's lots are not equal: "*His* sufferings … do not appear to have done him much harm" (434).

Emma perceives that women are prized not for "well-informed minds" but for their "beauty" and "sweetness of temper and manner, a very humble opinion of [themselves], and a great readiness to be pleased with other people": speaking of the malleable Harriet, she says to Mr. Knightley, "I am very much mistaken if your sex in general would not think such beauty and such temper, the highest claims a woman could possess" (67). This is certainly the case in her sister's marriage to Mr. John Knightley. He "wishes his boys to be active and hardy" (86), but has chosen a docile wife. Isabella is a "worshipping wife" with an "extreme sweetness of … temper" (100). Isabella, "passing her life with those she doated on, full of their merits, blind to their faults, and always innocently busy, might have been a model of right feminine happiness" (151). Similarly, Mrs. Weston, "like a sweet-tempered woman and a good wife" (275), knows to concur with her husband's opinions. Mrs. Elton's repeated joke about "my lord and master" (319, 497, 499) hits a serious note. Mr. Knightley, comparing Miss Taylor's life as a governess to her life as Mrs. Weston, concludes: "At any rate, it must be better to have only one to please, than two" (9). The "independence" of marriage is thus qualified: she "has been used to have two persons to please; she will now have but one. The chances are that she must be a gainer" (9).

In *Emma*, marriage is a system which objectifies women; Mr. Weston, for one, "had made his fortune, bought his house, and obtained his wife" (15). Emma thinks that Harriet's beauty is "foundation enough" (35) for marriage. The novel largely supports Emma's cynical view of marriage. When realizing that she is Mr. Elton's object, Emma surmises that he "only wanted to aggrandize and enrich himself; and if Miss Woodhouse of Hartfield, the heiress of thirty thousand pounds, were not quite so easily obtained as he had fancied, he would soon try for Miss Somebody else with twenty or with ten" (147). And he does. While not moving along quite as quickly as *Pride and Prejudice*'s Mr. Collins, who transfers his affections from Jane Bennet to Elizabeth Bennet to Charlotte Lucas within days, Mr. Elton secures Augusta Hawkins, and her "independent fortune, of so many thousands as would always be called ten" (194), within four weeks of being rejected by Emma.

"Never loth to be first" (76), Emma consequently has little interest in marriage: "I believe few married women are half as much mistress of their husband's house, as I am of Hartfield; and never, never could I expect to be so truly beloved and important; so always first and always right in any man's eyes as I am in my father's" (90–91). As Maureen M. Martin argues so convincingly, Emma's desire for singleness is rooted in her love of independence, and she does not develop an interest in marriage until realizing that "To remain queen, Emma must accept the King" (13), Mr. Knightley. In *Emma*, the marriage plot is framed by an agricultural

one; both nature and women yield to men, in the dual sense of submission and
production of children. Juliet McMaster notes that the novel "begins on the
wedding night of … Mrs. Weston, and virtually culminates with … the delivery
of her first child": "the time scheme of the novel is … in harmony with woman's
biological rhythms in conception, gestation and childbirth" ("Children in *Emma*"
62). While this plot can be read as delivering our heroine into maturity and
happiness, it is also laced with considerable anxiety. The novel opens with Miss
Taylor's marriage, and her "loss" brings "grief" and "gentle sorrow" to Emma
and her father (4). Mrs. Weston's pregnancy is a source of anticipated joy, but
brings "agitation" and fears for her "safe[ty]" (493). And while Mrs. Weston fares
well, Emma, Frank, and Jane all lose their mothers at a very young age; Frank at
two (103), Jane at three (174), and Emma early enough so that she only has "an
indistinct remembrance of her caresses" (3). The narrator's comment that "Human
nature is so well disposed towards those who are in interesting situations, that a
young person, who either marries or dies, is sure of being kindly spoken of" (194)
is a rather gloomy gloss on the novel's plot.

Earlier in this chapter I demonstrated that Austen's use of satirical humor spells
out the parallel position of women and animals in patriarchy. *Emma* continues this
satire. Stroup points to "a series of cruxes in which the distinction between people
and the agricultural products they create dissolves" (161). He lists Jane Fairfax's
likening of the governess trade to the "sale … of human flesh" (325), Frank
Churchill's speaking of Jane "as one would a blue ribbon winner: 'Did you ever
see such a skin'" (Stroup 161), and Emma's questioning if Mr. Knightley might not
be mistaken that Robert Martin had proposed again to Harriet, and been accepted:
"Did you not misunderstand him?—You were both talking of other things; of
business, shows of cattle, or new drills—and might not you, in the confusion of so
many subjects, mistake him?—It was not Harriet's hand that he was certain of—
it was the dimensions of some famous ox" (516–17). There are other examples
we can add. Mr. Knightley tries to dissuade Emma's matchmaking for Mr. Elton:
"Invite him to dinner, Emma, and help him to the best of the fish and chicken, but
leave him to chuse his own wife" (12). Speaking of Jane's engagement to Frank
cancelling her governess post, Mrs. Elton adapts John Gay's lines about a bull and
his favorite cow: "For when a lady's in the case, / You know all other things give
place" (495). And like Charlotte Lutterel, who complains of "Roasting, Broiling
and Stewing both the Meat and Myself" (*J* 146), the dependent Miss Bates feels
"quite roasted" (350) at the ball at the Crown Inn. What is important about all of
these comic disjunctions is that women are turned into animals and flesh. That
Robert Martin's renewed courtship of Harriet gets underway at Astley's (515),
which boasted equestrian shows and "variety acts such as … trained dogs, learned
pigs, and famous monkeys" (Joseph W. Donohue, qtd. in Gay, *Austen and Theatre*
190), further links the taming of animals and wives.[14]

---

[14] Austen reports to her sister a proposed visit to Astley's on August 23, 1796
(*Letters* 5).

Rather than idealizing Mr. Knightley's treatment of nature, Austen draws out its implications for social groups associated with nature: women who "submi[t]" (38) in marriage and the vagrants who fear punishment. While Mrs. Elton is often seen as a parody of Emma at her worst, she is also a commentary on Mr. Knightley's managerial style: her meddling in Jane Fairfax's future to the point of cruelty is ironically described by the narrator as "Mrs. Elton's knight-errantry" (304). There also are striking similarities between how Emma and Mr. Knightley view their social inferiors. Emma's plans for Harriet—"she would improve her" (23)— resonate with the improvement of landscape. Mr. Elton's comment is quite explicit in this regard: "She was a beautiful creature when she came to you, but … the attractions you have added are infinitely superior to what she received from nature" (43). The likening of Harriet to improvable nature is made explicit in Emma's drawing of Harriet: "she meant to throw in a little improvement to the figure, to give a little more height, and considerably more elegance" (48). The portrait also is set outdoors and appropriately places the "the naiveté of Miss Smith's manners" next to a tree (50).[15] Harriet is the raw material of nature, to be sculpted into culture by her social superiors. Mr. Knightley, too, speaks of Harriet's being "improved" (61) and of her turning out well "in good hands" (61, 65). Emma's plans for Harriet mirror Mr. Knightley's self-appointed license to "find fault" (9) with Emma: "I have blamed you, and lectured you, and you have borne it as no other woman in England would have borne it" (469). Emma "read[s] Harriet in the terms in which Mr. Knightley effectively, if implicitly, reads Emma" (Roulston 47). Moreover, it is significant that Mr. Knightley's pedagogical methods cause pain: after the Box Hill lesson Emma "felt the tears running down her cheeks almost all the way home" (409). Christine Roulston makes the excellent point that "Emma's mistreatment of Miss Bates, although it occurs only once, is a slightly more extreme version of John Knightley's mistreatment of his wife, in its disregard of social decorum. In each case, a form of social transgression is taking place, yet they are responded to in radically different ways" (53). While Mr. Knightley would never presume to correct his brother, Emma is a candidate for instruction.

For Mr. Knightley, women's education should confer "strength of mind" and "make a girl adapt herself rationally to the varieties of her situation in life" (39). Mr. Knightley uses "rational" here in the sense of submission to things as they are, rather than in Wollstonecraft's sense of equality between men and women as "rational creatures" (5:75). Mr. Knightley emphasizes sexual difference. In his view, Emma, "a nonsensical girl" (231), has an imagined "genius for foretelling and guessing" (38), "fancy and whim" (106), whereas he possesses judgement. Mr. Knightley, it seems, would agree with the idealization of restraint in Alexander Pope's lines on "wit and judgement" in *Essay on Criticism*: "The winged courser, like a gen'rous horse, / Shows most true mettle when you check his course" (1:86–87). Emma grants that "no doubt you were much my superior in judgement" when

---

[15] Britton Wenner makes an interesting comparison to Thomas Gainsborough's famous "Mr. and Mrs. Andrews": "Just as Gainsborough naturalizes Mrs. Andrews and the tree, Mr. Elton sees Harriet in the same way" (64).

she was a young child and Mr. Knightley was 16. But when she suggests that "the lapse of one-and-twenty years bring[s] our understandings a good deal nearer," Mr. Knightley retorts, "I have still the advantage of you by sixteen years' experience, and by not being a pretty young woman and a spoiled child" (106). It is hence Mr. Knightley's prerogative to correct Emma. Mr. Knightley wants Emma to be humbled: "I should like to see Emma in love, and in some doubt of a return; it would do her good" (41). Emma recognizes this impulse in Mr. Knightley's style of education: "You are very fond of bending little minds" (159). Emma's caricature of male authority—"standing up in the middle of the room ... speaking as loud as he could" (158)—holds considerable truth. Mr. Knightley does "Stand up, in tall indignation" (63), and, as Sulloway notes, he "invariably interrupts Emma with all the cool authority he exercises over Miss Bates and Mrs. Weston" (164).[16]

Linking agriculture and marriage as systems in which nature and women are born to submit, Austen further explores the symbolic value of food in man's mastery over nature. The connections between the hierarchy of food and social hierarchies is implicit in Mr. Knightley's arrangement of the strawberry party at Donwell: "The nature and the simplicity of gentlemen and ladies, with their servants and furniture, I think is best observed by meals within doors. When you are tired of eating strawberries in the garden, there shall be cold meat in the house" (386). Mr. Woodhouse's diet and its marginalization are key to the novel's analysis of food, that is, its cultural mediation and delineation of social hierarchy. Mr. Woodhouse, who dislikes wedding-cake (17), clearly is attuned to the symbolic meaning of food. He speaks directly and repeatedly on the importance of boiling meat and vegetables and of exercising moderation. His fondness for a "nice basin of gruel" (108) is a recurrent detail, and his diet is frequently marked by a refusal of meat, fish, and poultry. While Mr. Woodhouse does "consider our Hartfield pork ... so very superior to all other pork" (186), he cautions that even though it "is not like any other pork," it "still ... is pork" and should be "eaten very moderately of" (184). He prefers a "basin of thin gruel" to "minced chicken and scalloped oysters" (23). While gruel is sometimes made with meat, according to the OED, gruel with meat was specifically referred to as such: "gruel of beef," "gruel forced" (meaning enforced), "gruel of force," a telling phrase reflecting meat's symbolic meaning of domination. We can assume that Mr. Woodhouse's gruel is strictly oatmeal; indeed, the OED quotes Austen's novel as an example of usage of gruel in this sense. His offers of gruel are rejected by everyone except Isabella. When Mr. Woodhouse suggests, "My dear Emma, suppose we all have a little gruel," Emma "could not suppose any such thing, knowing, as she did, that both the Mr. Knightleys were as unpersuadable on that article as herself;—and two basins only were ordered" (108). While Mr. Woodhouse's "thin gruel" is perceived as unappetizing, when food is contested at Hartfield, more is at stake than individual taste. As Fiddes states, "our attitudes to different foods are conditioned by the associations which we invest in them" (30). While "the notion persists that what makes an item of food acceptable is some quality inherent in the thing itself ... the cultural controls on perception are

---

[16]   See Christine Roulston's analysis of gendered language in *Emma*.

precisely what needs to be analysed" (Mary Douglas, qtd. in Fiddes 30). Indeed, this was one of the arguments made in vegetarian tracts: meat tastes delicious because of the "force of human habits" and the "luxuries to which [humans] have been accustomed" (Newton 1). There is nothing innately tasteless or comic about gruel: it is just the way Mr. Woodhouse likes it—thin. But the context of Highbury thickens it with social meaning. How is its bad taste produced? While criticism has simply accepted the bad taste of gruel, we might ask, why does everyone besides Mr. Woodhouse and Isabella dislike gruel so much?

Mr. Woodhouse's diet receives a lot of negative attention in criticism, repeatedly citing it as one of his peculiarities and even linking it to his supposedly failed masculinity. Marvin Mudrick goes as far as claiming that Mr. Woodhouse is a "parasitic plant" (196) and "really an old woman" (192): "He has no single masculine trait" (192–93) and "is, in fact, an annoyance, with his gruel, his hypochondria" (195). Tony Tanner similarly describes Mr. Woodhouse as "emasculate" (*Austen* 180), a "travesty of a father," and for evidence points to the "bizarre fatuity" of his "rambl[ings]" (*Austen* 200) about food. And Lane comments that gruel "is not the stuff from which a healthy, enterprising, self-reliant population can be built—let alone a mighty empire founded and maintained" (*Jane Austen and Food* 155). Lisa Hopkins, in contrast, sees Mr. Woodhouse's dietary concerns as a form of aggression: he "tantalise[s] and terrorise[s] his neighbours" (65) and attempts to "exert … an iron control not only over his own digestive system but over those of all whom he can dominate socially" (64).[17] But this argument does not take into account the low status of gruel in the hierarchy of food and Mr. Woodhouse's failure to "persuade" others of its good taste. Emma "allowed her father to talk—but supplied her visitors in a much more satisfactory style" (24). The fact that his success is highly limited makes clear that it is the community that controls perceptions of the taste and value of food, not Mr. Woodhouse. The dinner of "apples and biscuits" satisfies him, but, as Miss Bates lets Emma know, it was a "disappointment" to Mrs. Bates:

> The baked apples and biscuits, excellent in their way, you know; but there was a delicate fricassee of sweetbread and some asparagus brought in at first, and good Mr. Woodhouse, not thinking the asparagus quite boiled enough, sent it all out again. Now there is nothing grandmama loves better than sweetbread and asparagus—so she was rather disappointed, but we agreed we would not speak of it to any body, for fear of its getting round to dear Miss Woodhouse, who would be so very much concerned. (356–57)

The absence of meat makes the meal inadequate; fruit and grain are excellent "only" in their way. Given the hierarchy of food and its connection to social hierarchy, it is not surprising that Mrs. Bates is disappointed about the "sweetbread"; she probably was looking forward to a more elaborate dinner than usual.

---

[17]   Gwen Hyman also notes that Mr. Woodhouse "attempts to choke everyone around him with gruel" (98).

Not writing off Mr. Woodhouse's preferences as "thoroughly unreasonable," Stroup grants Mr. Woodhouse's concern over "medical qualifications" and "the salting of pork" in the "age before refrigeration," but he nevertheless concludes that "beyond this point, we must confront his authentic weirdness" (156). What makes Mr. Woodhouse "weird" is his fear of nature: "nature is alien to him" and "Nothing is wholesome in its natural state for Mr. Woodhouse" (157).[18] Stroup does briefly mention Shelley and the debates on "health and ethics of diet" (157), but only to dismiss their relevance to Austen. The context of Shelley and other vegetarian discourses is relevant, I argue, for in Mr. Woodhouse's diet Austen imagines a less exploitative interaction with nature.

Mr. Woodhouse likes his food boiled, whether it be apples (256), asparagus (336), or pork: "if it is not over-salted, and if it is very thoroughly boiled ... and eaten very moderately of, with a boiled turnip, and a little carrot or parsnip, I do not consider it unwholesome" (184). Mr. Woodhouse is adamant that "No stomach can bear roast pork" (184). His preference for boiled meat and vegetables is not so much a withdrawal from nature as a discomfort with its domination. Deborah Lupton explains the gendering of food which is "easy to digest" versus "heavy" food "that needs sharp teeth to chew and break down" as corresponding to a masculine-feminine binary (107). Given the association of "heavy" food, such as roasted joints of meat, with masculine force, Mr. Woodhouse's boiled food marks him as feminine. His consistent advocacy of moderation and temperance has similar implications. He thinks passing the Muffin "round once" is "enough" (183) and he offers "a *little* bit of tart—a *very* little bit" and "*half* a glass of wine ... a *small* half glass—put in a tumbler of water" (24). While Mr. Knightley's agricultural model is to get as much from nature as possible, Mr. Woodhouse seems to want to take as little as possible. Vegetarian tracts spoke of the wastefulness of meat production. Lisa Hopkins argues that Mr. Woodhouse "reinforces" class difference (64) with his emphasis on small portions, "which, literally as well as metaphorically, belittles" his guests (65), but his emphasis on moderation does just the opposite. His diet attempts to level class and gender difference.

The lowness of Mr. Woodhouse's diet is matched by his abdication of patriarchal authority and his concern for those "lower" on the social hierarchy.[19]

---

[18]   Hyman, too, examines the historical dietary context and makes the point that Mr. Woodhouse's fears are partly legitimate (22, 24). Our conclusions differ, however: "Mr. Woodhouse ... uses gruel in his attempt to create a bounded, static, uncompromised, and uncompromising self: a body protected from the alimentary incursions and depredations of the industrial and scientific world, yet distanced from the uncontrollable, potentially radical implication of overly natural fare; a body that consumes only the known, the safe, the controllable, the civilized, that is never haunted by the unintended effects of foreign, undercooked, or insufficiently tamed fare" (33).

[19]   *Clueless*, Amy Heckerling's adaptation of *Emma*, transforms Mr. Woodhouse's quiet and retiring character into a litigation lawyer—which, as Cher explains to us, is "the scariest type of lawyer." Part of that transformation involves changing Mr. Woodhouse's diet; his high cholesterol level seems to indicate a diet rich in animal fat, and it is his

The narrator notes that the lowly Mrs. Goddard "formerly owed much to Mr. Woodhouse's kindness" (21). We are told that Mr. Woodhouse thoughtfully recommended James's daughter Hannah for a place nearby at the Westons' (7), facilitating his servants' family closeness. He is concerned about giving James "due notice" (344) about the additional work associated with the ball at the Crown Inn. In contrast, Mrs. Elton sees servants only in terms of her own status and their utility: "The man who fetches our letters every morning (one of our men, I forget his name) shall inquire for your's too and bring them to you" (319). Mr. Woodhouse also expresses concern for the horses several times (7, 99): "it is right to spare our horses when we can" (271–72). The novel does not cast this as an idle sentiment; later we are told of a "lame" horse (384) delaying the excursion to Box Hill, and of Frank's mare suffering "a cold," necessitating him taking a "Crown chaise" (417). These passages, which do not serve a plot function, are significant in their inclusion of animal sentience. Moreover, they vindicate Mr. Woodhouse's caring character in contrast to *Northanger Abbey*'s John Thorpe, who reasons that "nothing ruins horses so much as rest" (42).

Commentary on the novel has tended to let the comic aspects of Mr. Woodhouse's characterization overshadow his merits. He certainly has shortcomings: "his talents would not have recommended him at any time" and "he could not meet [Emma] in conversation, rational or playful" (5). I do not pretend to set him up as Austen's model of fatherhood, but seek to redress the balance. He is introduced by the narrator as "a most affectionate, indulgent father" (3) and "everywhere beloved for the friendliness of his heart and amiable temper" (5). He was "universally civil" (5)—no small praise in comparison to the likes of Mrs. Elton and her Mr. E, who do not have any redeeming features, or Mr. John Knightley, whose uneven temper is a source of anxiety for Emma. Mr. Woodhouse's dislike of matrimony is accounted for in the novel by his "hating change of every kind" (6) and has been pathologized by readers, but we might also relate it to his eschewal of masculine dominance and his attachment to his children: "My dear, pray do not make any more matches, they are silly things, and break up one's family circle grievously" (12). This attachment, of course, is no clear-cut matter; it is stifling at times for Emma, but, on the other hand, it compares favorably to Mr. Weston's giving up of his young son.[20] While Mr. Weston takes on the "saddle of mutton" (128) at his dinners, Mr. Woodhouse abdicates his role as carver: he "made the usual stipulation of not sitting at the bottom of the table himself" (314). And after the Christmas dinner at the Westons', he quickly leaves behind the men, their

---

daughter's role to rip meat sandwiches out of his hands and supply him with "low-fat" foods. Changing the character's diet is one of the ways in which *Clueless* reinscribes the traditional gender roles that Austen's novel unsettles.

[20]   Jim O'Hanlon's 2009 adaptation of *Emma* is noteworthy in its sympathetic portrayal of Mr. Woodhouse, played by Michael Gambon, as traumatized by the early loss of his wife and thus understandably anxious about the safety of those he loves. The adaptation also gestures towards the childhood trauma of Frank's adoption by the Churchills.

conversation and "wine" (131), to join the women in the drawing room. It is likely that Mr. Woodhouse was a kind husband; his comment that Emma "takes[s] after" her mother in her "clever[ness]" (83) suggests he did not choose a docile wife.

Finally, we do well to remember that Mr. Woodhouse's "hatred of change" facilitates the remarkable conclusion of Mr. Knightley's moving into Hartfield upon his marriage to Emma. The heroine does not have to leave her beloved home. Not exulting in the humbling of its heroine, the novel's final pages leave us with a highly complex renegotiation of male-female roles, in part because of Mr. Woodhouse's so-called "neurosis" (Lisa Hopkins 64). Mr. Woodhouse forms an important counterpoint to Mr. Knightley's view of nature in the novel, and one which the conclusion does not dismiss.

We have seen in Chapter 3 that *Persuasion*'s Captain Benwick is perceived as a "very odd young man" (141), in part because of his lack of interest in rural sport. Similarly, Mr. Woodhouse's masculinity is called into question because of his hesitancy to eat at the top of the food chain. It is striking that those male characters who forego dominance over nature also eschew dominance over women. Austen's refiguring of gender relationships is intricately connected to rethinking the human relationship to nature and animals. In "Sanditon," the subject of the next chapter, she creates a heroine independent of the marriage plot and a vision of nature independent of humans.

Chapter 6
Rock and Rain

> Charlotte … found amusement enough in standing at her ample, Venetian window, and looking over the miscellaneous foreground of unfinished buildings, waving linen, and tops of houses, to the sea, dancing and sparkling in sunshine and freshness. (*LM* 161)

The earliest readers of "Sanditon," the Austen family, recognized its unprecedented sense of place by giving the work, unnamed by Austen herself, the title by which it is now known. The title is unique among the other novels and short fictions, which are named after characters (*Emma*, "The Watsons," "Lady Susan"), estates (*Mansfield Park*, *Northanger Abbey*), or themes (*Sense and Sensibility*, *Pride and Prejudice*, *Persuasion*). E.M. Forster may have found "Sanditon" at times "stale"—"we realize with pain that we are listening to a slightly tiresome spinster, who has talked too much in the past to be silent unaided" (178)—but he did note its landscape as a significant change in direction. He wrote that Austen "hitherto regarded the face of the earth as a site for shrubberies and strawberry beds" (179), but here

> there is a queer taste … which is not easily defined: a double-flavoured taste—half topography, half romance. Sanditon is not like Lyme or Highbury or Northanger or the other places … . It exists in itself and for itself. Character-drawing, incident, and wit are on the decline, but topography comes to the front. (178)

Sanditon, as Barbara Britton Wenner observes, emerges as a character (103). And, as a character, nature is not a passive backdrop; nature is not only acted upon—it also acts.

This agency of nature is established in the text's first sentence: "A gentleman and lady travelling from Tunbridge … being induced by business to quit the high road, and attempt a very rough lane, were overturned in toiling up its long ascent—half rock, half sand" (*LM* 137). *Emma*'s Mr. John Knightley, in a fit of ill humor, seeks to vex Mr. Woodhouse with the prospect of his carriage being "blown over in the bleak part of the common field" (137), but in Austen's fiction carriages do not lose their ground until "Sanditon."[1] The overturning of the carriage is "Sanditon"'s opening move in its destabilization of the human-nature relationship and, I will argue, associated social hierarchies. While all of Austen's novels and short fictions begin with the specific mention of key players, "Sanditon" introduces its characters

---

[1]   In the juvenile "Love and Freindship," Edward and Augustus's phaeton "overturn[s]" (*J* 129).

in generic terms: "a gentleman and lady" (*LM* 137). Their mention is followed by references to a "driver" (*LM* 137), "several persons," "a gentlemanlike man," "haymakers," and "men, women and children" (*LM* 138). The first character finally to be named is Mr. Heywood; the "gentleman and lady" of the opening sentence are not distinguished as Mr. and Mrs. Parker until several pages later (*LM* 142). Human agents are characterized as generic types, almost like subsets of a species. They are dwarfed by the landscape (like the Parkers' overturned carriage) or subsumed within it—as in the grammar of this list: "the field, men, women and children" (*LM* 138). Human individuality is downplayed, as is human agency, in Austen's plotting of her text as a series of accidents. In contrast, the landscape is invested with agency: "the road ... expressing with a most intelligent portentous countenance that beyond it no wheels but cart wheels could safely proceed" (*LM* 137). Kathryn Sutherland, examining Austen's manuscript revision, notes there is an "oddly non-human investment in the scene": the road becomes "personified and animated ... to convey 'intelligent' information" (188) in its "intelligent portentous countenance," whereas in the earlier version, "the Change" in the road "seemed to say that beyond it no wheels but cart wheels had ever thought of proceeding" (188).[2] The revision personifies nature more directly.

If nature is a character with the capacity for expression, Mr. Parker consistently misreads it. Peter Knox-Shaw argues that the "main theme of *Sanditon* is quixotry" (250). Sir Edward Denham thinks of himself "quite in the line of the Lovelaces" (*LM* 184), and Diana, Susan, and Arthur Parker live by narratives of illness. Mr. Parker misreads newspaper advertisements and William Cowper's praise for rural simplicity in "The Truth" (*LM* 145), and he misreads nature, only deciphering those "intelligible characters" (*LM* 143) that fit into his "profitable speculation" (*LM* 146):

> Nature had marked [Sanditon] out—had spoken in most intelligible characters—the finest, purest sea breeze on the coast—acknowledged to be so—excellent bathing—fine hard sand—deep water ten yards from the shore—no mud—no weeds—no slimey rocks—never was there a place more palpably designed by Nature for the resort of the invalid—the very spot which thousands seemed in need of—the most desirable distance from London! One complete, measured mile nearer than East Bourne. (*LM* 143)

He reads nature as something to be "planned and built, and praised and puffed" (*LM* 146), and edits out, for example, "the yearly nuisance of its decaying vegetation.—Who can endure a cabbage bed in October?" (*LM* 156). Austen's text points to the natural processes that evade Mr. Parker's entrepreneurial drive. The comforts of the Parkers' new home are pointedly undercut. Passing by the Parkers' former residence in "a sheltered dip within two miles of the sea" (*LM* 155), Charlotte Heywood calls it a "very snug-looking place" (*LM* 155)—while Trafalgar House

---

[2]   Sutherland connects the revision to the "disturbing sense which runs throughout the fragment that life is being lived at a critical distance, as a second-order reality" (189–90).

is precariously perched on the cliffs and leaves its inhabitants exposed to the wind and sun. Mrs. Parker notes that their former neighbors in the valley "did not seem to feel the storms last winter at all ... when *we* had been literally rocked in our bed" (*LM* 157). In "Sanditon" nature is a force to be reckoned with. The Parkers resort to a "canvas awning" (*LM* 157) for protection.

Mr. Parker's attempt to make rock and sand yield at the text's dramatic opening also involves "constrain[ing]" humans and other animate beings. The carriage driver is "most unwilling." He "had grumbled and shaken his shoulders so much indeed, and pitied and cut his horses so sharply, that he might have been open to the suspicion of overturning them on purpose" (*LM* 137). Mr. Parker seeks to teach the mastery of nature to his sons; he agrees to a "parasol ... for little Mary ... or a large bonnet," but not for the boys: "I must say I would rather *them* run about in the sunshine than not. I am sure we agree my dear, in wishing our boys to be as hardy as possible" (*LM* 157).

Mr. Heywood is often held up as a positive ideal against the modern speculations of Mr. Palmer; the former lives in harmony with nature, the latter out of harmony. Joseph Kestner, for example, writes of the conflict "mirrored by their names": "*Hey/wood*, the traditional agrarian impulse; *Parker*, nature subdued and tamed by 'civilization'" or the "conflict as one between nature as itself ... represented by Heywood and nature as regularized ... illustrated by Parker, with his abusive utilitarianism" ("*Sanditon* or *The Brothers*" 162). But Willingden is no pastoral idyll.[3] For *both* Mr. Heywood and Mr. Parker, nature is there to be useful. Mr. Heywood's objection to seaside resorts is not that they spoil the countryside, but that they spoil the poor: "Bad things for a country;—sure to raise the price of provisions and make the poor good for nothing" (*LM* 142). When Mr. Parker mistakes one of the homes for that of the Surgeon, Mr. Heywood's reply is telling in its dismissiveness of those below him on the social scale: "as to that cottage, I can assure you Sir that it is in fact ... as indifferent a double tenement as any in the parish, and that my shepherd lives at one end, and three old women at the other" (*LM* 140). He does not individuate any of the "old women"; like the building, they are "indifferent." He views both nature and people in terms of utility.

In this context, it is significant that Austen delays the entrance of her heroine. Charlotte Heywood is not mentioned until the very end of the second chapter (*LM* 150), at which point she is singled out by her parents to accompany the Parkers because she is the oldest and "useful and obliging" (*LM* 150). She is also silent. She does not speak until the family home is behind her. Her first words open the fourth chapter (*LM* 155), almost one third of the way into the narrative. We see Charlotte's subjectivity only after she has left the parental home. One of "Sanditon"'s most famous passages is its heroine "standing at her ample, Venetian

---

[3]   The opening of "Henry and Eliza" suggests that the young Austen did not idealize agrarian life: "Sir George and Lady Harcourt were superintending the Labours of their Haymakers, rewarding the industry of some by smiles of approbation, and punishing the idleness of others, by a cudgel" (*J* 38).

window, and looking over the miscellaneous foreground of unfinished buildings, waving linen, and tops of houses, to the sea, dancing and sparkling in sunshine and freshness" (*LM* 161). It is a moment of "release" for the heroine, as Peter Knox-Shaw points out (246). Moreover, the moment links the liberty of the heroine with the liberty of nature. Charlotte looks beyond the human presence in the landscape to the sea and sky, which, "dancing and sparkling," are indifferent to human presence and are "beyond the control of Mr. Parker's and Lady Denham's speculation" (Curry, "New Kind of Pastoral" 167). While the human part of the landscape is connected to work, the sea cannot be reduced to an instrumental function. The non-instrumentality of the sea is matched by the independence of the heroine, who realizes "I must judge for myself" (*LM* 181), and the text's evasion of the marriage plot. The characterization of Charlotte marks a significant departure on Austen's part. Charlotte has no suitor; she is not in need of a lover-mentor; and she can easily see through wanna-be rakes like Sir Edward, who "was entitled (according to his view of society) to approach with high compliment and rhapsody on the slightest acquaintance" (*LM* 184) any woman he likes.

When Charlotte meets Sir Edward, she is taken in by him for less than a sentence: "She could not but think him a man of feeling—till he began to stagger her with the number of his quotations, and the bewilderment of some of his sentences" (*LM* 174). She "began to think him downright silly" (*LM* 176); he "had not a very clear brain" (*LM* 177). With his "cottage ornée" (*LM* 153), he is another version of *Sense and Sensibility*'s Robert Ferrars, who also is "excessively fond of a cottage" (285)—as a second home. Sir Edward, to impress Charlotte, offers a rhapsody on the "terrific grandeur of the ocean in a storm, its glassy surface in a calm, its gulls and its samphire, and the deep fathoms of its abysses, its quick vicissitudes, its direful deceptions, its mariners tempting it in sunshine and overwhelmed by the sudden tempest" (*LM* 174). It is telling that Sir Edward turns the ocean into a fickle, femininized figure who seduces and punishes those who worship her. Moreover, the panegyric on the sea is merely a lead-in to his subject proper: "woman" (*LM* 175) and "the sovereign impulses of illimitable ardour" (*LM* 176). Sir Edward objectifies both woman and nature. His fantasy of "carry[ing] Clara] off" to "the neighbourhood of Tombuctoo" (*LM* 184) brings together, as Curry points out, "two kinds of speculation: colonial trade in products seized from nature (gold, ivory) and the proposed sexual exploitation of Clara" ("New Kind of Pastoral" 173). We also see this overlap in Miss Lambe from the West Indies, whose name crystallizes the animalizing of women and exploited social groups that Austen explored in *Mansfield Park*. Miss Lambe is the site of fantasy for all the speculators; the Parkers imagine her as part of a large family of West Indians taking up lodgings, and Lady Denham imagines her as a gullible customer for "asses' milk" (*LM* 203). These fantasies of power are consistently undercut. Lady Denham "as to the animals … soon found that all her calculations to profit would be vain" (*LM* 203). Sir Edward thinks he has "serious designs" on Clara, but she "saw through him, and had not the least intention of being seduced" (*LM* 184). Sir Edward cannot do the damage of the likes of a Wickham, Henry Crawford, or John Willoughby.

Charlotte sees Sir Edward and others clearly. It is in this sense of possessing "intelligent or comprehending vision" (Curry, "New Kind of Pastoral" 173) that Charlotte is a speculator. In "Sanditon" the male gaze that objectifies landscape and women is disrupted. Barbara Britton Wenner comments on the final scene: "Charlotte enjoys a fair degree of safety, as well as freedom to see without being seen … . A female gaze penetrates this artificial landscape, with its park palings and plantings" (109). But the famous mist (the only mist in all of Austen) descending in the last two pages of "Sanditon" complicates this argument. Charlotte's vision is obscured by a "great thickness of air" (*LM* 208). Juliet McMaster compares "Sanditon" to the art of John Turner developing from realism into impressionism. While Charlotte does not need to move from blindness to insight, McMaster argues that

> clarity and accuracy of vision may not be enough … shrewd observation, even intelligent interpretation and penetration, still leave out something essential … . Charlotte's perspicacity, her ability to penetrate to some objective reality out there, seems ready to give way to some achieved consciousness of complexity, subjectivity, even inscrutability. ("The Watchers" 157)

It is also important that mist cannot be recruited to utility. Charlotte speculates that Sir Edward seeks the shroud of mist for his illicit meetings, but his plans for secrecy fall flat. The mist does not take on the desired shape, and Charlotte catches a glimpse of Sir Edward and Clara through one of the "vacant spaces" in the fence (*LM* 207) "in spite of the mist" (*LM* 208). The ephemerality of the mist evades the Enlightenment imperative to define and categorize nature. Mr. Palmer speaks of reading the characters of nature, but the mist is a reminder of the limits of the human ability to read, and control, nature.

Austen uses the quixotic theme in "Sanditon" to draw attention to the textuality of social conventions, including the textuality of the human relationship to nature. The speculators of "Sanditon" read nature along the lines of the human-nature dualism which subjugates nature for human ends. But the rock, sand, wind, and mist all are living presences, and evade human control. Much has been written in feminist theory about "the dualism of (western) patriarchal society that makes a distinction between humanity (man) and the natural world" and "the subordinate position of women in that dualism" (Mary Mellor 59). In "Sanditon" the human-nature dualism is destabilized, and this subversion extends to the social hierarchies it underpins. Austen creates in Charlotte Heywood an autonomous heroine not in need of male cultivation. "Sanditon" has a number of free agents, like the Parker singles (Arthur, Diana, Susan, and Sidney) and Lady Denham, who boasts: "I do not think I was ever overreached in my life; and that is a good deal for a woman to say that has been married twice" (*LM* 178).

In "Sanditon," humans are turned into "its" by the commodifying speculators, the narrative voice, and, as we have seen, the agency of nature. Mr. Parker speculates on the "effect" of "such a young man as Sidney, with his neat equipage and fashionable air": "many a respectable family, many a careful mother, many a pretty daughter, might *it* secure us, to the prejudice of East Bourne and Hastings" (*LM* 159; emphasis mine). The passage simultaneously inflates Sidney's importance (he will attract hundreds to Sanditon and be its competitive edge!) and reduces him to an object, and an interchangeable one at that: any young man "such … as" Sidney will do. The narrator also turns Lady Denham into an "it," as Susan Allen Ford points out: "in a kind of ironic justice [she] is transformed into a commodity herself: 'Every Neighbourhood should have a great lady.— The great Lady of Sanditon was Lady Denham'" (181). The demotion of human individuality and agency is also reflected in the fact that accidents propel the plot of "Sanditon." The carriage accident and Mr. Palmer's ankle injury lead to the friendship with the Heywoods. And it is accidental that the Parkers are on the road leading to the Heywoods' in the first place; they are off by "seven miles": Mr. Parker, on the hunt for a doctor to bring to Sanditon, misread the newspaper notice of a "dissolution of a partnership in the medical line" in Great Willingden: "All done in a moment;—the advertisements did not catch my eye till the last half hour of our being in town" (*LM* 139–40). Similarly, the origin of his investment in Sanditon is described in terms of chance: the place was chosen because of "some natural advantages in its position and some accidental circumstances" (*LM* 146). And the mistakes continue. There is the "accidental resemblance of names and circumstances" giving rise to false expectations—"The family from Surrey and the family from Camberwell were one and the same" (*LM* 200)—and Charlotte, by chance, catches a sight of Sir Edward and Clara (*LM* 208). The narrative structure undermines human agency and control.

In *Mansfield Park* Fanny mourns the cutting of an avenue of trees at Sotherton, and in *Sense and Sensibility* Elinor feels "provocation" and "censure" (257) at the clearing of trees at Norland Park to make room for a hothouse, but neither heroine is in a position to make her objections count; they occupy only the margins of estates, and the domination of the landscape goes unchecked. I have argued throughout this book that Austen's novels explore the dual oppression of women and nature. In her final work of fiction, Austen turns these hierarchies upside down. Nature is not so yielding as Mr. Parker would wish, and neither are women, contrary to Sir Edward's wishes. In "Sanditon," the evasion of the marriage plot and the autonomy of its heroine, with her solitary two-hour walks along the beach, are connected to the natural landscape, which evades human control.

Austen put aside "Sanditon" on March 18, 1817. Too ill to complete what would have been her seventh novel, she pursued its theme in her final work. Austen composed "When Winchester races first took their beginning" on July 15, 1817, three days before her death on July 18. The poem was very topical; the *Hampshire Chronicle* announced the Winchester Races for "horses, mares and geldings" on July 14 (Honan 401), and the next day Austen dictated the following verses to her sister, by her side during the last days of her illness:

> When Winchester races first took their beginning
> It is said the good people forgot their old Saint
> Not applying at all for the leave of S^t: Swithin
> And that William of Wykham's approval was faint.

The races however were fix'd and determin'd
The company met & the weather was charming
The Lords & the Ladies were sattin'd & ermin'd
And nobody saw any future alarming.

But when the old Saint was informed of these doings
He made but one Spring from his shrine to the roof
Of the Palace which now lies so sadly in ruins
And then he address'd them all standing aloof.

Oh, subjects rebellious, Oh Venta depraved
When once we are buried you think we are dead
But behold me Immortal.—By vice you're enslaved
You have sinn'd & must suffer.—Then further he said

These races & revels & dissolute measures
With which you're debasing a neighbouring Plain
Let them stand—you shall meet with your curse in your pleasures
Set off for your course, I'll pursue with *my* rain.

Ye cannot but know my command o'er July.
Henceforward I'll triumph in shewing my powers,
Shift your race as you will it shall never be dry
The curse upon Venta is July in showers. (*LM* 255)[4]

"When Winchester races first took their beginning" has not been accorded
the reverence usually given to authors' final words. Valerie Grosvenor
Myer, for example, writes, "It wasn't much better than her usual attempts at verse, but it
showed her sense of humour was still alive although she was fading fast" (236).
Austen's poetry, as a whole, has been given short shrift, relegated to the ephemera
of family entertainment.[5] Biographers commenting on the poem chiefly note
Austen's comic spirit, irrepressible even in the face of illness and death, and, to be
sure, this is remarkable (as is "Sanditon" for the same reason).

---

[4] Because the poem was untitled by Austen, and a manuscript in her hand does not
exist, there is considerable variation in the titles among various editions. R.W. Chapman
titled it "Venta, Written at Winchester on Tuesday the 15th July 1817"; Venta, Roman for
Winchester, also alludes to James Austen's poem on the death of his sister, "Venta! Within
thy sacred fane." David Selwyn, editor of *The Poetry of Jane Austen and the Austen Family*,
chooses a title, "Written at Winchester on Tuesday the 15th July 1817," which foregrounds
the poem's biographical context and undermines its status as a formal composition. Margaret
Anne Doody and Douglas Murray abbreviate the first line for a title. The Cambridge edition
uses the complete first line.

[5] David Selwyn writes: "The handful of poems written by Jane Austen—impromptu,
occasional, often arising from games—were the result not so much of the art which
produced her novels as of a tradition of family verse-writing inherited from her mother"
(*Jane Austen in Context* 59).

The poem, published not until 1906, also is a vivid instance of the Austen family's interventionism. In the 1818 "Biographical Notice of the Author" included with the posthumous publication of *Northanger Abbey* and *Persuasion*, Henry Austen mentions that "The day preceding her death she composed some stanzas replete with fancy and vigour" (328), but this reference was deleted in subsequent editions. The Austen family actively resisted publication of the poem. James Edward Austen-Leigh's *Memoir of Jane Austen* excluded the poem, a decision applauded by Caroline Austen:

> Tho' there are no reasons *ethical* or orthodox against the publication of these stanzas, there are reasons of taste—I never thought there was much point in them—they were good enough for a passing thought, but if she had lived she would probably soon have torn them up—however there is a much stronger objection to their being inserted in any memoir, than a want of literary merit—If put in at *all* they must have been introduced as the latest working of her mind … . The joke about the dead Saint, & Winchester races, all jumbled up together, would read badly as amongst the few details given, of the closing scene. (Qtd. in Le Faye 89–90)[6]

Given the emphasis on Austen's "thoroughly religious and devout" character (331) in the "Biographical Notice," it is not surprising that the poem was suppressed. As Emily Auerbach puts it, "Her family members would have liked 'dear Aunt Jane's' final burst of poetry to be a pious utterance. Instead, she wrote six stanzas of doggerel about a saint so hopping mad that he springs out of his shrine to berate the public for attending horse races rather than honoring him" (265). As is the case with the delayed publication of her early writings, the Austen family's concern about securing Austen's literary reputation as domestic novelist was paramount. But the subject matter of the horse races also must have played a part. The poem offers a decided comment on a sport which members of the Austen family regularly attended. David Selwyn is right in stating that Austen "seems to have been less enthusiastic about horse-racing than other members of her family," but does not account for why this might be so: "one might perhaps guess that her attitude towards it was one of tolerant amusement that people should subject themselves to the discomfort of a large crowd in uncertain weather merely for the pleasure of seeing which horse could run fastest" (*Jane Austen and Leisure* 113). The representations of sport which we have examined in this study point to a much more complex and political response on Austen's part.

We ought to listen to Austen's final words and take seriously the poem's treatment of the racing of animals, a subject which comes up in Austen's fiction as well. In *Mansfield Park*, the Newmarket Races are responsible for Tom Bertram's "dangerous illness": he "had gone from London with a party of young men to Newmarket, where a neglected fall, and a good deal of drinking, had brought on

---

[6]   See Le Faye's "Jane Austen's Verses and Lord Stanhope's Disappointment" for a full publication history of the poem.

a fever" (494). The poem offers a judgement on racing. Saint Swithin views the races as a "vice," as "dissolute," and as "debasing," and punishes the revelers with showers. It is important that the curse takes the form of a natural phenomenon; nature, through Saint Swithin, takes revenge on those who exploit nature. The poem denies the "ermin'd" lords and ladies their sport. The legend of Saint Swithin contains several elements useful to Austen's pitting of nature against sport. Saint Swithin's request for a simple burial site outside the cathedral associates him with nature and against social pomp. Further, according to *The Golden Legend*, Saint Swithin did not ride horses: "For he loved no pride, ne to ride on gay horses, ne to be praised ne flattered of the people." The Saint's refusal of the social privilege of riding connects with the poet in Cowper's *The Task* or, more generally, the Romantic poet, who hesitates to ride due to its class implications and due to concerns about animal cruelty and, instead, embraces pedestrianism. Auerbach poses the following question: "By selecting a specifically British saint who is annoyed by the dissolute behavior of the fashionable aristocracy, does she register an attack on her countrymen's secularism, pettiness, and class segregation?" (266). My answer is that the poem is a critique of the class system *and* the ways in which class and gender hierarchies are demarcated on the bodies of animals.

The site of the poem's composition—the two sisters working together inside Jane Austen's bedroom—reenacts the division that Austen consistently draws between sport and women in her fiction. Like Charlotte Heywood observing the social world of Sanditon at a distance, the speaker in the poem is removed from the "company" of "Lords and Ladies." In the context of Jane Austen's mocking irreverence towards the sporting world in her letters to Cassandra, and her fiction's sustained critique of sport, the poem is far from anomalous in Austen's oeuvre. Luckily for us, the Austen family's attempt to stage "the closing scene" failed, and we can read "When Winchester races first took their beginning" as Jane Austen's final take on sport, a subject of interest throughout her writing life.

A recent example of the Austen family's framing of "When Winchester races first took their beginning" can be found in *Life in the Country* (2005; 2008), which includes an Afterword by Joan Austen-Leigh and is co-edited by Freydis Jane Welland, the "great, great, great grand-niece to Jane Austen [who] carries on the literary tradition of her branch of the family—descendants of Jane Austen's eldest brother James—who in each generation has written about their beloved aunt Jane" (book jacket). *Life in the Country* pairs the silhouettes of James Edward Austen-Leigh, one of Austen's nephews, with quotations from Austen's novels and other writings. The assertion of parallels between the two is entrenched in the myth of the Austen family: as Maggie Lane writes in the short biographical sketch entitled "Jane Austen and Her Family," the Austens, "that most supporting and stimulating of extended families," was all Jane required: they "supplied all her emotional and intellectual needs" (n.pag.). While the collection purports to consist of "Quotations by Jane Austen and Silhouettes by Her Nephew," Jane Austen is so undistinguishable from her family that quotations from J.E. Austen-Leigh's *Memoir* and M.A. Austen-Leigh's *Personal Aspects of Jane Austen* are included in the written text as if Austen and her relatives are one and the same. Joan Klingel Ray claims that the art of nephew and aunt are similar in their "realism" and their use of detail (Jane Austen's "exquisite use of irony" on the one hand, and the "exquisite art of form" of her nephew's silhouettes on the other hand [n.pag.]). Further, we are told, "Jane Austen's lively text and James Edward's astute observations of nature combine in a way that illustrates their perspective on life in the English countryside" (Welland and Sutherland, "Preface" [n.pag.]). The pairings construct a seamless relationship between J.E. Austen-Leigh's enthusiasm for country sports (evident in his *Recollections of the Early Days of the Vine Hunt*) and Austen's writing. For example, the concluding description of Willoughby's fate—"he lived to exert, and frequently to enjoy himself. ... In his breed of horses and dogs, and in sporting of every kind, he found no inconsiderable degree of domestic felicity"— is paired with a silhouette of a foxhunt (n.pag.). Given that the editorial apparatus stresses James Edward's "love" of sport, all irony and critique on his aunt's part in her description of Willoughby's enjoyment is lost. Passages from *Mansfield Park* that speak of sport are similarly flattened by silhouettes which celebrate the sport. A silhouette of three riders in rapid movement is paired with three lines from "When Winchester races first took their beginning." The selected quotation does not capture Austen's treatment of the races, nor even the basic "events" of the poem, for all is well and the delights of the sport are about to begin:

> When Winchester races first took their beginning ...
> The races however were fix'd and determin'd
> The company met & the weather was charming (n.pag.)

The idealization of the sporting world in *Life in the Country* puts Jane Austen in the service of the very ideologies she consistently opposed in her writing. A similar process is at work in the contemporary film and television adaptations of Austen's novels, discussed in the Conclusion.

Conclusion

The late twentieth- and early twenty-first-century film and television adaptations of Jane Austen's novels are rich in scenic appeal. In contrast to earlier adaptations, they move Austen's characters "out of the Drawing Room, onto the Lawn," to use Rachel M. Brownstein's phrase (13). While this shift draws welcome attention to the novels' natural settings, the films tend to back away from the politics of nature in Austen, instead delivering a "nostalgic geography of a lost English society" (Crang 111) or a "souvenir England" (James Thompson 25). Elisabeth Ellington states that "most" of the adaptations "can be read as tributes to the English countryside and nostalgia for a bygone lifestyle" (92), and cites the films' exclusion of the history of Enclosure Acts and their "social and economic upheaval" (93).[1] Similarly, the films idealize rural sport and set their handsome hunters amidst lush and atmospheric landscape. Willoughby's entrance in Emma Thompson's screenplay for Ang Lee's *Sense and Sensibility* is a case in point: "Crash! Through the mist breaks a huge white horse. Astride sits an Adonis in hunting gear" (85). In Austen's novel, Willoughby's entrance is less dramatic: "A gentleman carrying a gun, with two pointers playing round him, was passing up the hill and within a few yards of Marianne, when her accident happened. He put down his gun and ran to her assistance" (50). This is not to evaluate the adaptations in terms of their faithfulness to Austen. Rather, as film theorist Christopher Orr argues, "lapses of fidelity … are of interest … as a means of reconstructing the film's … ideology": "a film adaptation is a product of the culture that created it and thus an expression of the ideological forces operative in that culture at a specific historical moment" (73). My point, then, is that "lapses of fidelity" in the representation of rural sport contribute to shaping Austen for a particular ideological purpose. Critics, such as Julian North, posit that the adaptations have made Austen "something of a conservative icon in popular culture: a canonical author whose life and work signify English national heritage and all that implies of the past as an idyll of village life in a pre-industrial society, of traditional class and gender hierarchies, sexual propriety and Christian values" (North 38).[2] While I do not wish to deny the textual complexities of the films (Devoney Looser is right to say that the adaptations do not "simply toll … neoconservative bells" ["Feminist Implications" 159]), the rewriting of Austen's depiction of hunting is conspicuous and oddly continuous with the early reception of Austen.

---

[1]   She also notes, however, that the films "argue for … a landscape that is worth preserving" and "productions of Jane Austen (and other classic British authors from Shakespeare to the Brontës …) benefit from an ecocritical reading which can place filmmakers' use of nature and landscape in the context of the current nature conservancy movement" (108).

[2]   See Harriet Margolis on "branding Jane" (26).

As we saw in the Introduction, nineteenth- and early twentieth-century readers of Jane Austen saw her primarily in domestic terms and isolated her from contemporary debates about nature and animals. This critical tradition has had a long legacy. Alongside the elision of Austen's participation in Romantic-era debates about animals and nature, the novels continue to circulate, especially in popular culture, primarily as romances whose heroines find happiness in marriage to men who happen to be rich, or rich enough. I have argued that Austen's engagement with contemporary debates about nature is integral to her feminism. As I hope to have shown, the unease of Austen's marriage plots is connected to her exposition of women treated as animals in patriarchy. It is thus not accidental that the films' emphasis on romance is coupled with an erasure of Austen's critique of sport. In fact, the "harlequinization of Jane Austen's novels" (Kaplan, "Mass Marketing" 178) requires the idealization of rural sport.

For example, Ang Lee's *Sense and Sensibility*, based on Emma Thompson's screenplay, inverts the novel's connections between hunting and the exploitation of women, which we examined in Chapter 2, and instead presents a connection between hunting and romance. Part of the film's building up of Colonel Brandon as romantic hero involves turning him into a hunter to echo Willoughby. Colonel Brandon and Sir John Middleton are shown at the Keeper's Lodge in Barton Park "cleaning their guns in companionable silence—a habit left over from army days," when Sir John attempts to encourage his friend's feelings for Marianne: "A man like you—in his prime—she'd be a most fortunate young lady." But Colonel Brandon retorts that Marianne would "no more think of me than she would of *you*, John" (Emma Thompson 75). The very next scene emphasizes the difference between the two men. It shows the melancholy Colonel Brandon "strid[ing] along in hunting gear, a gun slung under one arm, his dog trotting behind him with a duck clamped between its jaws. The bulrushes catch his eye and he slows, then stops. He stands for a moment deep in thought. Then he takes his hunting knife, cuts one and walks off contemplatively" (Emma Thompson 76). Presumably he is reminiscing about the erotically charged moment in which he assists Marianne cutting the bulrushes: "Her knife is blunt ... . [He] wordlessly offers her his hunting knife. Oddly nervous, Marianne takes it ... . The Colonel's gaze follows her movements as if held by a magnet" (Emma Thompson 75). The film's montage of these three scenes characterizes hunting as an emotional, reflective, and romantic activity— precisely the opposite to how Austen characterizes sport. The 2008 adaptation of *Sense and Sensibility*, directed by John Alexander, builds on the representation of sport in Lee's film. Linda Hutcheon, in *A Theory of Adaptation*, points out that "multiple versions exist laterally, not vertically" and that "other earlier adaptations may, in fact, be just as important as contexts for some adaptations as any 'original'" (xiii). This certainly seems to be the case for the 2008 television series, which rewrites scenes originating in Lee's film. Like its 1995 precursor, the 2008 version connects sport with romance and it develops a connection to education. We see this particularly in the montage of Marianne playing the piano and Colonel Brandon shooting. While Austen's Colonel Brandon "paid her ... the compliment of attention" (41), the adaptation amplifies his musical knowledge so that he can recognize Marianne changing the tempo of a particular movement. He also gives her a challenging piece of sheet music ("You overestimate my abilities," responds Marianne), and we see her labor to learn it. This Brandon clearly is the lover-mentor. Interspersed with the scenes of Marianne practicing at the piano (and Colonel Brandon looking on) are scenes of Colonel Brandon, with his dogs, returning from an evidently successful shooting excursion (he carries a number of dead birds). Colonel Brandon is placed in a position of cultured authority over nature, animals, and Marianne. The overlay of sport and courtship is played out again in the scene of Sir John and Colonel Brandon shooting together. Sir John gives his friend courtship advice: "bide your time … and then she'll see that the old dog has some life in him yet." The scene leaves the viewer in little doubt of Colonel Brandon's ultimate success: "I don't think I've ever seen you aim a gun and miss," says the good-natured Sir John, who, predictably, misses every shot. In a later scene, also not based on the novel, Sir John offers Robert Ferrars hunting and shooting privileges at Barton Park, but they are refused: "I'm not enamoured of country sports." The film thus plays into the claim that sport is integral to the virtues of country life. In Austen's novels, however, participation in rural sport is not delineated along city versus country lines; urbanites like Henry Crawford are as keen shooters as country gentlemen. Rather, participation in rural sport is connected to the abuse of women.

Pride and Prejudice, as we have seen, is unique in the Austen canon for associating both hero and heroine with nature, and its landscape descriptions have been well translated in recent adaptations. The 1995 adaptation of *Pride and Prejudice*, directed by Simon Langton, emphasizes Elizabeth's and Darcy's relationships to nature. We see Darcy, played by Colin Firth, talking to Mrs. Gardiner about a particular chestnut tree they both admire in Lambton, and some of us (à la Helen Fielding's Bridget Jones) fondly remember him diving into the lake at Pemberley. Darcy catches sight of Elizabeth playing tug with a dog at Netherfield. And on one of her many walks, she stops to admire a soaring flock of birds. These added scenes communicate the novel's kinship between hero and heroine. However, the representation of rural sport deviates from Austen's. The adaptation's opening scene is of Darcy and Bingley galloping through the landscape; the soundtrack of horns suggests that they are hunting. Darcy and Bingley's sporting activities are emphasized throughout. They are shown shooting at Netherfield, and their return is framed as a beautiful dusk scene, rich in sounds of birds and crickets, making their sport part of nature. When Elizabeth reads Darcy's letter of explanation, the narration of Darcy and Wickham's childhood and their "playing together" is supplemented with scenes of them fishing. The film connects Darcy's love of nature to a long-held love of rural sport, thus undoing Austen's critique, which pits the two in opposition.

The 2005 adaptation of *Pride and Prejudice*, by Joe Wright, plays up the English countryside and places its hero and heroine in nature even more than the 1995 version, but it, too, is inconsistent with Austen's critique of sport. In the film Elizabeth wishes Darcy "fine weather" for shooting, but the novel associates women's comments on sport with their compliance to men; Austen has Mrs. Bennet and Lydia, not Elizabeth, take an interest in men's sport. The crucial moment of Darcy offering fishing privileges to Mr. Gardiner also hits a discordant note: "Can I persuade you to accompany me to the lake this afternoon? It is very well stocked and its occupants left in peace far too long." This line sits ill with the film's presentation of Darcy as the introspective, sensitive hero; and fishing, rather than a bridge between the classes, is marked here as aggression towards nature and compromises the novel's description of Pemberley as a place where "natural beauty had been so little counteracted" (271). In this regard, Cyril Coke's 1979 adaptation, based on a screenplay by Fay Weldon, captures more of the novel's spirit. Its Mr. Hurst declares, "I prefer shooting to fishing. I cannot understand a man who likes fishing." Here, the significance of Darcy's fishing is registered—it sets him apart from other men. Moreover, Mr. Hurst's fondness for shooting is pointedly opposed to an appreciation of nature. When Mrs. Hurst announces, "I find mountains to be very dull. They lack refinement," her equally foolish husband agrees: "I can't abide a mountain." Roger Michell's *Persuasion* perhaps comes closest to Austen's representation of sport. One of its scenes depicts the Uppercross party on a shooting expedition: servants are employed to scare up the fowl while Charles Musgrove and Wentworth pull the triggers. As Carol M. Dole comments, the scene "is less notable for proving our hero to be a good shot than for exposing the purely recreational and rather silly nature of the hunt, as beaters are shown at the labor of producing easy shots for their masters" (61). The tableau also draws attention to gender roles: the men shoot while the women in attendance politely applaud each successful shot.

The representation of rural sport has been central to my analysis of Jane Austen's work. As we have seen, sport's underlying ethos of mastery over nature also plays itself out in the novels' depiction of agriculture, landscape improvements, and animal captivity. At the very end of her career, in "Sanditon" and "When Winchester races first took their beginning," Austen focussed explicitly on a nature that resists human control. These texts do not so much mark a departure as they highlight themes that are continuous in her work. *Emma*'s Mr. Elton, on the way to the Christmas party at the Randalls', may enthuse about "the use of a sheepskin for carriages"—"One is so fenced and guarded from the weather, that not a breath of air can find its way unpermitted. Weather becomes absolutely of no consequence" (123), but that very night the weather brings Highbury to a halt for a few days, "the ground covered with snow, and the atmosphere in that unsettled state between frost and thaw" (150). We are pointedly reminded that nature is not simply there for humans. Throughout her work, Austen subjects anthropocentrism to feminist analysis: those who dominate nature and animals also oppress those lower in the social hierarchy. When we listen to Austen's description of herself as a "wild beast" (*Letters* 212), we can begin to understand that Austen's case for women is connected to the eighteenth- and early nineteenth-century case for animals.

Works Cited

Adams, Carol J. *The Sexual Politics of Meat: A Feminist-Vegetarian Critical Theory*. New York: Continuum, 1990.

Adams, Carol J., and Josephine Donovan. Introduction. *Animals & Women: Feminist Theoretical Explorations*. Durham: Duke University Press, 1995. 1–8.

Agamben, Giorgio. *The Open: Man and Animal*. Trans. Kevin Attell. Stanford: Stanford University Press, 2004.

Alexander, John, dir. *Sense and Sensibility*. BBC, 2008.

Altomari, Lisa. "Jane Austen and Her Outdoors." *Persuasions: The Jane Austen Journal* 12 (1990): 50–53.

Auerbach, Emily. *Searching for Jane Austen*. Madison: University of Wisconsin Press, 2004.

Austen, Henry. "Biographical Notice of the Author." *Persuasion*. Ed. Janet Todd and Antje Blank. Cambridge: Cambridge University Press, 2006. 326-32.

Austen, James. "To Edward on the Death of His First Pony." *The Poetry of Jane Austen and the Austen Family*. Ed. David Selwyn. Iowa City: University of Iowa Press, 1997. 42–45.

Austen, Jane. *The Cambridge Edition of the Works of Jane Austen*. 9 vols. Gen. Ed. Janet Todd. Cambridge: Cambridge University Press, 2005-2008.

———. *Letters*. Ed. Deirdre Le Faye. 3rd ed. Oxford: Oxford University Press, 1995.

Austen-Leigh, James Edward. *A Memoir of Jane Austen*. Oxford: Clarendon Press, 1963.

———. *Recollections of the Early Days of the Vine Hunt and of its Founder William John Chute, Esq., M.P. of the Vine together with Brief Notices of the Adjoining Hunts by a Sexagenarian*. London: Spottiswoode, 1865.

Austen-Leigh, Mary Augusta. *Personal Aspects of Jane Austen*. London: J. Murray, 1920.

Austen-Leigh, William, Richard Arthur Austen-Leigh, and Deirdre Le Faye. *Jane Austen: A Family Record*. London: British Library, 1989.

Barker-Benfield, G.J. *The Culture of Sensibility: Sex and Society in Eighteenth-Century Britain*. Chicago: University of Chicago Press, 1992.

Bate, Jonathan. *The Song of the Earth*. London: Picador, 2000.

Bentham, Jeremy. *An Introduction to the Principles of Morals and Legislation*. Ed. J.H. Burns and H.L.A. Hart. Oxford: Clarendon Press, 1996.

Berger, John. *About Looking*. New York: Pantheon, 1980.

Blackwell, Mark, ed. *The Secret Life of Things: Animals, Objects, and It-Narratives in Eighteenth-Century England*. Lewisburg: Bucknell University Press, 2007.

———. "The Thing about Fanny Price." 2005 MLA Convention, Washington, DC. 28 December, 2005.

Bluestone, George. *Novels into Film*. Los Angeles: University of California Press, 1966.

Bodenheimer, Rosemarie. "Looking at the Landscape in Jane Austen." *Studies in English Literature* 21.4 (1981): 605–23.

Boonin-Vail, David. "The Vegetarian Savage: Rousseau's Critique of Meat-Eating." *Environmental Ethics* 15.1 (1993): 75–84.

Boulukos, George E. "The Politics of Silence: *Mansfield Park* and the Amelioration of Slavery." *Novel: A Forum on Fiction* 39.3 (2006): 361–83.

Bowerbank, Sylvia. *Speaking for Nature: Women and Ecologies of Early Modern England*. Baltimore: Johns Hopkins University Press, 2004.

Bradbrook, Frank W. *Jane Austen and Her Predecessors*. Cambridge: Cambridge University Press, 1966.

Brantlinger, Patrick. *The Rule of Darkness: British Literature and Imperialism, 1830–1914*. Ithaca: Cornell University Press, 1988.

Braunschneider, Theresa. "The Lady and the Lapdog: Mixed Ethnicity in Constantinople, Fashionable Pets in Britain." *Humans and Other Animals in Eighteenth-Century British Culture: Representation, Hybridity, Ethics*. Ed. Frank Palmeri. Aldershot: Ashgate, 2006. 31–48.

Britton Wenner, Barbara. *Prospect and Refuge in the Landscape of Jane Austen*. Aldershot: Ashgate, 2006.

Brodey, Inger Sigrun. "Papas and Ha-has: Rebellion, Authority, and Landscaping in *Mansfield Park*." *Persuasions: The Jane Austen Journal* 17 (1995): 90–96.

Brown, Laura. *Fables of Modernity: Literature and Culture in the English Eighteenth Century*. Ithaca: Cornell University Press, 2001.

———. *Homeless Dogs and Melancholy Apes: Humans and Other Animals in the Modern Literary Imagination*. Ithaca: Cornell University Press, 2010.

Brownstein, Rachel M. "Out of the Drawing Room, Onto the Lawn." *Jane Austen in Hollywood*. Ed. Linda Troost and Sayre Greenfield. 2nd ed. Lexington: University Press of Kentucky, 2001. 13–21.

Burney, Fanny. *Camilla, or A Picture of Youth*. Ed. Edward A. Bloom and Lillian Bloom. Oxford: Oxford University Press, 1983.

———. *The Wanderer; Or, Female Difficulties*. Oxford: Oxford University Press, 1991.

Butler, Marilyn. *Jane Austen and the War of Ideas*. Oxford: Clarendon Press, 1975.

Byron, George Gordon. *The Complete Poetical Works*. Ed. Jerome McGann. 7 vols. Oxford: Clarendon Press, 1980–1993.

Canovan, Margaret. "Rousseau's Two Concepts of Citizenship." *Women in Western Political Philosophy: Kant to Nietzsche*. Ed. Ellen Kennedy and Susan Mendus. New York: St. Martin's Press, 1987. 78–105.

Cartmill, Matt. *A View to a Death in the Morning: Hunting and Nature through History*. Cambridge, MA: Harvard University Press, 1993.

Cavalieri, Paola. *The Animal Question: Why Non-Human Animals Deserve Human Rights*. Trans. Catherine Woolard. Oxford: Oxford University Press, 2002.

Chapin, Lisbeth. "Shelley's Great Chain of Being: From 'blind worms' to 'new-fledged eagles.'" *Humans and Other Animals in Eighteenth-Century British Culture: Representation, Hybridity, Ethics*. Ed. Frank Palmeri. Aldershot: Ashgate, 2006. 153–68.

Chapman, R.W., ed. *Minor Works*. Vol. 6 of *The Novels of Jane Austen*. 3ʳᵈ ed. Oxford: Oxford University Press, 1988.

Cole, Lucinda, ed. Spec. issue of *The Eighteenth Century: Theory and Interpretation* 52.1 (2011): 1–106.

Coleridge, Samuel Taylor. *The Complete Poetical Works of Samuel Taylor Coleridge*. 2 vols. Ed. Ernest Hartley Coleridge. Oxford: Clarendon, 1912.

Coke, Cyril, dir. *Pride and Prejudice*. BBC, 1979.

Cowper, William. "Epitaphium Alterum." Vol. 2 of *The Poems of William Cowper*. Ed. John D. Baird and Charles Ryskamp. Oxford: Clarendon Press, 1995. 20–21.

———. "Epitaph on a Hare." Vol. 2 of *The Poems of William Cowper*. Ed. John D. Baird and Charles Ryskamp. Oxford: Clarendon Press, 1995. 19–20.

———. *The Gentleman's Magazine*, June 1784. Vol. 5 of *The Letters and Prose Writings of William Cowper*. Ed. James King and Charles Ryskamp. Oxford: Clarendon Press, 1986. 40–44.

———. "The Progress of Error." Vol. 1 of *The Poems of William Cowper*. Ed. John D. Baird and Charles Ryskamp. Oxford: Clarendon Press, 1980. 262–79.

———. *The Task*. Vol. 2 of *The Poems of William Cowper*. Ed. John D. Baird and Charles Ryskamp. Oxford: Clarendon Press, 1995. 113–263.

Crang, Mike. "Placing Jane Austen, Displacing England: Touring between Book, History, and Nation." *Jane Austen and Co.: Remaking the Past in Contemporary Culture*. Ed. Suzanne R. Pucci and James Thompson. Albany: State University of New York Press, 2003. 111–30.

Curry, Mary Jane. "A New Kind of Pastoral: Anti-Development Satire in *Sanditon*." *Persuasions: The Jane Austen Journal* 19 (1997): 167–76.

———. "'Not a Day Went by Without a Solitary Walk': Elizabeth's Pastoral World." *Persuasions: The Jane Austen Journal* 22 (2000): 175–86.

Dean, Richard. *An Essay on the Future Life of Brutes, Introduced with Observations upon Evil, its Nature and Origin*. 2 vols. *Animal Rights and Souls in the Eighteenth Century*. Vol. 2. Ed. Aaron Garrett. Bristol: Thoemmes, 2000.

Dekoven, Marianne. "Why Animals Now?" *PMLA* 124.2 (2009): 361–69.

Deresiewicz, William. "Community and Cognition in *Pride and Prejudice*." *ELH* 64.2 (1997): 503–35.

———. *Jane Austen and the Romantic Poets*. New York: Columbia University Press, 2004.

Derrida, Jacques. *The Animal That Therefore I Am*. Trans. David Wills. New York: Fordham University Press, 2008.

Deuchar, Stephen. *Sporting Art in Eighteenth-Century England: A Social and Political History*. New Haven: Yale University Press, 1988.

Dole, Carol M. "Austen, Class, and the American Market." *Jane Austen in Hollywood*. Ed. Linda Troost and Sayre Greenfield. 2nd ed. Lexington: University of Kentucky Press, 2001. 58–78.

Donald, Diana. *Picturing Animals in Britain 1750–1850*. New Haven: Yale University Press, 2007.

Donovan, Josephine. "Animal Rights and Feminist Theory." *Signs: Journal of Women in Culture and Society* 15.2 (1990): 350–75.

Doody, Margaret Anne. Introduction. *Sense and Sensibility*. Oxford: Oxford University Press, 1990.

Doody, Margaret Anne and Douglas Murray, ed. *Catharine and Other Writings*. Oxford: Oxford University Press, 1993.

Duckworth, Alistair. *The Improvement of the Estate*. Baltimore: Johns Hopkins University Press, 1994.

———. "Nature." *The Jane Austen Handbook*. Ed. J. David Grey. London: Athlone, 1986. 317–19.

Ellington, Elisabeth H. "'A Correct Taste in Landscape': Pemberley as Fetish and Commodity." *Jane Austen in Hollywood*. Ed. Linda Troost and Sayre Greenfield. 2nd ed. Lexington: University Press of Kentucky, 2001. 90–110.

Ellis, Markman. "Suffering Things: Lapdogs, Slaves, and Counter-Sensibility." *The Secret Life of Things: Animals, Objects, and It-Narratives in Eighteenth-Century England*. Lewisburg: Bucknell University Press, 2007. 92–113.

Ferguson, Moira. *Animal Advocacy and Englishwomen, 1780–1900: Patriots, Nation, and Empire*. Ann Arbor: University of Michigan Press, 1998.

———. *Colonialism and Gender Relations from Mary Wollstonecraft to Jamaica Kincaid: East Caribbean Connections*. New York: Columbia University Press, 1993.

Fiddes, Nick. *Meat: A Natural Symbol*. London: Routledge, 1991.

Foer, Jonathan Safran. *Eating Animals*. New York: Little Brown, 2009.

Ford, Susan Allen. "The Romance of Business and the Business of Romance: The Circulating Library and Novel-Reading in *Sanditon*." *Persuasions: The Jane Austen Journal* 19 (1997): 177–86.

Forster, E.M. *Abinger Harvest*. 1936. London: Edward Arnold, 1953.

Fosso, Kurt. "'Sweet Influences': Animals and Social Cohesion in Wordsworth and Coleridge, 1794–1800." *Isle: Interdisciplinary Studies in Literature and Environment* 6.2 (1999): 1–20.

Fox, Michael Allen. *Deep Vegetarianism*. Philadelphia: Temple University Press, 1999.

Fraiman, Susan. "Jane Austen and Edward Said: Gender, Culture, and Imperialism." *Critical Inquiry* 21.4 (1995): 805–21.

Fudge, Erica. *Pets*. Stocksfield: Acumen, 2008.

Galperin, William H. *The Historical Jane Austen*. Philadelphia: University of Pennsylvania Press, 2003.

Gardner, Catherine. "Catharine Macaulay's 'Letters on Education': Odd but Equal." *Hypatia* 13.1 (1998): 118–37.

Garrett, Aaron. Introduction. Vol. 1 of *Animal Rights and Souls in the Eighteenth Century*. 6 vols. Bristol: Thoemmes, 2000. vii–xxvi.

Gay, Penny. "A Changing View: Jane Austen's Landscape." *Sydney Studies in English* 15: 47–62.

———. *Jane Austen and the Theatre*. Cambridge: Cambridge University Press, 2002.

Graham, Peter W. *Jane Austen & Charles Darwin: Naturalists and Novelists*. Aldershot: Ashgate, 2008.

Gregerson, Jon. *Vegetarianism: A History*. Fremont: Jain, 1994.

Grey, J. David. "Pets and Animals." *The Jane Austen Companion*. Ed. J. David Grey. Houndmills: Macmillan, 1986. 324-25.

Guerrini, Anita. "A Diet for a Sensitive Soul: Vegetarianism in Eighteenth-Century Britain." *Eighteenth-Century Life* 23.2 (1999): 34–42.

Halperin, John. *The Life of Jane Austen*. Baltimore: Johns Hopkins University Press, 1984.

———. "The Worlds of *Emma*: Jane Austen and Cowper." *Jane Austen: Bicentenary Essays*. Ed. John Halperin. Cambridge: Cambridge University Press, 1975. 197–206.

Haraway, Donna J. *Simians, Cyborgs, and Women: The Reinvention of Nature*. New York: Routledge, 1991.

Hardy, Barbara. "The Objects in *Mansfield Park*." *Jane Austen: Bicentenary Essays*. Ed. John Halperin. Cambridge: Cambridge University Press, 1975. 180–96.

Harris, Jocelyn. *Jane Austen's Art of Memory*. Cambridge: Cambridge University Press, 1989.

Heckerling, Amy, dir. *Clueless*. Paramount Pictures, 1995.

Heydt-Stevenson, Jill. *Austen's Unbecoming Conjunctions: Subversive Laughter, Embodied History*. Basingstoke: Palgrave, 2005.

———. "Liberty, Connection, and Tyranny: The Novels of Jane Austen and the Aesthetic Movement of the Picturesque." *Lessons of Romanticism: A Critical Companion*. Ed. Thomas Pfau and Robert F. Gleckner. Durham: Duke University Press, 1998. 261–79.

Hickman, Peggy. "Food and Drink." *The Jane Austen Handbook*. Ed. J. David Grey. London: Athlone, 1986. 160–64.

Hildrop, John. *Free Thoughts Upon the Brute Creation*. London: R. Minors, 1742.

Hill, Bridget. "The Links between Mary Wollstonecraft and Catharine Macaulay: New Evidence." *Women's History Review* 4.2 (1995): 177–92.

Hogarth, William. *Engravings by Hogarth*. Ed. Sean Shesgreen. New York: Dover, 1973.

Honan, Park. *Jane Austen: Her Life*. New York: St. Martin's, 1987.

Hopkins, Lisa. "Food and Growth in *Emma*." *Women's Writing* 5.1 (1998): 61–70.

Hopkins, Robert. "General Tilney and Affairs of State: The Political Gothic of *Northanger Abbey*." *Philological Quarterly* 57 (1978): 213–24.

Hothem, Thomas. "The Picturesque and the Production of Space: Suburban Ideology in Austen." *European Romantic Review* 31.2 (220): 49–62.

Hutcheon, Linda. *A Theory of Adaptation*. New York: Routledge, 2006.

Hyman, Gwen. *Making a Man: Gentlemanly Appetites in the Nineteenth-Century British Novel*. Athens: Ohio University Press, 2009.

Itzkowitz, David C. *Peculiar Privilege: A Social History of English Foxhunting, 1753–1885*. Hassocks: Harvester Press, 1977.

Jarvis, Robin. *Romantic Writing and Pedestrian Travel*. Basingstoke: Macmillan, 1997.

Johnson, Claudia L. *Jane Austen: Women, Politics, and the Novel*. Chicago: Chicago University Press, 1988.

Jones, Owain. "Un(ethical) Geographies of Human/Non-Human Relations: Encounters, Collectives and Spaces." *Animal Spaces, Beastly Places: New Geographies of Human-Animal Relations*. Ed. Chris Philo and Chris Wilbert. London: Routledge, 2000. 268–91.

Jones, Vivien, ed. *Pride and Prejudice*. London: Penguin, 1996.

Kaplan, Deborah. "Female Friendship and Epistolary Form: *Lady Susan* and the Development of Jane Austen's Fiction." *Criticism: A Quarterly for Literature and the Arts* 29.2 (1987): 163–78.

———. *Jane Austen Among Women*. Baltimore: Johns Hopkins University Press, 1992.

———. "Mass Marketing Jane Austen: Men, Women, and Courtship in Two of the Recent Films." *Persuasions: The Jane Austen Journal* 18 (1996): 171–81.

Kean, Hilda. *Animal Rights: Political and Social Change in Britain since 1800*. London: Reaktion, 1998.

Kenyon-Jones, Christine. *Kindred Brutes: Animals in Romantic-Period Writing*. Aldershot: Ashgate, 2001.

Kern, Robert. "Ecocriticism: What Is It Good For?" *Isle: Interdisciplinary Studies in Literature and Environment* 7.1 (2000): 9–32.

Kestner, Joseph. "Jane Austen: The Tradition of the English Romantic Novel, 1800–1832." *The Wordsworth Circle* 7.4 (1976): 297–311.

———. "*Sanditon* or *The Brothers*: Nature into Art." *Papers on Language and Literature: A Journal for Scholars and Critics of Language and Literature* 12 (1976): 161–66.

Kheel, Marti. "License to Kill: An Ecofeminist Critique of Hunters' Discourse." *Women & Animals: Feminist Theoretical Explorations*. Ed. Carol J. Adams and Josephine Donovan. Durham: Duke University Press, 1995. 85–125.

Kirkham, Margaret. *Jane Austen, Feminism and Fiction*. New York: Methuen, 1986.

Kneedler, Susan. "The New Romance in *Pride and Prejudice*." *Approaches to Teaching Austen's* Pride and Prejudice. Ed. Marcia McClintock Folsom. New York: MLA, 1993. 152–66.

Knox-Shaw, Peter. *Jane Austen and the Enlightenment*. Cambridge: Cambridge University Press, 2004.

Kulisheck, Patricia Jo. "Every Body Does Not Hunt." *Persuasions: The Jane Austen Journal* 8 (1986): 20–24.

Landry, Donna. *The Invention of the Countryside: Hunting, Walking and Ecology in English Literature, 1671–1831*. Houndmills: Palgrave, 2001.

———. "Learning to Ride at Mansfield Park." *The Postcolonial Jane Austen*. Ed. You-Me Park and Rajeswari Sunder Rajan. London: Routledge, 2000. 56–73.

Lane, Maggie. *Jane Austen and Food*. London: Hambledon Press, 1995.

———. "Jane Austen and Her Family." *Life in the Country with Quotations by Jane Austen and Silhouettes by Her Nephew James Edward Austen-Leigh*. Ed. Freydis Jane Welland and Eileen Sutherland. London: British Library, 2008.

Lange, Lynda. Introduction. *Feminist Interpretations of Jean-Jacques Rousseau*. Ed. Lynda Lange. Pennsylvania: Pennsylvania State University Press, 2002. 1–23.

Langton, Simon, dir. *Pride and Prejudice*. BBC and A&E, 1995.

Lascelles, Mary. *Jane Austen and Her Art*. Oxford: Clarendon Press, 1939.

Lau, Beth. "Jane Austen and John Keats: Negative Capability, Romance and Reality." *Keats-Shelley Journal* 55 (2006): 81–110.

———. "Jane Austen, *Pride and Prejudice*." *A Companion to Romanticism*. Ed. Duncan Wu. Oxford: Blackwell, 1998. 219–22.

———. "Placing Jane Austen in the Romantic Period: Self and Solitude in the Works of Austen and the Male Romantic Poets." *European Romantic Review* 15.2 (2004): 255–67.

———. "The Uses and Abuses of Imagination in Jane Austen and the Romantic Poets. *Fellow Romantics: Male and Female British Writers, 1790–1835*. Ed. Beth Lau. Burlington: Ashgate, 2009. 179–210.

Lawrence, John. *A Philosophical and Practical Treatise on Horses and on the Moral Duties of Men towards the Brute Creation*. 2 vols. London: Longman, 1796–1798.

Lee, Ang, dir. *Sense and Sensibility*. Columbia, 1995.

Le Faye, Deirdre. "Jane Austen's Verses and Lord Stanhope's Disappointment." *The Book Collector* 37.1 (1988): 86–91.

Life in the Country with Quotations by Jane Austen and Silhouettes by her Nephew James Edward Austen-Leigh. Ed. Freydis Jane Welland and Eileen Sutherland. London: British Library, 2008.

Litvak, Joseph. *Strange Gourmets: Sophistication, Theory, and the Novel*. Durham: Duke University Press, 1997.

Litz, Walton A. *Jane Austen: A Study of Her Artistic Development*. London: Chatto and Windus, 1965.

Looser, Devoney. "Feminist Implications of the Silver Screen Austen." *Jane Austen in Hollywood*. Ed. Linda Troost and Sayre Greenfield. 2nd ed. Lexington: University Press of Kentucky, 2011. 158–76.

———. "'Those Historical Laurels which Once Graced My Brow are Now in Their Wane': Catharine Macaulay's Last Years and Legacy." *Studies in Romanticism* 42 (2003): 203–25.

Lupton, Deborah. *Food, the Body and the Self*. London: Sage, 1996.

Macaulay, Catharine. *Letters on Education*. London: C. Dilly, 1790.

MacKenzie, John M. *The Empire of Nature: Hunting, Conservation and British Imperialism.* Manchester: Manchester University Press, 1988.

Maehle, Andreas Holger. "Cruelty and Kindness to the 'Brute Creation': Stability and Change in the Ethics of the Man-Animal Relationship, 1600–1850." *Animals and Human Society: Changing Perspectives.* Ed. Aubrey Manning and James Serpell. London: Routledge, 1994. 81–105.

Malamud, Randy. *Reading Zoos: Representations of Animals and Captivity.* New York: New York University Press, 1998.

Malcolmson, Robert W. *Popular Recreations in English Society, 1700–1850.* Cambridge: Cambridge University Press, 1973.

Malins, Edward. *English Landscaping and Literature: 1660–1840.* London: Oxford University Press, 1966.

Margolis, Harriet. "Janeite Culture: What Does the Name 'Jane Austen' Authorize?" *Jane Austen on Screen.* Ed. Gina Macdonald and Andrew F. Macdonald. Cambridge: Cambridge University Press, 2003. 22–43.

Martin, Maureen M. "What Does Emma Want? Sovereignty and Sexuality in Austen's *Emma.*" *Nineteenth-Century Feminisms* 3 (2000): 10–24.

McFarlane, Brian. *Novel to Film: An Introduction to the Theory of Adaptation.* Oxford: Clarendon Press, 1996.

McKenzie-Stearns, Precious. "Lady Bertram's Lapdog: The Empire Rests in *Mansfield Park.*" *Notes and Queries* December 2005: 450–51.

McMaster, Juliet. "The Children in *Emma.*" *Persuasions: The Jane Austen Journal* 14 (1990): 61–67.

———. "The Watchers of *Sanditon.*" *Persuasions: The Jane Austen Journal* 19 (1997): 149–59.

Mee, Jon. "Austen's Treacherous Ivory: Female Patriotism, Domestic Ideology, and Empire." *The Postcolonial Jane Austen.* Ed. You-Me Park and Rajeswari Sunder Rajan. London: Routledge, 2000. 74–92.

Mellor, Anne K. *Mothers of the Nation: Women's Political Writing in England, 1780–1830.* Bloomington: Indiana University Press, 2000.

———. "Why Women Didn't Like Romanticism: The Views of Jane Austen and Mary Shelley." *The Romantics and Us: Essays on Literature and Culture.* Ed. Gene W. Ruoff. London: Rutgers University Press, 1990.

Mellor, Mary. *Feminism & Ecology.* New York: New York University Press, 1997.

Meyersohn, Marylea. "The Duets of *Pride and Prejudice.*" *Approaches to Teaching Austen's* Pride and Prejudice. Ed. Marcia McClintock Folsom. New York: MLA, 1993. 148–51.

Michell, Roger, dir. *Persuasion.* BBC, 1995.

Mortensen, Peter. "Taking Animals Seriously: William Wordsworth and the Claims of Ecological Romanticism." *Orbis Litterarum* 55 (2000): 296–310.

Morton, Timothy. Introduction. Vol. 1 of *Radical Food: The Culture and Politics of Eating and Drinking 1790–1820.* 3 vols. London: Routledge, 2000. 1–32.

———. *Shelley and the Revolution in Taste: The Body and the Natural World.* Cambridge: Cambridge: University Press, 1994.

Moss, Sarah. "Fetching Broth from Hartfield: Sustaining the Body Politic in Jane Austen's *Emma*." *Eating Culture: The Poetics and Politics of Food.* Ed. Tobias Döring, Markus Heide, and Susanne Mühleisen. Heidelberg: Universitätsverlag, 2003. 195–206.

Mudrick, Marvin. *Jane Austen: Irony as Defense and Discovery.* Princeton: Princeton University Press, 1952.

Mukherjee, Meenakshi. *Jane Austen.* London: Macmillan, 1991.

Mullan, Bob, and Garry Marvin. *Zoo Culture: The Book about Watching People Watch Animals.* 2nd ed. Chicago: University of Illinois Press, 1999.

Munsche, P.B. *Gentlemen and Poachers: The English Game Laws, 1671–1831.* Cambridge: Cambridge University Press, 1981.

Myer, Valerie Grosvenor. *Jane Austen: Obstinate Heart.* New York: Arcade, 1997.

Nash, Richard. "Animal Nomenclature: Facing Other Animals." *Humans and Other Animals in Eighteenth-Century British Culture: Representation, Hybridity, Ethics.* Ed. Frank Palmeri. Aldershot: Ashgate, 2006. 101–18.

Neill, Edward. *The Politics of Jane Austen.* London: Macmillan, 1999.

Newton, John Frank. *The Return to Nature, Or, A Defence of the Vegetable Regimen; With Some Account Of An Experiment Made During the Last Three or Four Years in the Author's Family.* London: T. Cadell, 1811.

Nicholson, George. *On Food.* 1803. *Radical Food: The Culture and Politics of Eating and Drinking 1790–1820.* Vol. 1. Ed. Timothy Morton. London: Routledge, 2000. 41–142.

———. *On the Primeval Diet of Man; Arguments in Favour of Vegetable Food; On Man's Conduct to Animals.* 1801. Ed. Rod Preece. Lewiston: Edwin Mellen Press, 1999.

Nokes, David. *Jane Austen: A Life.* Berkeley: University of California Press, 1997.

North, Julian. "Conservative Austen, radical Austen: *Sense and Sensibility* from text to screen." *Adaptations: From Text to Screen, Screen to Text.* Ed. Deborah Cartmell and Imelda Whelehan. London: Routledge, 1999. 38–50.

O'Connor, Erin. "Preface for a Post-Postcolonial Criticism." *Victorian Studies* 45.2 (2003): 217–46.

Oerlemans, Onno. *Romanticism and the Materiality of Nature.* Toronto: University of Toronto Press, 2002.

O'Hanlon, Jim, dir. *Emma.* BBC, 2009.

Okin, Susan Moller. *Women in Western Political Thought.* Princeton: Princeton University Press, 1979.

Orr, Christopher. "The Discourse on Adaptation. *Wide Angle* 6.2 (1984): 72–76.

Oswald, John. *The Cry of Nature; Or, An Appeal to Mercy and to Justice, on Behalf of the Persecuted Animals.* London: J. Johnson, 1791.

Palmer, Sally B. "Slipping the Leash: Lady Bertram's Lapdog." *Persuasions: The Jane Austen Journal On-Line* 25.1 (2004).

Palmeri, Frank, ed. *Humans and Other Animals in Eighteenth-Century British Culture: Representation, Hybridity, Ethics.* Aldershot: Ashgate, 2006.

Pearson, Jacqueline. *Women's Reading in Britain, 1750–1835: A Dangerous Recreation.* Cambridge: Cambridge University Press, 1999.

138 *Jane Austen and Animals*

Perkins, David. "Cowper's Hares." *Eighteenth-Century Life* 20.2 (1996): 57–69.
———. *Romanticism and Animal Rights*. Cambridge: Cambridge University Press, 2003.
Pickard, Richard. "Environmentalism and 'Best Husbandry': Cutting Down Trees in Augustan Poetry." *Lumen* 17 (1998): 103–26.
———. "The Sexual Politics of Landscape: Augustan Women Poets and Environmentalism." Canadian Society for Eighteenth-Century Studies Conference. Victoria, BC. 17 Oct. 1996.
Pinch, Adela. *Strange Fits of Passion: Epistemologies of Emotion, Hume to Austen*. Stanford: Stanford University Press, 1996.
Plasa, Carl. *Textual Politics from Slavery to Postcolonialism: Race and Indentification*. Houndmills: Macmillan, 2000.
Plumb, J.H. "The Acceptance of Modernity." *The Birth of a Consumer Society: The Commercialization of Eighteenth-Century England*. Ed. Neil McKendrick, John Brewer, and J.H. Plumb. London: Hutchinson, 1982. 316–34.
———. "The Commercialization of Leisure in Eighteenth-Century England." *The Birth of a Consumer Society: The Commercialization of Eighteenth-Century England*. Ed. Neil McKendrick, John Brewer, and J.H. Plumb. London: Hutchinson, 1982. 265–86.
Plumwood, Val. "Nature, Self, and Gender: Feminism, Environmental Philosophy, and the Critique of Rationalism." *Hypatia: A Journal of Feminist Philosophy* 6.1 (1991): 3–27.
Pope, Alexander. *Pope: Poetical Works*. Ed. Herbert Davis. Oxford: Oxford University Press, 1978.
Preece, Rod. *Awe for the Tiger, Love for the Lamb: A Chronicle of Sensibility to Animals*. Vancouver: University of British Columbia Press, 2002.
Primatt, Humphrey. *A Dissertation on the Duty of Mercy and Sin of Cruelty to Brute Animals. Animal Rights and Souls in the Eighteenth Century*. Vol. 3. Ed. Aaron Garrett. Bristol: Thoemmes Press, 2000.
Ray, Joan Klingel. "The Silhouette Art of James Edward Austen-Leigh." *Life in the Country with Quotations by Jane Austen and Silhouettes by her Nephew James Edward Austen-Leigh*. Ed. Freydis Jane Welland and Eileen Sutherland. London: British Library, 2008.
Ritson, Joseph. *An Essay on Abstinence from Animal Food as a Moral Duty*. London: Richard Phillips, 1802.
Ritvo, Harriet. "Animals in Nineteenth-Century Britain: Complicated Attitudes and Competing Categories." *Animals and Human Society: Changing Perspectives*. Ed. Aubrey Manning and James Serpell. London: Routledge, 1994. 106–26.
———. "The Emergence of Modern Pet-Keeping." *Animals and People Sharing the World*. Ed. Andrew N. Rowan. Hanover: University Press of New England, 1988.
Rizzo, Betty. "Equivocations of Gender and Rank: Eighteenth-Century Sporting Women." *Eighteenth-Century Life* 26.1 (2002): 70–93.

Robbins, Louise. *Elephant Slaves and Pampered Parrots: Exotic Animals in Eighteenth-Century Paris*. Baltimore: Johns Hopkins University Press, 2002.

Rolston, Holmes III. *Environmental Ethics: Duties to and Values in the Natural World*. Philadelphia: Temple University Press, 1988.

Roulston, Christine. "Discourse, Gender, and Gossip: Some Reflections on Bakhtin and *Emma*." *Ambiguous Discourse: Feminist Narratology and British Women Writers*. Ed. Kathy Mezei. Chapel Hill: University of North Carolina Press, 1996. 40–65.

Rousseau, Jean-Jacques. *Discourse on the Origin and Foundations of Inequality Among Men. The Basic Political Writings*. Trans. and ed. Donald A. Cress. Indianapolis: Hackett, 1987. 23–109.

———. *Emile or On Education*. Trans. Allan Bloom. New York: Basic Books, 1979.

Ruoff, Gene W, ed. Spec. issue of *Wordsworth Circle* 7.4 (1976): 290–356.

Ryder, Richard. *Animal Revolution: Changing Attitudes Towards Speciesism*. Cambridge: Basil Blackwell, 1989.

Said, Edward W. *Culture and Imperialism*. New York: Knopf, 1993.

Sales, Roger. "In Face of All the Servants: Spectators and Spies in Austen with Special Reference to the 1995 Adaptation of *Persuasion*." *Janeites: Austen's Disciples and Devotees*. Ed. Deidre Lynch. Princeton: Princeton University Press, 2000. 188–205.

Schotland, Sara D. "Man as Brute and Beast as Exemplar: Man and Animals in Wordsworth's Poetry." *New Perspectives on the Eighteenth Century* 7.1 (2010): 3–18.

Schwartz, Joel. *The Sexual Politics of Jean-Jacques Rousseau*. Chicago: University of Chicago Press, 1984.

Seeber, Barbara K. "'Does not it make you think of Cowper?' Rural Sport in Jane Austen and Her Contemporaries." *Fellow Romantics: Male and Female British Writers, 1790–1835*. Ed. Beth Lau. Burlington: Ashgate, 2009. 159–77.

———. "'I sympathize in their pains and pleasures': Women and Animals in Mary Wollstonecraft." *Animal Subjects: An Ethical Reader in a Posthuman World*. Ed. Jodey Castricano. Waterloo, Ontario: Wilfrid Laurier University Press, 2008. 223–40.

Selwyn, David. *Jane Austen and Leisure*. London: Hambledon Press, 1999.

———. "Poetry." *Jane Austen in Context*. Ed. Janet Todd. Cambridge: Cambridge University Press, 2005. 59–67.

———, ed. *The Poetry of Jane Austen and the Austen Family*. Iowa City: University of Iowa Press, 1997.

Senior, Matthew. "The Ménagerie and the Labyrinthe: Animals at Versailles, 1662–1792." *Renaissance Beasts: Of Animals, Humans, and Other Wonderful Creatures*. Ed. Erica Fudge. Chicago: University of Illinois Press, 2004. 208–32.

Sewell, Anna. *Black Beauty*. New York: Penguin, 2011.

Shannon, Laurie. "The Eight Animals in Shakespeare; or, Before the Human." *PMLA* 124.2 (2009): 472–79.

Shell, Marc. "The Family Pet." *Representations* 15 (1986): 121–53.

Shelley, Percy Bysshe. "On the Game Laws." *The Prose Works of Percy Bysshe Shelley*. Vol. 1. Ed E.B. Murray. Oxford: Clarendon Press, 1993. 280–81.

———. "On the Vegetable System of Diet." *The Complete Works of Percy Bysshe Shelley*. Vol. 6. Ed. Roger Ingpen and Walter E. Peck. London: Ernest Benn, 1965. 335–44.

———."A Vindication of Natural Diet." 1813. *The Complete Works of Percy Bysshe Shelley*. Vol. 6. Ed. Roger Ingpen and Walter E. Peck. London: Ernest Benn, 1965. 5–20.

Shevelow, Kathryn. *For the Love of Animals: The Rise of the Animal Protection Movement*. New York: Henry Holt, 2008.

Simons, John. *Animal Rights and the Politics of Literary Representation*. Houndmills: Palgrave, 2002.

Singer, Peter. *Animal Liberation: A New Ethics for Our Treatment of Animals*. New York: Avon, 1975.

Snyder, William C. "Mother Nature's Other Natures: Landscape in Women's Writing, 1770–1830." *Women's Studies* 21.2 (1992): 143–62.

Southam, B.C. *Jane Austen and the Navy*. London: Hambledon and London, 2000.

———, ed. *Jane Austen: The Critical Heritage*. 2 vols. London: Routledge, 1968.

Spiegel, Marjorie. *The Dreaded Comparison: Human and Animal Slavery*. Rev. ed. New York: Mirror Books, 1996.

Spivak, Gayatri Chakravorty. "Three Women's Texts and a Critique of Imperialism." *Critical Inquiry* 12.1 (1985): 243–61.

Spongberg, Mary. "Jane Austen and the *History of England*." *Journal of Women's History* 23.1 (2011): 56–80.

Stroup, William. "I Live out of the World: The Problem of Nature in *Emma*." *Wordsworth Circle* 28.3 (1997): 155–62.

Stuart, Tristram. *The Bloodless Revolution: A Cultural History of Vegetarianism from 1600 to Modern Times*. New York: Norton, 2006.

Sulloway, Alison. *Jane Austen and the Province of Womanhood*. Philadelphia: University of Pennsylvania Press, 1989.

Sutherland, Eileen. "Dining at the Great House: Food and Drink in the Time of Jane Austen." *Persuasions: The Jane Austen Journal* 12 (1990): 88–98.

Sutherland, John. *Can Jane Eyre Be Happy? More Puzzles in Classic Fiction*. Oxford: Oxford University Press, 1997.

Sutherland, Kathryn. *Jane Austen's Textual Lives: From Aeschylus to Bollywood*. Oxford: Oxford University Press, 2005.

Tague, Ingrid H. "Dead Pets: Satire and Sentiment in British Elegies and Epitaphs for Animals." *Eighteenth-Century Studies* 41.3 (2008): 289–306.

Tanner, Tony. *Jane Austen*. London: Macmillan, 1986.

———. "A Very Fine Cop." *TLS* 23, June, 1995.

Thomas, Keith. *Man and the Natural World: A History of the Modern Sensibility*. New York: Pantheon, 1983.

Thomas, Richard H. *The Politics of Hunting*. Aldershot: Gower, 1983.

Thompson, Emma. *Sense & Sensibility: The Screenplay & Diaries*. London: Bloomsbury, 1995.

Thompson, James. "How to Do Things with Austen." *Jane Austen and Co.: Remaking the Past in Contemporary Culture*. Ed. Suzanne R. Pucci and James Thompson. Albany: State University of New York Press, 2003. 13–32.

Tomalin, Claire. *Jane Austen: A Life*. London: Penguin, 1998.

Toohey, Elizabeth. "*Emma* and the Countryside: Weather and a Place for a Walk." *Persuasions: The Jane Austen Journal* 21 (1999): 44–52.

Trickett, Rachel. "Cowper, Wordsworth, and the Animal Fable." *The Review of English Studies* 34.136 (1983): 471–80.

Tuan, Yi-Fu. *Dominance and Affection: The Making of Pets*. New Haven: Yale University Press, 1984.

Tuite, Clara. "Domestic Retrenchment and Imperial Expansion: The Property Plots of *Mansfield Park*." *The Postcolonial Jane Austen*. Ed. You-Me Park and Rajeswari Sunder Rajan. London: Routledge, 2000. 93–115.

Twigg, Julia. "Vegetarianism and the Meanings of Meat." *The Sociology of Food and Eating: Essays on the Sociological Significance of Food*. Aldershot: Gower, 1983.

Vitali, Theodore. "Sport Hunting: Moral or Immoral?" *Environmental Ethics* 12 (1990): 69–82.

Waldau, Paul. *Animal Rights: What Everyone Needs to Know*. Oxford: Oxford University Press, 2011.

Wallace, Tara Goshal. "*Sense and Sensibility* and the Problem of Feminine Authority." *Eighteenth-Century Fiction* 4.2 (1992): 149–63.

Warren, Karen J. "The Power and the Promise of Ecological Feminism." *Environmental Ethics* 12.2 (1990): 125–46.

Weinsheimer, Joel. "Jane Austen's Anthropocentrism." *Jane Austen Today*. Ed. Joel Weinsheimer. Athens: University of Georgia Press, 1975. 128–41.

White, Gabrielle D.V. *Jane Austen in the Context of Abolition: 'A Fling at the Slave Trade.'* Houndmills: Palgrave Macmillan, 2006.

Williams, Raymond. *The Country and the City*. New York: Oxford University Press, 1973.

Wilson, Alexander. *The Culture of Nature: North American Landscape from Disney to the Exxon Valdez*. Toronto: Between the Lines, 1991.

Wiltshire, John. "Decolonising *Mansfield Park*." *Essays in Criticism* LIII.4 (2003): 303–22.

———. Introduction. *Mansfield Park*. Ed. John Wiltshire. Cambridge: Cambridge University Press, 2005. xxv–lxxxiv.

———. *Jane Austen and the Body*. Cambridge: Cambridge University Press, 1992.

Wolfe, Cary. *Animal Rites: American Culture, the Discourse of Species, and Posthumanist Theory*. Chicago: Chicago University Press, 2003.

Wolloch, Nathaniel. "Rousseau and the Love of Animals." *Philosophy and Literature* 32.2 (2008): 293–302.

Wollstonecraft, Mary. *The Works of Mary Wollstonecraft*. Ed. Marilyn Butler and Janet Todd. 7 vols. London: Pickering and Chatto, 1989.

Woolf, Virginia. *The Common Reader*. New York: Harcourt, Brace & World, 1925.

———. *Flush*. Oxford: Oxford University Press, 1998.

Wordsworth, William. "Hart-Leap Well." *William Wordsworth*. Ed. Stephen Gill. Oxford: Oxford University Press, 1984. 168–73.

Wright, Joe, dir. *Pride & Prejudice*. Focus Features, 2005.

Wyett, Jodi L. "The Lap of Luxury: Lapdogs, Literature, and Social Meaning in the 'Long' Eighteenth Century." *LIT: Literature Interpretation Theory* 10.4 (2000): 275–301.

Yeazell, Ruth Bernard. *Fictions of Modesty: Women and Courtship in the English Novel*. Chicago: University of Chicago Press, 1991.

Young, Thomas. *An Essay on Humanity to Animals. Animal Rights and Souls in the Eighteenth Century*. Vol. 5. Ed. Aaron Garrett. Bristol: Thoemmes Press, 2000.

Index